GOING HIGHER

OXYGEN, MAN, AND MOUNTAINS

GOING HIGHER

OXYGEN, MAN, AND MOUNTAINS

FOURTH EDITION

CHARLES HOUSTON, M.D.

THE
MOUNTAINEERS

Published by
The Mountaineers
1001 SW Klickitat Way, Suite 201
Seattle, WA 98134

Fourth edition, 1998

First published in 1980 as *Going Higher: The Story of Man and Altitude*. Revised 1983, 1987.

Published simultaneously in Great Britain by Swan Hill Press, an imprint of Airlife Publishing Ltd., 101 Longden Road, Shrewsbury, England SY3 9EB

Manufactured in the United States of America

Edited by Kris Fulsaas
Illustrations by Gary Nelson, except as noted
Cover, book design, and layout by Alice C. Merrill

Cover photograph © Galen Rowell

Library of Congress Cataloging-in-Publication Data
Houston, Charles S.
    Going Higher : oxygen, man, and mountains / Charles Houston. — 4th ed.
            p.   cm.
        "First published in 1980 as Going Higher : the story of man and altitude. Revised 1983, 1987"—CIP t.p. verso.
        Includes bibliographical references and index.
        ISBN 0-89886-580-8
        1. Mountaineering—Physiological aspects. 2. Altitude, Influence of. I. Title
RC1220.M6H68   1998
616.9'893—dc21
                                                                98-19462
                                                                CIP

♻ Printed on recycled paper

CONTENTS

LIST OF ILLUSTRATIONS

PREFACE

A happy mixture of mountains and medicine has filled my life. Climbing was my game, medicine my work, and I loved both. As I climbed higher, the medical problems on mountains became more and more interesting. Now that I can no longer climb, what began as a love of mountains has grown into a passion to learn about oxygen and what happens when we don't have enough of it— and so, back to medicine and physiology and physics.

Twenty years ago I wrote my first book about altitude illnesses because many mountaineers were getting sick and some were dying, and many simply didn't understand why. Much has changed since then. Not only have we learned a great deal more about lack of oxygen, but technology has enormously increased our ability to learn even more. In this, the fourth revision of the small original book, I've tried to update what we know.

Because the earlier editions of this book are long out of print, I have rewritten almost the whole book. I felt a certain urgency because the world-wide fascination with the 1996 tragedy on Mount Everest seems only to have increased the attraction of high mountains, a siren song that is likely to lure the less experienced to heights they should not attempt.

Although what may happen to people on mountains is the central theme of this book, there are many other causes of lack of oxygen— hypoxia—than high altitude. Far more people are hypoxic from illness at sea level than are victims of mountain sickness. So I have tried to show how the lessons we can learn from high altitude can help us to understand certain illnesses at sea level.

Only a few thousand people are interested in very high mountains, while many *millions* experience lack of oxygen at *low* altitude due to illness, injury, or unusual events. So I've described how hypoxia may complicate other problems and how it may perhaps be better managed—if we know more about it!

Because we can learn so much from the past, I have tried to use the past as a mirror to the future, and I've tried to make this book a record of how we learned about air and how it is carried by the moving blood to all parts of the body. From this I describe mountain sickness and wellness, and what happens to the people who go to the mountains. I've chosen information that will interest the curious reader, whether patient or doctor, scientist, climber, skier, or anyone with an inquiring mind. This is not a medical text. Unavoidably, I must use some medical jargon here and there, but I've tried to make it understandable to nonscientists. I'm really writing about the interrelationships between oxygen, man, and mountains.

ACKNOWLEDGMENTS

In preparing this book I've been blessed with help from many people wiser and more knowledgeable than I am, and it's a privilege to thank them here. Of course most of the medical facts come from the books and papers written by hundreds of persons, living and dead, whom I don't know. All who study and define science owe this great debt to those who went before; I've tried to recognize them.

For reading and correcting the whole book or pieces of it, I owe special thanks to Peter Hackett, David Kaminsky, Bruce Paton, and Brownie Schoene. Al Cymerman, Chuck Fulco, Ben Levine, Lorna Moore, Geoff Tabin, and Mike Wiedman made helpful comments from their special expertise. Plinio Prioreschi opened a whole area of ancient history for me. Most of the case reports are from my collection of letters and stories mountaineers and others have sent me over the last thirty years!

Finally, the raw manuscript was read and revised at The Mountaineers by Uma Kukathas, and then even more drastically edited by Kris Fulsaas. Between them they have made it a much better book than I ever could have done alone. I owe them both heartfelt thanks—and also for suffering my impatience.

Most of the book is new, though facts that haven't changed over the years have been taken from my out-of-print 1987 edition.

My hope is that this will enable many more people to enjoy high mountains, and more doctors to understand what lack of oxygen can do to individuals anywhere, any time.

INTRODUCTION

The growing numbers of tourists, trekkers, and mountaineers have not only increased interest in mountain sickness, but also enable us to study the pathophysiology of hypoxia more comprehensively. Unusual cases of altitude-related illness attract new insights, and wonderful new instruments and techniques make possible studies that were beyond our reach only a few years ago. As we use new tools and concepts, we see more instances where they may be relevant to lack of oxygen from everyday illnesses at sea level, as well.

This book shows how our knowledge of the air around us and the functions of heart and lungs has evolved over thousands of years, at first slowly and with mistakes, then more and more rapidly and accurately. The constellation of facts we know today is bewildering and so large that comprehending how they relate to one another becomes more and more difficult.

Though I've received lots of help from friends and from extensive reading, I am very keenly aware of shortcomings, and obviously I'm solely responsible for mistakes in facts that I haven't fully mastered. Unfortunately, too, I have had to omit many important concepts and observations. To make this book most understandable (and I hope helpful) to the nonscientist, I've taken liberties—not with facts but with explanations—here and there. But in places I often had to resort to medispeak because I know many doctors will read this, and I want to be as scientifically accurate as possible for those practicing doctors who may want to know more about the physiology of mountain sickness.

So in places the text is too simple; in others it may seem too technical. I don't apologize for this!

A special note about anecdotes. I've included a large number of true stories about what happened to people who went to the mountains and suffered. Like any good scientist, I know that anecdotes rarely have statistical validity; in order to find the truth, rigorously controlled studies are needed. On the other hand, anecdotes are snapshots of the real world. Sometimes they lead us in new and important directions. Often they mean nothing. Humans have a great weakness for *post hoc propter hoc* reasoning. I recognize the limitations of this, but I believe these true stories can teach us a great deal. And quite often a certain event really did result from such-and-such a cause.

Most of these anecdotes and case histories are based on letters and conversations I've had over the years with many different people who had many different problems. Other reports are excerpted from published sources, and I've shown the source in each case; those readers who want more scientific information can find these sources in the Bibliography at the back of the book. To distinguish case histories and anecdotes from excerpts that *are* derived from published sources, the former are set in italics.

It has been a great deal of fun and hard work to research this material and to explain it accurately as well as briefly. I was determined to make this book "a good read," but only you can decide how well I have succeeded.

Enjoy the mountains; they have beauty and wisdom for us if we approach them with humility, respect, and knowledge.

About This Book

I've divided the book into four parts, each with several chapters. Because there is so much to learn from the past, I've included in each part snapshots of how and when we learned basic facts.

Part I deals with the atmosphere around us and our forebears' gradual realization of its weight and extent. Oxygen is the smaller and only essential part of air, so I've traced how we came to learn that oxygen is indispensable for life, not only for humans, but for nearly every living organism.

In **Part II** I trace how we draw in and exhale air and where it goes in our body. Respiration is inseparable from circulation, and they are intertwined both in their history and their functions. Moving air and moving blood serve several purposes, but the most important is to provide food and fuel to the cells. In the third chapter of Part II, I summarize how the living cell—the secret of life itself—works.

Part III addresses the main topic of this book: mountain sickness. Here also the history is fascinating and important, as is how mountain sickness fits with respiration and circulation. First I describe the most frequent forms of mountain sickness and what we know about their pathophysiology. Then I look at some of the less common but important problems due to lack of oxygen at altitude. The last but in some ways the most interesting part of this section is a brief look at how we become short of oxygen in our everyday lives. This is a large subject related to mountain sickness, but not yet fully explored.

In **Part IV** I cover the processes by which our bodies "learn" to survive with a lack of oxygen, which, if it began rapidly, would be fatal. Acclima-

tization saves us, not only on mountains but, wonderfully, during gradually developing lung and heart conditions that threaten our oxygen supply. The lives of those who summit the highest mountains depend on acclimatization. I include here the unresolved issues of training for athletic competition, and the questions of who can and who should not go to high altitude.

Other chapters in Part IV cover prevention and treatment of mountain sicknesses, differences (where they exist) between genders and ages, and the important subject of environmental hazards other than hypoxia that threaten mountaineers at great altitude.

A glossary of the more frequently used medical terms is found at the back of the book, to make the denser scientific material easier to grasp. For those with special interest in the past, I include an appendix that contains brief biographies of some of the most important—and sometimes least known—of the people who brought us what we know.

Some may want to explore the medical facts and theories more deeply, so I include a list of specially helpful books and articles for further reading. Some of the works cited in the Bibliography are sources for the excerpts found throughout the book. The World Wide Web provides a much more complete High Altitude Bibliography, which can be searched by author, date, title, or keywords. There's also a mass of material on the Web about oxygen and mountain sickness and wellness. Unfortunately, quite a bit of it is inaccurate, incomplete, or totally misleading. After you've read this book, you will be better able, I hope, to sort out the good from the bad advice about high altitude.

PART I

Understanding the Atmosphere

The Air About Us

IN MAY 1996 THE TRAGEDY UNFOLDING HIGH ON MOUNT EVEREST WAS watched on television with shocked fascination by millions of people around the world.

During that ten-day period, more than eighty-eight men and women from several countries and their Sherpas were somewhere on the mountain; of these, forty were caught in a furious storm near the top of Mount Everest, on the "ordinary" route. Eight had reached the summit and were on their way down, a few were still pushing toward the top but were tired and moving slowly, while others had halted, delayed by the slowly moving crowd at the crux of the final climb, or too exhausted to go on. Around midnight on May 10, most had reached safety in their high camp, but some were missing. During the night, two rescuers (one a doctor) made desperate rescue sorties and found two of the missing; both were unconscious and covered with ice; both were barely breathing. In the black, stormy night the exhausted rescuers decided that the two were too near death to be saved, and they did not have strength to carry them down. Six hours later one of them, a male pathologist, staggered into camp; next day they found the other, a small woman, dead where the rescuers had found her. Four others had also died higher up. Twelve died during the first part of May, nine in the furious storm.

This was not the first, nor likely to be the last, high-mountain tragedy. In fact Everest 1996 was eerily like an equally bad disaster ten years before on K2, the second-highest mountain in the world.

In June and July 1986, eighty men and women from twelve countries attempted K2 on different routes. By August 10, twenty-seven had reached the summit and thirteen had died, many while descending the "ordinary" route, the Abruzzi Ridge. The worst of the awfulness played out between August 2 and 10 when, despite worsening weather, some had pushed on toward the summit and were lost near the top when a severe storm struck.

Other parties had changed their plans, leading them to use the tents and supplies of others. When those descending climbers, already exhausted, tried to find refuge in their own already overcrowded tents, some were refused. At this point, language barriers led to major misunderstandings, and differences in philosophy or ethics arose. It was bitterly cold, shelter was inadequate, food and drink were scarce, and what little togetherness there had been in a crowd of mostly strangers disappeared. Some started down and survived, but others fell. Most of those who decided to wait for better weather died. By the end of the storm, half of those who had been in the ill-fated camp were dead.

In 1986 there were no satellites sending instant news and live photographs from K2 around the world. No celebrities or journalists phoned or faxed news while other climbers struggled for their lives. The full story of K2 1986 was slow to reach the public and the shock was muted.

As one reads the often conflicting reports about K2, it seems incredible that the same terrible mistakes of 1986 would be repeated on Everest only a decade later. On the other hand, given the competitive force that drives climbers despite the overwhelming impact of the high-mountain environment, perhaps this later tragedy was inevitable and, sadly, may even be repeated, as had happened only twelve years before the K2 deaths.

In 1974 the Russian Mountaineering Federation invited mountaineers to a base camp in the seldom visited Pamirs. One hundred and sixty leading climbers from twelve countries assembled that summer and during several weeks climbed many of those great mountains (22,000–24,600 feet). A severe storm trapped twenty climbers in various camps on Pic Lenin. Eight Russian women pushed to the summit despite the storm and camped there at 23,460 feet. For four days they were battered by 70-mile-per-hour winds and temperatures far below zero. Their inadequate tents were shredded; they could not melt snow for water or cook their food. They had no supplementary oxygen. One by one, they died from the terrible combined stresses, talking ever more feebly by radio to those at Base Camp, who were powerless to help them. By the time the storm abated, all eight had died; a dozen others, trapped lower on the mountain, escaped. Before the tragedy ended, six others were dead.

The unique opportunity to climb in a magnificent, remote, and little-known mountain range may have tempted some climbers to push too hard despite dangerous avalanche conditions (which killed several) and in the face of a coming storm. The Russian women were inspired by national and women's pride to continue to the summit even in bad weather. Their courage and strength are an extraordinary testament, though it cost them their lives.

Even earlier, when big-time Himalayan mountaineering was in its infancy, nine men died when national pride led another expedition to ignore the basics:

In 1934 a party of ten elite German climbers and thirty Sherpas were high on Nanga Parbat (26,100 feet). Their supply line was overextended when a major storm came on them, dumping 8 feet of snow in six days. As supplies and strength dwindled, climbers tried to get down to safety as best each one could. They struggled through the immense snow alone or in pairs. When the storm finally ended, three German climbers and six Sherpas had died of exhaustion. Two Sherpas, who might have made it to safety, had opted to stay with their sahibs and died with them. Far from acknowledging the awful disaster, the returning climbers were greeted as national German heroes.

These and other less-known tragedies were mainly due to lack of oxygen in the atmosphere at high altitudes. We call this *hypoxia,* or, less accurately, *anoxia* or *anoxemia.* Its subtle impact has caused many deaths not only on mountains but near sea level too. We have learned about oxygen and its lack slowly over centuries.

△ △ △

LOOKING TO THE SKY ON A CLEAR DAY, it's easy to understand why our distant ancestors were puzzled by what could be out there. At night they saw tiny lights and a large one that moved and changed; in daylight the sun also moved and changed. But what and where were these objects, and what, if anything, surrounded them?

Sometimes clouds and fog, rain or snow, and wind could be seen and felt, but how did these natural phenomena relate to the invisible, impalpable, tasteless stuff they breathed and without which they could not live? On clear days they could see forever into the void—and wonder. Today science can tell us a thousand things about the atmosphere in which we live, but our forebears could only look and speculate.

Two thousand years ago, the Chinese recognized that an uninterrupted supply of "good" air was necessary to support most life. During the age of the Pharaohs, Egyptian physicians described the pathways through which air entered and left the chest. The Greco-Roman philosopher-scientists, building on such beliefs, taught that the purpose of breathing was to cool the "innate heat" of the heart.

In the fifth century B.C., Anaximenes of Miletus proposed that *aer* was an invisible spirit that was sometimes manifested when it condensed into water vapor or mist. He saw this as a divine and universal living spirit. As the ancients had, he suggested that this invisible stuff sustains the soul that animates life, and introduced the name *pneuma* for it. Erasistratus later expanded this concept to found the Pneumatic school. A few centuries later the word *pneuma* was being used for the mixture of air and blood that sustained life and was found in both arteries and veins.

THE KLEPSYDRA

History does not tell us just what mathematician, explorer, and inventor Empedocles had in mind when he used this curious jar almost 500 years before the Christian era. But whatever his purpose, he did in fact show that the atmosphere had weight. He showed that when the vessel, with one small hole in the top (the view on the right in Figure 1) and several small holes in the bottom (the view on the left), was held under water with the hole in the top closed, water could not enter until the top was opened. Conversely, once the vessel was filled and the top closed, when he held it in air, water would not flow out—because, as we now recognize, the weight of the air prevented a vacuum from being formed in the jar. This did not persuade doubters until a more impressive demonstration was done 2,000 years later by Gaspar Berti.

Figure 1. *The klepsydra: bottom of vessel* (left); *top of vessel* (right)

The term *klepsydra* is commonly used to describe an ancient "water-clock," but it was also the name of a device for collecting a small amount of liquid from a large container. The great experimentalist Empedocles in the fifth century B.C., apparently saw something more in a *klepsydra* (see Figure 1). Inadvertently or not, he showed that a vacuum could exist—a concept that was, and would be for centuries, contrary to accepted beliefs. His little experiment led him to state that air had weight and therefore substance. Thus he laid the groundwork for understanding the atmosphere.

Aristotle, who lived and taught in the fourth century B.C., and was one of the greatest of the philosopher-scientists, used observation and experience rather than theory to define what he saw about him. Looking toward the heavens, he could not conceive that space could be empty, because then it would have no dimensions. Light could not penetrate a space that did not exist and therefore could not be visible through a vacuum—but he could see the distant stars and therefore space was not a vacuum. Thus he differed with Empedocles about the nature of air even while agreeing that "In its own place, every body has weight except fire, even air. . . . It is proof of this that an inflated bladder weighs more than an empty one."

A century later, Strato(n) of Lampsacus theorized that everything—solids, liquids, gases, even light rays—consisted of particles separated by "void," and the heavier the substance, the less "void" it contained. He showed that a "void" could be produced by sucking air out of a closed container, and thus took another step toward the concept of a vacuum.

During the next few centuries, philosophers of the Pneumatic school advanced more theories, but with little or no experimental evidence. Another school, the "Atomists," came very close to describing the atomic theory we know today.

To us, swept along in the frantic expansion of knowledge, it seems strange that it took our ancestors so many centuries to understand such basics. But remember, only a few score scholars were involved, and their resources were limited. In fact it is really a marvel that they laid such a broad base for what we do know today.

Aristotle's writings pervaded European thought for 1,500 years. Many of his principles were accepted without question and slowly became fundamental to the religious doctrine of the time, which held that the universe was static and perfect. Aristotle had been vague about the possibility of a vacuum, but much later the Roman Catholic Church denied the existence of a vacuum, and all that this implied, even while conceding that if God wanted to create a vacuum He could certainly do so. Those who differed were heretics.

The Nature of Air

These views prevailed for many centuries. The universe was made of four elements—fire, water, earth, and air. Although the importance of air to life was recognized, its nature was unknown and debatable. In the late sixteenth century, as the Age of Enlightenment began, a remarkable series of new ideas blossomed like spring flowers after the long winter of the Dark Ages. A few short years opened the way for exciting studies of air and altitude.

A big step came when the vague idea suggested by Aristotle and Empedocles—that air had substance—was brilliantly restated in 1618 by a young student, Isaac Beeckman, who wrote in his doctoral thesis: "It happens that air, in the manner of water, presses upon things and compresses them according to the depth of the super-incumbent air." Beeckman and others opened new windows on the natural world. From his bold pronouncement it followed that air must be flexible and could be expanded, even far enough to create a vacuum.

This put Beeckman in direct conflict with the Catholic Church and also with the distinguished Galileo Galilei, who accepted Aristotle's somewhat ambiguous position that air had weight, even while arguing that a vacuum could not exist. Beeckman persisted: Air did weigh something, and it was also elastic and compressible. His career suffered from this heresy, but he was twenty years ahead of a monumental experiment that would show his intuitive statement to be correct. Soon after, others began to challenge the Church and Aristotle with direct experiments.

Creation of a Vacuum

One of the early challenges came from Giovanni Baliani, who made an experiment with a long hose. When the hose was filled with water and extended from a tub of water over a small elevation, it acted as a siphon, drawing water from the higher end, sending it over the rise, and discharging it at the lower. But if the elevation was too high, the siphon failed and water simply ran out of each end. Baliani described this in a long letter to Galileo in 1630, implying that the weight of the air pushed the column of water up the hose, but could not do so if the siphon were too high. Galileo had a different explanation because he still would not accept the idea that a vacuum could exist. Three months later, Baliani wrote again, clearly stating his agreement with Beeckman, and added, "The higher you go in the air, the lighter it is." He concluded that the siphon failure was due to the formation of a vacuum in the hose.

The first firm proof that air had weight came from a young Italian mathematician and astronomer, Gaspar Berti. Berti was modest and left little record of what he did or why, so we rely on his philosopher friend Emmanuel Maignan, who described the great experiment that Berti did in Rome between 1640 and 1642 (see Figure 2B), in the presence of a handful of friends, all scientists, all churchmen. They too wrote accounts, differing only slightly in details.

From his experiment (see sidebar, overleaf), Berti concluded that there must be a vacuum between the water and the upper sealed end of the tube, which was exactly what he hoped to show was present in order to convince Galileo of the existence of a vacuum. But, more importantly, Berti had made the first barometer!

Little publicity attended this epoch-making demonstration, but word soon reached physicist Evangelista Torricelli, a devoted student of Galileo's. He immediately recognized its importance and took the next great step: He substituted mercury for water, which reduced the necessary length of the tube from 34 feet to 40 inches. Mathematician René Descartes later added a scale—which converted the device into a measuring instrument.

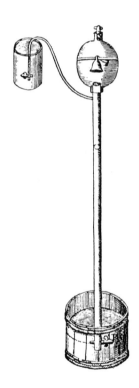

Figure 2A. *Gaspar Berti's barometer, ca. 1642*

THE FIRST BAROMETER

Gaspar Berti wanted to prove to Galileo that a vacuum could exist. Probably he knew about Giovanni Baliani's demonstration (ca. 1630) of the limitations of a siphon, and planned his own experiment a decade later to prove Baliani right. He erected a long leaden pipe against the wall of his house and filled it with water. The pipe was closed by a stopcock at the bottom end, which was then immersed in a tub of water. The upper end was then filled with water and then closed with a stopcock, and the lower stopcock opened (see Figure 2A). Supported by the atmospheric pressure on the water in the tub, water in the pipe fell in the tube to a level some 34 feet above the level in the lower reservoir, leaving a vacuum at the top, which he demonstrated by closing the lower stopcock and opening the upper stopcock.

W. E. K. Middleton wrote a scholarly book, *The History of the Barometer*, about this first experiment, showing how Galileo's student Evangelista Torricelli recognized its importance and went on to make the barometer we know today, using mercury instead of water. Berti had made his point and went back to his mathematics, leaving credit for this great accomplishment to Torricelli. Robert Boyle, of London's newly formed Royal Society, quickly made a number of different models using glassware (see Figure 2B), and foresaw how useful the device might be in predicting weather.

The Barometer

In a famous letter dated June 11, 1644, Torricelli took another step toward understanding altitude, referring to Berti's experiment:

I have already hinted to you that some sort of philosophical experiment was being done concerning the vacuum; not simply to produce a vacuum, but to make an instrument which might show the changes in the air, now heavier and coarser, now lighter and more subtle . . . above the peaks of very high mountains air begins to be very pure, and of very much less weight . . . [than at sea level].

Torricelli went further in an experiment planned to determine the nature of the vacuum at the upper end of the tube: He placed a mouse in the lower reservoir of his barometer and allowed it to swim up through the mercury to the empty space. The mouse died, but it was not clear whether from struggling through the mercury or because of the vacuum at the top. He tried fish and butterflies and other animals with little success. Others quickly made different models of his barometer and did many ingenious experiments.

Once he accepted the firm evidence of atmospheric pressure, Torricelli suggested that he might be able to observe (and perhaps predict) changes in weather, as Robert Boyle would do a few years later. He described the atmosphere, which he estimated might be 50 miles thick, in words almost identical to Beeckman's:

> We live submerged at the bottom of an ocean of elementary air which is known by incontestable experiments to have weight, and so much weight, that the heaviest part near the surface of the earth weighs about one four hundredth as much as water. . . .

Torricelli's prestige and his rapid-fire studies did attract notice among scientists, and very quickly an unseemly competition for recognition began. New players appeared, claiming to have had the idea first, or to have told Berti what to do. One Viviani Magni demonstrated the barometer in Poland, claiming it had been his idea in the first place. National pride was at stake, and French scientists claimed the honor for the city of Rouen. The squabble spread to other countries; charges of forgery and falsification of documents flew back and forth. It was all unfortunately similar to the competition among some scientific communities today.

Still more evidence for understanding the effect of altitude was needed, solid proof that air was really thinner and weighed less on mountains, as Giovanni Baliani had predicted. Just who pressed for the definitive experiment remains unclear; it may have sprung from a demonstration of the barometer that was staged by physicists Pierre Petit and Blaise Pascal (who had a flair for the dramatic). Among the audience was Pascal's brother-in-law, Florin Perier.

A few years after Berti's experiment, Perier carried a Torricellian barometer up a small mountain, the Puy de Dôme, and after carefully preparing his control observations at the foot of the mountain, showed that the mercury was lower on the summit (see Figure 3). The importance of this neat little project immediately prompted other claimants for priority, one of whom, already widely known, may have suggested the idea—but Perier did the necessary work before others. Perhaps Perier realized that this was a great moment in the history of science, and his astonishment suggests that he really did not expect it—and his nicely designed experiment was quite unbiased! But whose idea was it?

Young Blaise Pascal, already a distinguished mathematician, claimed credit for the idea in a letter to Perier, the date of which has been challenged.

Figure 2B. *Robert Boyle's barometer, 1665*

AIR WEIGHS LESS THE HIGHER ONE GOES

On September 18, 1648, Florin Perier filled two Torricellian barometers with redistilled mercury (to remove all air) and meticulously compared the readings in the courtyard of a monastery at the foot of a small mountain, the Puy de Dôme (3,500 feet). With him were several distinguished local citizens to attest to the experiment. Leaving a monk, Father Chastin, to record the readings at the monastery, the party carried one barometer up the path, pausing halfway up and again at the top to measure the height of the mercury. Between the readings at the bottom and the top of the mountain, Perier later wrote that "there was a difference of 3 inches and one and a half lines which ravished us all with admiration and astonishment and surprised us so much that for our own satisfaction we wished to repeat it"—which of course they did.

When they returned to the monastery, Father Chastin assured them that the level of the mercury had not changed, and indeed it showed the same as in the instrument brought back from the summit.

Figure 3. *Perier uses a Torricellian barometer*

Descartes might also have done so, and certainly the idea had been around for some time. Anonymous pamphlets were published, dates of documents were altered; it was all quite nasty for several years and has surfaced now and then ever since. Only one fact is unquestioned: Florin Perier did the work.

Priority in science is a will-o'-the-wisp; few great ideas have sprung fully hatched from a single person, and all of us learn from the work of those who have gone before. As Lucan wrote at the start of the Christian era: "Even pygmies, placed on the shoulders of giants, can see further than the giants can." The exact sequence of events from 1640 to 1645, who did what when, and whose ideas inspired successive steps, are debatable and not terribly important. Torricelli gave us the mercury barometer by using Berti's demonstration, and his device, with many refinements, is the basic instrument we use today, and it is quite fitting that his name should be remembered in the units of measurement—torr. But at the same time, let us honor and respect Gaspar Berti for his imaginative and almost forgotten experiment, and honor Florin Perier as well.

There it is in the span of one short decade—proof that a vacuum could exist, recognition of the weight of the atmosphere, and invention of a sensitive instrument with which to measure atmospheric pressure. Word of these experiments spread rapidly through Europe.

The Royal Society

In 1645 a small group of men soon to become imperishably famous, calling themselves "The Invisible College," met in London to discuss scientific subjects. Soon they were meeting regularly, and by 1660 were chartered as The Royal Society. They began studies of the atmosphere, recognizing that the experimental *proof* by Berti and Torricelli had established that air had weight and, equally important, that a vacuum could be produced with a new kind of pump.

Otto von Guericke, Mayor of Magdeburg in Bavaria (later made baron), had built a pump with which he sucked water out of wine barrels, and found that the weight of the atmosphere caused these to collapse. In 1654, in a dramatic demonstration of atmospheric pressure, he fitted together two copper hemispheres, carefully made to be airtight, and then pumped the air out of the sphere. Then he showed that two teams of horses could not pull the hemispheres apart until the vacuum inside the sphere was released—because of the weight of the atmosphere.

Robert Boyle, a prime mover in the new Royal Society, asked his assistant Robert Hooke to improve on von Guericke's pump. Hooke was curator of the Society and charged with bringing to the meetings several new experiments each week.

The *Proceedings of the Royal Society of London* during an incredibly productive five years are a fascinating record of many ingenious and imaginative experiments of many kinds. The Society heard tales from travelers and examined strange minerals, plants, and animals. They were an extraordinary group of scholars. Many of their experiments used the "New Pneumatical Engine" to examine all sorts of animals, snakes, insects, fish, and materials like wood and cork and rock in a vacuum.

One of the most significant glimpses into the future came when a mouse and a lighted candle were placed under a bell jar, which was then evacuated. Over and over again Hooke and Boyle found that the candle went out a short time before the mouse died. This led to the mistaken belief that life and combustion were fueled differently.

After many experiments on animals, plants, and nonliving materials, in

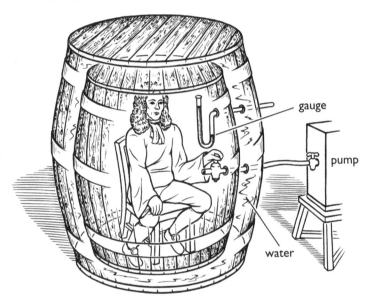

Figure 4. *Hooke's barrel*

THE FIRST DECOMPRESSION CHAMBER

In 1654 Otto von Guericke's vacuum pump attracted immediate attention, and Fellows of the young Royal Society commissioned the curator, Robert Hooke, to build an improved model. After many years of experiments in the vacuum made possible by the pump, Hooke was asked to make a vessel large enough to hold a man. After some time, he described this to the Society, and in 1671 demonstrated its use in his home. Watched by several other members, he entered the barrel, an assistant operated the pump, and Hooke was "taken up" about 4,000 feet. Considering what had happened to animals under an evacuated bell jar, this was rather brave, and so far as I have found, the barrel was not used again.

December 1670 Hooke proposed to make a vessel large enough to hold a man, from which air could be extracted with his pump. There was some delay, but on February 2, 1671, Hooke reported in the *Proceedings of the Royal Society of London*:

> . . . that the air-vessel for a man to fit in was ready. . . . Being asked how it was contrived, he said that it consisted of two tubs, one included in the other; the one to hold a man, the other filled with water thereby to keep it staunch; with tops to put on with cement, or to take off; one of them having a gage to see to what degree the air is rarefied; as also a cock to be turned by the person who sits in the vessel.

Finally Hooke entertained the members of the Society in his rooms to demonstrate the device. He entered the inner barrel, the outer one sealing it with water, and one-tenth of the air was extracted by his pump. This "took him up" to about 4,000 feet, and he noticed no discomfort save for slight pressure in his ears when the experiment was ended. The first human study in a decompression chamber had been completed. It was a courageous experiment, in view of what had been learned from mice and other forms of life, and perhaps it is not surprising that there seems to be no record of its being repeated for a hundred years.

Composition of Air

By 1660 Boyle had repeated Berti's experiment and had made many types of Torricellian barometers. He knew all about the Perier/Torricelli experiment and probably had read descriptions of the symptoms suffered by Jesuit missionaries Father Alonzo Ovalde and Father Jose Acosta while crossing the high Andes (see Chapter 6, AMS: Acute Mountain Sickness). He corresponded with many other travelers who had been on high mountains. All this confirmed Perier's observation that air was thinner the higher one went, but did little to answer the question of what substance in air was necessary for life or combustion. Boyle tried to explain:

> . . . the atmospherical air consists of three different kinds of corpuscles . . . first these numberless particles . . . in the form of vapors . . . the second more subtle consists of those exceedingly minute atoms, the magnetic effluvia of earth . . . the third sort is its characteristic and essential property, I mean permanently elastic parts.

Boyle did not continue these studies, which might have led him to discover oxygen, but John Mayow, a lawyer turned physician and a prominent member of the Royal Society, picked up Boyle's theory and suggested that the atmosphere consisted of two kinds of gases, one of which he called "nitro-aerial particles," which were necessary for the support of life and combustion. The other would not support either life or combustion. He showed this by burning a candle under a bell jar sealed with water, and watched the water level rise in the bell jar as the candle slowly went out. Then he showed that a mouse confined in a small bell jar consumed the air in the jar, and soon died.

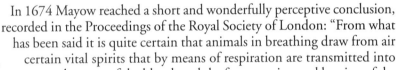

LIFE CANNOT EXIST IN A VACUUM

The vacuum pump was used to examine anything that caught the fancy of the Fellows of the Royal Society: stones, fish, wood, minerals, liquids, and a great variety of living animals. In the mid-1600s, John Mayow found that a mouse could not live very long in the evacuated bell jar, concluding that something in air was essential to life. But proof would not come for a hundred years.

Figure 5. *Bell jar and mouse*

In 1674 Mayow reached a short and wonderfully perceptive conclusion, recorded in the Proceedings of the Royal Society of London: "From what has been said it is quite certain that animals in breathing draw from air certain vital spirits that by means of respiration are transmitted into the mass of the blood, and the fermentation and heating of the blood are produced by it."

Some believe that Mayow deserves credit for so clearly showing the necessity for life and combustion of a "vital substance" (which would be christened "oxygene" 150 years later). Alas, to history he remains in the background—but a major player.

Despite wars, famine, plagues, and other difficulties that made travel slow and uncertain, word of new ideas and discoveries did spread throughout Europe surprisingly fast. In Denmark Olaus Borrichius (aka Ole Borch) also theorized that air contained a special life-giving substance and in 1678 actually isolated oxygen from the decomposition of potassium nitrate—but he did not appreciate the importance of what he had done and remains unrecognized.

Carbon Dioxide

Much earlier in the seventeenth century a restless, unorthodox Belgian scholar, Johann Baptista Van Helmont, had coined a new word, *gas,* to describe a substance different from solids and liquids. He made carbon dioxide by dripping acid over limestone, and showed that this was the same gas which, heavier than air, pooled in the bottom of a famous cave (La Grotte de Cane) in Italy, where dogs who entered perished but their taller masters survived. He went on to show that his new gas would extinguish fire and would not support life. It was still too early to relate this to combustion.

A century later Joseph Black found that what he christened "fixed aire" was formed by burning charcoal. Furthermore, in an ingenious experiment, he arranged for the air exhaled by 1,500 people during ten hours inside a church at a religious gathering to pass through a ceiling vent and over rags saturated with limewater. By weighing the calcium carbonates thus formed, he showed that the expired gases contained what he called "fixed aire"; it was carbon dioxide. Thus, even before oxygen was isolated, the gas exhaled during respiration and generated by combustion, and presumably by bodily functions too, had been identified.

The next step would be to determine what this "aerial spirit" or "vital essence" really was, and to connect it clearly with combustion of inert materials, and with the metabolism of living animals.

△

Oxygen
THE VITAL ESSENCE

ONCE THE EXISTENCE OF A VACUUM AND PROOF THAT AIR HAD WEIGHT HAD been demonstrated by Berti, Torricelli, and Perier in the seventeenth century, the composition of the atmosphere began to attract more attention. By the middle of the eighteenth century, it had become clear that air, or some part of it, was essential for life. In fact that essential part had been isolated several times during the previous 200 years (and even earlier)— though it was not recognized as such. Finally came the climactic experiment, by a British clergyman, Joseph Priestley, who wrote in his laboratory notes on November 21, 1774:

> I procured a mouse and put it into a glass vessel containing two ounce measures of the air obtained from mercuris calcinatus. Had it been common air, a full grown mouse such as this was would have lived in it about a quarter of an hour. In this air, however, my mouse lived a full half hour.
>
> I did not certainly conclude that this air was any better because, though one mouse would live only a quarter of an hour in a given quantity of air, I knew it was not impossible but that another mouse might have lived in it for half an hour. [So I] procured another mouse and putting it into less than two ounce measures of air extracted from mercuris calcinatus . . . I found it lived three quarters of an hour. Being now fully satisfied of the goodness of this kind of superior air I proceeded to measure that degree of purity with as much accuracy as I could.

This is the first clear and unequivocal description of how essential for life is the unique substance we now know as oxygen.

Long before this, however, in A.D. 756, a Chinese scientist, Nao Hoa, had generated a "purified" air by heating potassium nitrate to produce oxygen, but history does not tell us whether he did anything with it. Pliny the Elder wrote in his *Natural History* that Roman well-diggers would lower a lighted lamp into the well, deciding that if the lamp went out, the air was dangerous for them to breathe. Anticipating Robert Boyle by 150 years, Leonardo Da Vinci recognized that "air" in which fire would not burn would not support life either.

Alchemists in the sixteenth and seventeenth centuries, trying to change base metals into gold, had released oxygen by heating mercuric oxide, potassium nitrate, or lead oxide, but although they saw that this "gas" supported fire and life, few seem to have asked why: Their interests lay in other directions. The "philosopher's stone" they sought would not only miraculously cure disease but also make them wealthy; the "gas" was only a distraction.

Phlogiston

While the brilliant members of the fledgling Royal Society were exploring the relationship of air to fire and life, Danish chemist Georg Stahl proposed a theory that all combustible materials contained an impalpable substance, which his followers called *phlogiston,* or "fire substance," that enabled them to burn. But this idea was hard to sell, because some substances weighed more *after* they were burned. So his followers decided that phlogiston must have a property the opposite of weight—levity—which was what made the substance heavier when phlogiston was consumed or escaped during combustion. This seems rather absurd today, but it captured the minds of many scientists for a century.

Sixty years earlier, Jean Rey was puzzled by his own finding that some matter (he used tin) heated in air gained weight. He proposed that this was due to air, which somehow became "adhesive" and clung to the substance as it burned. Like the ancient Chinese and many alchemists, Ole Borch also had isolated oxygen, but he too has been forgotten.

Finally, between 1770 and 1773 Swedish pharmacist Carl Scheele, in an extraordinary and systematic series of experiments, not only generated a special gas but had the boldness to challenge the popular "phlogiston" theory, which did not endear him to his elders. He noted that his new gas supported life as well as combustion, and at first called this gas "vitriol air" but soon changed the name to "fire air."

During the same period in Paris, Antoine-Laurent Lavoisier, a young chemist from a well-to-do family, had been looking at oxidation of inorganic substances, and perhaps was interested in phlogiston. In 1772 he sent a letter to the French Academy describing this work, but asking that the letter be sealed until he was ready to publish.

On September 30, 1774, Scheele wrote Lavoisier thanking him for a book and added a description of his experiment. Scheele asked Lavoisier to repeat it, using his much larger burning glass to "reduce" silver carbonate in a bell jar sealed with water containing quick lime to combine with the "fixed air" (carbon dioxide), some of which he expected would be generated. Scheele did not tell Lavoisier what he had learned about this new gas, but explained that he sent him the information " . . . so that you will see how much air is produced by this reduction and whether a lighted candle can carry on its flame, and animals live in it," as Scheele already had found.

HOW TO MAKE OXYGEN

Over the centuries many alchemists had extracted a gas from different substances, but none realized that the gas was far more important than the precious metals they were trying to make. Among those who did, Swede Carl Scheele in the 1770s began studying the properties of a gas he extracted from silver carbonate. He soon showed that this gas would support life and fire in a confined space, and sought help from prominent French chemist Antoine-Laurent Lavoisier, who had a very powerful magnifying glass with which he could concentrate the sun's rays to create a higher temperature than in a conventional furnace. Scheele asked Lavoisier to use this lens to make the new gas, to confirm Scheele's own observations.

Figure 6. *Lavoisier's compound lens.* (From *Oeuvres de Lavoisier, Tome III [mémoires de chimie et de physique]*. Paris: imprimerie impériale, 1865, planche 9. Reproduced with permission.)

Oxygen Recognized

Joseph Priestley, who had been studying a gas formed from fermentation, visited Lavoisier in October 1774, and the two probably discussed Scheele's letter. Both seemed to sense that something important was close at hand, because right after their meeting they each hurried home to isolate the new gas using slightly different methods.

On Saturday, November 19, 1774, Priestley set up the crucial experiment, but on Sunday he was occupied at church, and not until Monday did he actually generate oxygen, as described in the preceding section. Excited by what he had done with the mouse, he took another step, as a good scientist would, and in his lab notes added an appealing personal note:

> My reader will not wonder that, after having ascertained the superior goodness of dephlogisticated air by mice living in it and the other tests mentioned, I should have the curiosity to taste it myself. I have gratified that curiosity, by breathing it, drawing it through a glass siphon, and, by this means I reduced a large jar full of it to the standard or common air. The feeling of it to my lungs was not sensibly different from that of common air but I fancied my breast felt peculiarly light and easy for some time afterwards. Who can tell but that in time this air may become a fashionable article in luxury. Hitherto only two mice and myself have had the privilege of breathing it.

It didn't take long for his prediction to come true: Within two years, others throughout Europe were using the new gas to treat many different conditions but with predictably mixed results.

Priestley described his work to the Royal Society in a letter dated March 15, 1775, which was accepted and formally read to the Society on March 23. This was the first formal announcement of the isolation of oxygen.

Five weeks later, on April 26, 1775, Lavoisier read to the French Academy his own paper describing oxygen. The existence of oxygen had been confirmed. There followed years of controversy, but debating who was first to "discover" oxygen is irrelevant. There is ample honor for both of these men, but their unsung predecessors should not be forgotten.

Then Lavoisier went further; he placed guinea-pigs in pure oxygen and found that they died from a "burning fever and an inflammatory illness." He soon concluded that "Healthy air is therefore composed of a good proportion between vital air (oxygen) and atmospheric moffete (nitrogen); . . . when there is an excess of vital air the animal undergoes a severe illness; when it is lacking, death is almost instantaneous." Others quickly confirmed the toxicity of pure oxygen.

Scheele also continued his studies, and at about this same time recognized the importance of his new gas, writing:

. . . our atmosphere consists of two very different kinds of air: the one is called corrupted air, because it is dangerous and fatal as well to living animals as to vegetables; it constitutes the greatest part of our atmosphere. The other is called pure air, fire air. This kind of air is salutary, supports respiration, and consequently the circulation; without it we could form no distinct idea, either of fire, or how it is kindled. It constitutes but the smallest part of the whole atmosphere. Now as we know this air is of the most immediate necessity for the support of our health.

Unfortunately his book was delayed for two years by a dilatory publisher and appeared after Priestley and Lavoisier had published their papers, so Scheele has not shared in their fame. But he continued his work, and a few years later stated that air always consisted of the same percentage (27 percent) of "fire air." This puzzled him; because both combustion and respiration consumed oxygen and formed "corrupted air," he had expected that the composition of air would vary from place to place, but he reached no conclusion about why it did not!

Oxygen From Plants

Even before he isolated his "dephlogisticated air," Priestley had started some pioneering studies with plants, the great importance of which would soon be recognized (see Figures 7 and 8). His was the first demonstration that plants can convert carbon dioxide into oxygen.

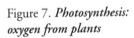

Figure 7. *Photosynthesis: oxygen from plants*

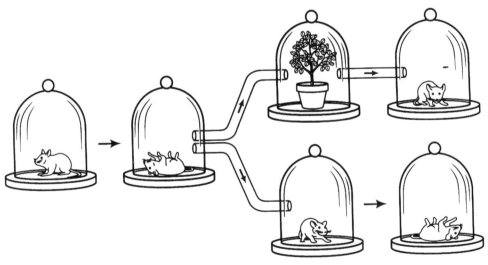

In Paris Benjamin Franklin, envoy from the rebellious American colonies, hearing about these experiments with plants, wrote several letters to friends calling Priestley's experiment very important, and adding:

> I hope this will give some check to the rage of destroying trees that grow near houses, which has accompanied our late improvements in gardening. . . . We Americans have everywhere our country habitations in the midst of woods, and no people on earth enjoy better health or are more prolific.

Priestley's experiment of growing mint in "corrupted" air led in a few years to an equally momentous discovery by Jan Ingenhousz, a Dutch physician who showed that green plants can isolate oxygen from "common aire" when exposed to sunlight—the first demonstration of photosynthesis.

Ingenhousz also advocated the use of Priestley's new gas for treatment of various illnesses, as did many other physicians hurrying to demonstrate Priestley's prediction that this pure air would become fashionable. Thomas Beddoes, a leading proponent of therapeutic oxygen, expected considerable benefit from oxygen in a variety of diseases, and founded a Pneumatic Institute in England, with Humphrey Davy as superintendent. Davy soon moved into other major studies for which he was later knighted. Others used the new gas for asthma, tuberculosis, and many other illnesses, with predictably variable success, before the fad subsided.

PLANTS CAN CONVERT BAD AIR TO GOOD AIR

Joseph Priestley was a very careful researcher who understood the importance of controls in his experiments. Three years before he isolated oxygen, he did a well-planned experiment that was almost as important in the broad scheme of life. From his lab notes: "On the 17th of August, 1771, I put a sprig of mint into a quantity of air, in which a candle had burned out, and found on the 27th of the same month [that] another candle burned perfectly well in it. . . . I took a quantity of air made thoroughly noxious by mice breathing and dying in it, and divided it into two parts; one of which I put into a phial immersed in water, and into the other . . . I put a sprig of mint. . . . and after eight or nine days I found that a mouse lived perfectly well in that part of the air in which the sprig of mint had grown, but died the moment it was put into the other part of the same original quantity of air, and which I had kept in the very same exposure, but without any plant growing in it." The fact that green plants can convert carbon dioxide into oxygen makes life possible for all animals on this earth today.

Oxygen as a Component of Air

By the end of the eighteenth century, the phlogiston theory was effectively dead, though a few scientists—among them, surprisingly, Priestley—never completely abandoned it; and the composition of air had been approximated. The next question was whether Scheele was right that air everywhere contained the same amount of "oxygene," or did it vary from place to place? Priestley and others soon devised tests to measure the proportion of oxygen in air, and most found that it was the same everywhere, but in his lab notes Priestley wrote:

> Doctor Ingenhousz discovered that the atmosphere at Vienna contains a greater proportion of vital air than in Holland and to this he attributes the remarkable increase in appetite felt by strangers on their arrival in Vienna.

Lavoisier too relied on imperfect analytical methods when he reported that the percentage of oxygen was 18.5 percent at floor level but 25 percent at ceiling level in a hospital ward, and he urged that society be alerted to these health hazards.

Lavoisier would be executed during the Reign of Terror in 1794, along with thirty-two "ex-nobles and former Farmers tried and convicted of conspiracy against the State." Priestley at first defended the principles of the French Revolution, but was disenchanted by the extremism during the Reign of Terror. A mob destroyed his laboratory, and two years later his anti-revolutionary sentiments led him to flee to Philadelphia, where he lived for the next ten years.

These two, building on those who had gone before, established the importance of oxygen. Like others before them, they asked why, if combustion and life were equally dependent on oxygen, did not the heat generated in living tissues consume them as it did other substances when they were ignited? It would be almost another hundred years before this question was answered.

In a short decade, several brilliant men had put one more piece of the puzzle of air, fire, and life on the table, but a few more pieces were needed before the relationship of oxygen to altitude sickness would be understood. How did life-supporting oxygen enter lungs and blood to be carried throughout the body? In the next two chapters I describe breathing and circulation and the substance that carries the essential gas.

PART II

How Our Body Gets Oxygen

$\triangle$

Moving Air
RESPIRATION

EVERYTHING WE DO—THINKING OR DREAMING, RUNNING OR CLIMBING mountains, eating, getting angry or making love—all require an uninterrupted supply of this "vital spirit"—oxygen—to release the energy to breathe, to pump the blood, move the muscles, secrete hormones, and excrete wastes.

Lavoisier named it "oxygene." Scheele, Boyle, Priestley, and forgotten others made it clear that all animals required it to live, to "burn" foodstuffs that fuel every activity, much as a candle must have air in order to burn. This wasn't really new: Long before these great men, the Chinese recognized that a continuing supply of "good" air was necessary to support most life.

Respiration brings air into the body, and the beating heart propels oxygen in blood to all parts of the body through the circulation. Breathing and moving blood are—as they must be—beautifully coordinated.

During the age of the Pharaohs, Egyptian physicians accurately described the respiratory tract through which air was drawn into the chest. Centuries later Greco-Roman philosopher-scientists taught that the purpose of breathing was to cool the "innate heat" of the heart. They developed various theories about how air entered the blood, mixing with it to form *pneuma,* which could be found in both arteries and veins.

Galen, the best-known physician at the start of the Christian era, described the process of breathing. His explanation is sometimes vague because, even though he could not accept the notion of a vacuum, he did believe that air was drawn into the lungs by expansion of the chest, and supported this concept by showing that the lungs collapsed when the chest was opened. For the next 1,500 years, Galen's theory went unchallenged.

Then in 1640 Gaspar Berti's demonstration of a vacuum, showing that air had weight, revived interest in Galen's theory that during inspiration the thorax actively expanded, so that air was pushed into the lungs by the weight of the atmosphere. When the thoracic muscles and diaphragm relaxed, Galen saw that the expanded thorax returned to its relaxed position, and air flowed out. "Sucked in" or "pushed in"—it's a fine but important distinction. During his studies in 1674 of the vital spirit in air, John Mayow described the process of breathing, and wrote in the *Proceedings of the Royal Society of London*:

> With respect then to the entrance of air into the lungs, I think it is to be maintained that it is caused . . . by the pressure of the atmosphere. For as the air, on account of the superincumbent atmosphere . . . rushes into all empty places . . . it follows that air passes through the nostrils and the trachea up to the bronchia. . . . When the inner sides of the thorax . . . are drawn outwards by muscles . . . and the space in the thorax is enlarged, the air which is nearest the bronchio-inlets . . . rushes under the full pressure of the atmosphere into the cavities of the lungs. . . . From this we conclude that the lungs are distended by air rushing in, and that they do not expand of themselves, as some have supposed.

Sylvius, aka Franciscus de la Boe had written much the same thing in 1660:

> The lungs do not move naturally of their own motion but they follow the motion of the thorax and the diaphragm. . . . The lungs are not expanded because they are filled with air, they are filled with air because they are expanded.

Another pioneer, mathematics professor Giovanni Borelli, friend and disciple of Galileo, applied his imagination and talent to physiology and also recognized that breathing air was essential for life in animals. Borelli made the new and important observation that air dissolved in water could pass through certain membranes, and thus pioneered the principles of the diffusion of gases, which are basic in respiration.

These theories were beginning steps toward understanding how the essential part of air moves from the surrounding atmosphere, into the lungs, and onward toward the living cells. Today we call this the oxygen transport system: the process of acquiring, transporting, delivering, and using oxygen.

The Oxygen Transport System

Oxygen is acquired by breathing in air, to fill the lungs, from which oxygen will diffuse into the blood. Oxygen is transported by the flowing blood, in which oxygen is loosely combined with the red pigment called *hemoglobin*. Oxygen is delivered when the large blood vessels, dividing into ever smaller ones, end in capillaries barely large enough for the red cells to tumble through. There oxygen leaves hemoglobin and diffuses both into the fluid-filled tissue around our living cells and into the cells themselves. Utilization of oxygen—for which the whole system is organized—takes place in tiny parts (*mitochondria)* inside each cell. There oxygen is used to release energy, which takes many forms depending on the type of cell.

The oxygen transport system is beautifully suited to its task. It is flexible and can double its capacity by changes in each stage, swiftly responsive to many feedback loops. It is specially designed to carry oxygen unless interfered with by a rare alien such as carbon monoxide or cyanide. It has multiple checks and balances and redundant control points that function so smoothly, we are seldom aware of them. And it is multi-tasked: Respiration partnered with blood maintains a constant body temperature, stable acidity, and a suitable level of body water. Blood carries free passengers such as hormones (messenger substances) and enzymes (catalysts), as well as essential foods, as well as others like alcohol. Blood also carries away wastes such as the products of metabolism.

THE OXYGEN TRANSPORT SYSTEM

My good friend John Sutton used a deceptively simple diagram to show how oxygen is taken in and dispersed throughout the body. Inhaling brings air deep into the lungs (acquisition), where oxygen diffuses into the lung capillaries. Diffusion is defined by several factors. Arrived in the blood, oxygen is picked up by red blood cells (transportation), and its carriage is limited by the amount of circulating hemoglobin and its affinity for oxygen. The amount of oxygenated blood pumped by the heart is a function of blood pressure and the heart rate and stroke output (which together comprise cardiac output); these are controlled by several nervous impulses from within the heart as well as elsewhere in the body. After passing through increasingly smaller and widely branching blood vessels (delivery), blood carries oxygen into the capillary network throughout the body for diffusion into each living cell. The amount of oxygen delivered is affected by the blood flow in the capillary net and by the oxygen partial pressure, which dictates passage through capillary wall and cell membrane. Finally, the living cells everywhere in the body receive oxygen (utilization), more or less according to demand. In muscle a pigment resembling hemogolobin (*myoglobin)* is an extra safeguard against hypoxia by holding in reserve some oxygen until urgently needed. Other organs must take what they are given, but that is dictated too according to demand, as sensed by the nervous system.

Less appreciated but just as important as the transport of oxygen is carriage of carbon dioxide in the opposite direction—from cells to blood to lungs and outside air. Carbon dioxide is dissolved in the liquid portion of blood (plasma) and diffuses twenty times as rapidly as oxygen; some moves from the interstitial fluid and cells directly out through the skin, unlike oxygen, which does not enter or leave through skin.

The easy mobility of carbon dioxide enables rapid adjustment of the acidity of blood and tissues. If blood becomes too acid, we automatically breathe more deeply or faster to eliminate more carbon dioxide, which, dissolved in water, is a weak acid. Or, should we err on the alkaline side, our breathing tends to slow, and we hold back this weak acid.

To understand the human body's successful response to the stresses of high altitude, we need to look at each part of the oxygen transport system— acquisition, transportation, delivery, and utilization—as well as transport and discharge of carbon dioxide. Each responds individually and to the responses of the others as well.

Figure 8. *The oxygen transport system*

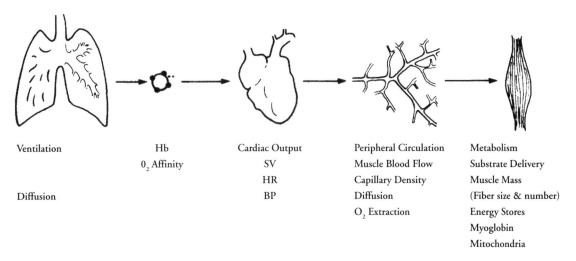

Ventilation	Hb	Cardiac Output	Peripheral Circulation	Metabolism
	O_2 Affinity	SV	Muscle Blood Flow	Substrate Delivery
		HR	Capillary Density	Muscle Mass
Diffusion		BP	Diffusion	(Fiber size & number)
			O_2 Extraction	Energy Stores
				Myoglobin
				Mitochondria

Acquisition: Mechanics of Breathing

Breathing in and breathing out is the first step in the oxygen transport system. For shorthand we call this *respiration* or *ventilation,* and, as Mayow pointed out, it's a purely mechanical function that, absent illness or injury, is automatic as well.

The chest is separated from the abdominal cavity by a great platelike muscle, the diaphragm, which Galen recognized was activated by the phrenic nerve from the brain. When relaxed, the diaphragm is domed upward into the chest cavity; when the diaphragm contracts, it flattens, enlarging the chest cavity. Simultaneously, small muscles positioned diagonally between the ribs contract, spreading the ribs and also enlarging the chest. Then air is pushed in by atmospheric pressure, and when the intercostal muscles and diaphragm relax, the chest wall (*thorax*), which is quite elastic, relaxes and becomes smaller; this is expiration.

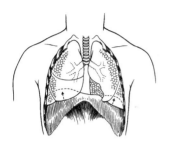

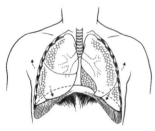

Figure 9. *The mechanics of breathing*

> ## THE MECHANICS OF BREATHING
> Even though he did not admit that a vacuum could exist, Galen taught that air was *drawn* into the lungs by the expansion of the thorax. His somewhat murky explanation was accepted for many centuries. Once a vacuum had been demonstrated, it became clear that air was *pushed* into the lungs when the chest expanded, creating a slight vacuum. This is accomplished by contraction of the diaphragm, which is domed upward when relaxed (during expiration). Flattening of this platelike muscle, together with contraction of short muscles diagonally placed between the ribs, enlarges the volume of the chest, making a vacuum that air rushes in to fill (*inspiration*). Relaxation of these muscles allows the elastic chest wall to contract, driving air out (expiration).

As outside air rushes in through the nose or mouth, it is warmed to body temperature and rapidly saturated with water vapor from the moist mucous lining of these passages. By the time air reaches the windpipe (trachea), it is warm and wet, otherwise it would chill and dry the delicate lung tissues.

The trachea splits into the two main *bronchi,* which in turn divide into smaller and smaller *bronchioles* that finally lead into the air cells (*alveoli*), where gas transfer takes place. In the adult lung there are about 300 million alveoli, whose total membrane lining has a combined area almost the size of a tennis court. Arrived in the alveoli, oxygen must pass into the lung capillaries—and carbon dioxide pass out—through the membrane enclosing each alveolus.

From Lungs to Blood: Diffusion of Gases
Borelli had demonstrated that air could pass through such a membrane, and it could be assumed that oxygen could do so. Soon it became necessary to ask a new question: If carbon dioxide was carried in the blood, and oxygen inhaled into the lung, could the two gases pass the lung membrane at the same time in opposite directions? Much later, in 1808, John Dalton provided the answer: "When a vessel contains a mixture of such elastic fluids (gases), each acts independently on the vessel . . . just as if the other were absent. . . . "

This was the crucial law of partial pressures, which said that the passage of a gas or gases through a membrane was dependent (among other things) on the difference in the pressure of each gas on the opposite sides of the membrane. Of course Dalton's law wasn't known in the seventeenth century, but those early workers recognized intuitively that it applied to the alveolar walls: Oxygen could pass into blood at the same time that carbon dioxide was passing out of it. Note that the partial pressure of nitrogen is the same on each side of all these membranes because it is inert and takes no part in body processes.

Scheele and others had shown that air everywhere on earth is made up of about 21 percent oxygen and the remainder is mostly nitrogen with traces of other gases. Today, by Dalton's law we easily calculate that the partial pressure of oxygen in air at sea level (barometric pressure 760 torr) is 20.93 percent of 760 torr, or roughly 160 torr. At 18,000 feet, where barometric pressure is half that at sea level, oxygen partial pressure is 20.93 percent of 380 torr, or about 80 torr. Dalton's law enables us to think of *oxygen partial pressure* and *partial pressure of carbon dioxide* and to use these in mathematical equations. We can think of oxygen as having "high" pressure in outside air, lower pressure in the lungs where it is diluted with carbon dioxide and water vapor, and still lower pressure by the time it has reached the cells. This we call the oxygen cascade.

The Oxygen Cascade

When we breathe in, the entering air mixes with the outgoing and has already picked up water vapor, which—like any other gas—has a partial pressure. This is 47 torr at body temperature, because air is fully saturated with water in the upper trachea. Together carbon dioxide and water vapor deep in the lungs reduce the partial pressure of oxygen there to about 100–110 torr (see Figure 10).

At each stage in oxygen's journey from outside air to lungs, into blood and on into cells, its partial pressure decreases. It is by minimizing the loss at each stage of the oxygen cascade that man is able to live and work at altitudes (or in environments) where the oxygen pressure is very low. This is the first part of acclimatization, and without changes in the oxygen cascade we could not survive at high altitude.

Between outside air and the depths of the lungs comes the first "drop" in the oxygen cascade (from atmospheric to alveolar oxygen). We decrease this drop by breathing faster and/or more deeply, bringing more fresh air deep into the lungs. But we can't reach ambient oxygen pressure because carbon dioxide is constantly entering the lungs, and because water vapor pressure is constant.

When we breathe in, oxygen moves through the trachea and bronchial tubes into the alveoli. Once in the innermost parts of the lung, oxygen must diffuse from alveolus into lung capillary. First it passes through the lining of the alveolus (the alveolar *epithelium* and *basement membrane*), then through the loose *interstitial space*, and finally through the capillary basement membrane and capillary *endothelium* and into the red blood cell. The single layer of cells lining the alveoli, and those lining the adjacent capillaries, are joined tightly together and are programmed to permit diffusion by oxygen, carbon dioxide, and some other gases, but not liquids or large molecular substances.

THE OXYGEN CASCADE

The partial pressure of oxygen in the air we breathe (atmospheric oxygen) decreases markedly in the lungs, where it mixes with water vapor and carbon dioxide (alveolar oxygen), and falls further during passage from the lungs into the blood (arterial oxygen). There's a further drop in the tissue capillaries (capillary oxygen) and during passage into the cells (mixed venous oxygen). It's convenient to compare this to a waterfall or cascade. The first drop (from atmospheric to alveolar) is by far the greatest, but is also the most sensitive to change: As ventilation increases, alveolar oxygen more closely approaches that of inhaled air (atmospheric oxygen). Obviously this improves oxygenation all the way to the cells. Increased breathing is the first and most important part of adjustment—and later acclimatization—to hypoxia.

Next, under normal conditions there is only a slight drop in oxygen as it passes from alveolus to blood (arterial oxygen). Finally, as blood courses into ever smaller vessels the oxygen pressure drops until, close to its destination, the oxygen pressure in blood (capillary oxygen) is only slightly higher than in the cells it is feeding.

At increasing altitudes, the changes of acclimatization decrease the oxygen pressure at almost every stage, as shown here in Figure 10.

Carbon dioxide moves in the opposite direction, from a high partial pressure in cells, into the capillary blood as it moves toward the venous capillaries and into larger and larger veins back to the heart and thence to the lungs, where its partial pressure is low.

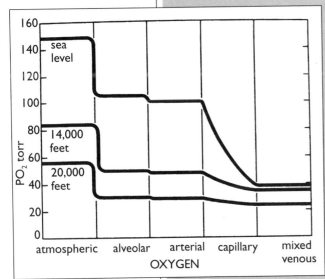

Figure 10. *The oxygen cascade*

The Aveolar-arterial Gradient

Passage through these layers causes another small drop in pressure, the second in the oxygen cascade, which we call the *Alveolar-arterial,* or *A-a, gradient.*

So large is the alveolar surface area that oxygen diffuses rapidly through the alveolar walls at sea level, where its partial pressure is much higher than in blood arriving in the lungs. Diffusion is complete in less than a half second at sea level, while a red blood cell takes eight-tenths of a second to traverse the capillary adjoining the alveolus. Transit or exposure time is not a limiting factor in loading oxygen into blood at sea level, though it may become so at very high altitude, or during prolonged and extreme exertion.

The normal resting A-a gradient in youth is 2–5 torr but it increases to 10–15 torr in old age. Usually—but not always—the A-a gradient increases during moderate or intense exercise. The few direct measurements of the gradient at extreme altitude show that it decreased to near zero at rest, but increased sharply with exertion.

Transportation: Blood Cells

The red cell is a selfless and versatile carrier: It has little need for the oxygen it carries and uses very little, which makes it a very efficient carrier. There is little drop in oxygen partial pressure while blood carries it to its destinations. In the arterial stage of the cascade, very little oxygen pressure is lost between the fluid portion of blood (plasma) and the red blood cell. The cascade is almost flat. (See Chapter 4, Moving Blood: Circulation, for more about blood cells.)

Delivery and Utilization: Capillaries and Cells

The final stage in the oxygen cascade is arrival in the capillaries, which spread everywhere through the body to deliver food and oxygen to living cells. From these tiny vessels, oxygen diffuses into the fluid in the interstitial space in which cells live and, thence, through another set of membranes, into the cell where the oxygen is utilized. The tissue capillaries do not have a muscular coat but are lined with endothelia in which the single cells are not tightly joined and have gaps between them, permitting passage of large molecules.

The major "purpose" of moving air and blood is to ensure an adequate supply of nutrients and oxygen in, as well as removal of carbon dioxide and other wastes from, the tissues. Direct measurement of the oxygen within living cells has only recently become possible and its wider application may change some of what we believe to be facts today. Almost a century ago, distinguished Swedish physiologist Christian Bohr described an integrative method to estimate tissue oxygenation; Joseph Barcroft, who became one of the pioneers in altitude research and wrote about his work and thoughts in a delightful style, carried it a step further, writing:

The mean tissue pO_2 is that pressure which, if it prevailed throughout the length of all the capillaries of the body, would not alter the quantity of oxygen diffusing from the capillaries to tissues from the quantity diffusing under actual physiological conditions.

This is based on the likely assumption that capillary oxygen is always higher than that in the cells. The formula gives a reasonably reliable indicator of how well (or poorly) the tissues are oxygenated. It's a practical approach to estimating the degree of hypoxia.

From Lungs to Blood, Revisited

Let us return briefly to the oxygen cascade between lungs and blood—the A-a oxygen gradient. As we measure it, this reflects the overall difference between alveolar and arterial oxygen pressures—it's an average for all parts of both lungs. We know that in different parts of the lung, the gradient is likely to be different depending on several important influences.

For one thing, the top (*apex*) of the lung is not as well ventilated as the rest of the lung. If there's some local obstruction like pneumonia in a part of the lung, that area may receive less air than normal lung tissue, while its blood flow is normal or even increased. If the alveolar walls are thickened by illness or swelling, oxygen passage from alveolus to blood will be slowed and the A-a gradient increased. On the circulatory side, blood flow may be impeded by any of several causes—by constriction or by small blood clots, for example—while ventilation is normal.

These are examples of imbalance or inequality between alveolar ventilation and circulation, which we call *ventilation-perfusion mismatch.* When mismatch exists, it can only increase the A-a gradient. Mismatch also results when some blood goes through vessels that bypass alveoli. These are called *shunts,* because blood transits the lung without being exposed to oxygen. Shunts occur in many people, but they are usually unimportant, although in extreme circumstances they may seriously hamper oxygen transport.

Early in the twentieth century, the neat oxygen diffusion theory was challenged by a major question: Does oxygen move through the alveolar-capillary barrier *only by diffusion,* or does the alveolar membrane *actively secrete* oxygen from lung to blood? Wouldn't it seem reasonable that for such an absolutely vital substance as oxygen, some additional protection—a fail-safe mechanism—should exist? Might oxygen actually be secreted from lung to blood in special circumstances, making the the A-a gradient negative?

After oxygen lack due to decreased barometric pressure had been shown to be the cause of mountain sickness, this question became even more compelling: Perhaps the answer would explain why some persons became ill while others did not. Finding the answer is an interesting story.

Oxygen Secretion Theory

In 1892 Christian Bohr confirmed earlier work by Baptiste Biot showing that the swim bladders of fish contained a very high concentration of oxygen; this appeared to violate Dalton's law and could be explained only by active oxygen secretion of oxygen from blood into the swim bladder.

Physiologist John Haldane and his assistant, Lorrain Smith, already studying how oxygen moved from lungs into blood, visited Bohr in 1894 and were intrigued by his suggestion that similar secretion might occur through the mammalian alveolar walls. To test this hypothesis, Haldane and Smith measured the oxygen pressure in their own alveolar air, calculated the arterial oxygen pressure using a carbon monoxide technique, and found the alveolar oxygen pressure lower than the arterial.

But by then Bohr's students Auguste and Marie Krogh had devised a more accurate method for measuring blood oxygen by equilibrating a bubble of air with blood and analyzing the oxygen in the bubble. With this technique they could not confirm their respected professor's findings. Reluctantly they published a series of brilliant papers in 1910 and started a famous controversy by their unequivocal statement: "The passage of [oxygen] and the elimination of carbon dioxide in the lungs takes place by diffusion and by diffusion alone."

Haldane and Smith's experiments led them to dispute the Kroghs' diffusion theory. In 1910 at a meeting in Vienna, Haldane met a young American, Yandell Henderson, who suggested that the summit of Pikes Peak in Colorado would be an ideal location to detect oxygen secretion if it took place. The following year Haldane and Henderson, with Englishmen Gordon Douglas and Edward Schneider, went to Pikes Peak to study acclimatization, including measuring oxygen pressure in alveolar air, and using the carbon monoxide method to estimate oxygen in arterial blood at rest and after exertion.

On Pikes Peak they found the calculated arterial oxygen pressure was always higher than the alveolar, which convinced Haldane that active oxygen secretion was a specific function of the lung that enabled humans to tolerate altitude. He proposed that differences between individuals in their susceptibility to mountain sickness were due to different degrees of secretion. His later studies did not shake this belief, even when confronted with contrary evidence collected by his former colleague, Joseph Barcroft.

Barcroft had begun his scientific career by studying the metabolism of salivary glands, and in 1901, together with Haldane, developed a method for measuring gases in small amounts of liquid. He found that the partial pressure of oxygen in saliva was higher than in the capillary blood in the salivary gland. At first he could explain this observation only by active oxygen secretion. Several years later, however, his study of factors changing the shape of the hemoglobin dissociation curve, and thus the oxygen content of blood, led him to re-examine his data and to renounce oxygen secretion in this instance.

Barcroft was called up in World War I to treat pulmonary edema caused by the military use of chlorine gas, but soon after the Armistice he returned to studies of other causes of hypoxia—such as high altitude. Because of his work with salivary glands, he did not accept oxygen secretion, but challenging the attractive oxygen secretion theory meant opposing his senior, Haldane, and trying to repeat his studies.

To do so, in 1920 Barcroft spent ten days in a sealed glass room where the oxygen was gradually decreased to the partial pressure equivalent of 18,000 feet. Using a method developed a few years earlier by Stadie, a physician at the Rockefeller Institute, Barcroft had a large needle (*cannula*) tied into his radial artery (which, as he wrote matter of factly, "of course had to be sacrificed"). Through this cannula he drew arterial blood and was able to measure oxygen directly at the same time that he collected his alveolar air sample. His data showed that his alveolar oxygen pressure was higher than the arterial.

Haldane countered that Barcroft had studied only himself, and when he was sick (perhaps from altitude?) at that. Haldane repeated and corrected his own studies, and argued that although secretion might not occur during rest or at normal atmospheric pressure, it was one of the means by which man adjusted or acclimatized to altitude. He correlated his data with clinical observations of those who had been sick or well on Pikes Peak but, again, he did not measure arterial oxygen directly.

The argument raged, of course in gentlemanly terms. Barcroft and a strong team went to Cerro de Pasco (14,200 feet) in Peru and, along with much other work, repeated the alveolar-arterial studies on themselves and on well-acclimatized altitude residents. Once again the alveolar air always contained a higher oxygen pressure than the arterial blood, even in the well-adapted natives. Haldane was wrong. This ended the oxygen secretion theory.

There remains, however, the faint possibility that at extreme altitude, the arterial blood may be slightly higher than the alveolar in acclimatized man. After all, there's the precedent in the swim bladder of fish . . .

Automatic Control of Breathing

From examination of the oxygen cascade it's obvious that we can best increase the partial pressure of oxygen in blood by improving alveolar ventilation—that is, by more efficient breathing. We are seldom conscious of our breathing because it is dictated by stimuli we only dimly perceive. The automatic control of breathing is one of the more fascinating chapters in human physiology and of course it is crucial to staying well at altitude and at sea level.

We know that strenuous exertion, sudden excitement, fear, passion, or even stepping under a cold shower makes us breathe faster or deeper, or both, even though there may not be any immediate, obvious demand for more oxygen. We know that during sleep our breathing becomes shallow, often irregular, and consequently our lungs are less well ventilated—an important effect at high altitude. How and where are these changes dictated?

It's obvious that strenuous exertion or fear-induced preparation for fight or flight require more than the customary supply of oxygen. Exertion calls for increased breathing to get rid of the accumulating carbon dioxide or lactic acid, or by stimuli to the brain from the working muscles. Fear is a more subtle stimulus: Breathing increases even before the demand for oxygen increases. A cold shower stimulates the skin nerve endings that direct blood flow to the skin and, again in anticipation, this calls for more breathing. Passion has both physical and emotional stimuli to greater effort and greater need for oxygen.

We also know that hypoxia *per se* stimulates breathing—this is an early and effective response to altitude (or a few other causes of oxygen lack). It's reasonable to expect that hypoxia would initiate instructions to breathe more deeply. It's also reasonable to expect that when carbon dioxide accumulates, breathing would be increased in order to wash out the excess. In fact, accumulation of carbon dioxide is a more powerful respiratory stimulant than is mild lack of oxygen: When you hold your breath at sea level, it is accumulation of carbon dioxide rather than lack of oxygen that forces you to breathe again.

Oxygen Sensors: The Carotid Bodies

Lack of oxygen in the arterial blood leaving the heart stimulates a small group of cells strategically sited along the carotid arteries on each side of the neck and richly supplied with blood vessels. These two collections of specialized cells are called the *carotid bodies*. When they sense a fall in blood oxygen, they send a signal to the brain, which in turn signals the respiratory muscles (chest and diaphragm) to increase rate and/or depth of breathing. Because oxygen is so crucial to life, the carotid bodies are a major first line of defense against an early threat of hypoxia.

Thirty years ago there was a fad to treat severe asthma by removal of one—and often both—carotid bodies. Nowhere is the resilience of the body better illustrated than by the continued survival of these patients; most stayed well, but a few were reported to have difficulty above 5,000 feet, possibly because they did not respond to hypoxia with adequate hyperventilation.

In some people, or under special circumstances, the center in the medulla, which controls how respiration responds to lack of oxygen, is less sensitive than normal. This is the hypoxic ventilatory response or HVR. Whether this is solely a fault in the carotid body or somewhere else in the neurotransmitter system is not clear. As a result of blunting, ventilation does not increase appropriately to the degree of oxygen lack.

The Brain's Respiratory Center

Although both lack of oxygen and excess carbon dioxide stimulate breathing, decreased carbon dioxide (but not excess of oxygen) slows breathing, while accumulation of excess carbon dioxide increases breathing. These and other stimuli are read by a collection of chemo-sensitive cells in the midbrain, called the respiratory center, from which appropriate corrective signals are sent by the brain. Like the thermostat in a house, which turns on the furnace when the temperature falls and turns it off when the house is too hot, the respiratory center responds to carbon dioxide and to changes in acidity of blood. The center also stimulates breathing under some conditions of hypoxia; it is an additional fail-safe device that protects those who have lost the function of their carotid bodies for some reason. The whole control system is exquisitely sensitive and versatile, responsive to blood and to spinal fluid (which is influenced, though slowly, by changes in the blood).

The carotid bodies and the respiratory center share most of the responsibility for maintaining the status quo of blood gases. They are critically important at high altitude.

Once oxygen has arrived in the lungs and diffused from the alveoli into the capillaries, it forms a loose bond with a substance in red blood cells and is propelled by the beating heart throughout the body.

Moving Blood
CIRCULATION

BREATHING IN AND OUT WOULD NOT BE VERY USEFUL WITHOUT SOME WAY to carry oxygen from lungs to the hungry cells, and to remove carbon dioxide. Wondrous though the whole process of breathing is, the circulatory system seems even more amazing.

It's fascinating to see how studies of the atmosphere gradually taught us more and more about breathing and the circulation and, from this, about high altitude and wellness or illness on mountains. The past can be our greatest teacher—if only we will listen.

A Chinese medical text, written early in the first century B.C. and quoted in Needham's book of Chinese history, gives a pretty good description of the circulation of the blood, even if the times and distances are a bit off. Though various translations differ, and portions of the text suggest that air was mixed together with blood in the vessels, it's a remarkable statement from the distant past:

> . . . the heart regulates all the blood in the body . . . the blood current flows continuously in a circle and never stops . . . a circle with no beginning and no end. Blood flows six inches with one respiration making a complete circuit of the body about fifty times in fourteen hours. . . .

Even earlier, in fact five centuries before Christ, the remarkable philosopher-scientist Empedocles, about whom much myth and some truth has survived, compared the circulation of the blood to the ebb and flow of the tides. Aristotle took the next step, observing that there were two types of blood, a "spiritual," which was purified by passing through the lungs, and a "venous," which moved through the rest of the body. He was the first to describe the branching of arteries and of veins from large to smaller and smaller, but, like his contemporaries, he thought the veins carried blood, while the arteries were filled with *pneuma,* a mixture of air and blood.

He was almost correct. Had he made the simple observations that Fabricius and William Harvey would make a thousand years later, he might have taken a giant stride and described how blood actually flows from heart to lungs, from lungs to body, and back to the heart and again to the lungs. But he did not, and instead he taught that there were two separate circulations. Much later Galen hypothesized how these were connected, mixing the two circulations. Galen had many opportunities to study anatomy, including the heart, lungs, and blood vessels. He was official surgeon for the gladiators, whose terrible wounds often exposed the functioning organs, and he also did many experiments on living animals.

Galen's Circulation Studies

Galen was the best-known and most influential physician of the Greco-Roman school, and made many fundamental studies by animal vivisection. He saw that the heart valves allow passage in only one direction, and he accepted the ancient belief that it was essential to life for air and blood to be distributed to all parts of the body—as of course it is. He thought that during respiration, air flowed from the lungs into the left side of the heart, where it both fueled and cooled the "innate heat" which was life itself. There air mixed with blood to form *pneuma,* which was then pumped through the arteries, which " . . . in the whole body . . . communicate with the veins and exchange air and blood with them through extremely fine invisible openings," as Galen is quoted in an article by D. Fleming.

But his dissections had shown that the arteries and veins contained only blood and no air. He escaped this quandary by some complicated speculations about anastomoses of arteries and veins in the lungs as well as elsewhere, and by postulating tiny pores between the two ventricles of the heart. He also believed that air entered arteries through the skin. Even though Galen did not fully understand the circulation in the lungs, his anatomical studies left an enduring and influential legacy to those who would later define the heart and circulation.

In 1553 Michael Servetus challenged Galen's dictum, defied the church, was charged with heresy, and was burned at the stake. Only a few copies of his great anatomical book survived, and show that he was convinced that blood flowed through the lungs to the heart, out to the body, and back through the heart to the lungs. He had no way to see or demonstrate the capillaries in the lung through which venous blood passes, becomes saturated with oxygen, and returns to the heart. Those connections were still to be found. Since most copies of his revolutionary book were burned with him, it's unlikely that William Harvey, whose work came less than a century later, saw one.

Then Belgian anatomist Andreas Vesalius challenged Galen more subtly:

"We are driven to wonder at the handiwork of the Almighty, by means of which blood from the right into the left ventricle sweats through passages which escape human vision." Vesalius also implied that air did not flow in blood vessels, but instead was bound to blood, but he never fully grasped what this meant to respiration and circulation.

In the thirteenth century, a Persian physician, Ibn-al-Nafis, stated that the blood followed the course we know today, and that the purpose of the lungs was to purify the blood. His theory was remarkably accurate, not only because he was forbidden by his religion to perform dissections, but also because he attributed "purification of the blood" to a process (oxygenation) that would not be discovered for four more centuries.

In 1524 other pioneers like Matteo Realdo Colombo and Renaldo Cesalpino, now largely forgotten, were also teaching correctly most of the pathways traveled by blood. For many centuries these and many other unknown scientists labored to understand the heart and circulation, and each contributed some small piece of the puzzle. William Harvey deserves the honor of solving the puzzle, not because he made a great new discovery, but because he had the genius to put together the observations of many others, and was able to explain, eloquently but simply, how the human circulation works.

Almost certainly Harvey did not know of Ibn-al-Nafis's work, which was published in Arabic and not discovered until 1924. Nor is it likely that he saw Servetus's book. Harvey buttressed his argument by calculating that in one hour the heart pumped blood weighing more than three times the weight of the entire body. Like Vesalius, he applied a simple tourniquet to the arm and showed that the veins contained valves that permitted blood to flow in only one direction. As Galen had done, he showed that valves in the heart also allowed only one-way blood flow. His synthesis was so masterful that it seemed no one could challenge him, but old beliefs die hard, and he was harshly attacked at home and abroad. Though stung, he refused to respond. Most of his contemporaries supported him, and he won acceptance from those who mattered most. Harvey was physician to Charles I, and later to James I; in 1628, prefaced with a letter to King Charles, his famous book *De Motu Cordis* was published. In it he wrote:

> Since calculations and visual observations have confirmed all my suspicions, to wit that the blood is passed through the lungs and the heart by the pulsations of the ventricles, is forcibly ejected to all parts of the body, therein steals into the veins and the porosities of the flesh, flows everywhere back through those very veins from the circumference to the center, from small veins into larger ones, and thence comes at last into the vena cava and to the auricle of the heart . . . I am forced to conclude that . . . the blood is driven around with an unceasing circular sort of movement.

This is what some of his predecessors had fumbled with, and Harvey sorted through many bits of information to prove it. Four years after Harvey's death, Marcello Malpighi, using the newly developed microscope, was able to add the missing bit when he saw the tiny capillaries (which Harvey called "porosities"), confirming Harvey's speculations. With this demonstration, Harvey's description of the continuity of the vessels that carry blood through the lungs and to all parts of the body was complete and confirmed.

The Heart

Central to circulation, of course, is the heart, celebrated by poets and lovers; but, as physiologists know, it is nothing but a tireless mechanical pump. If it has emotional or spiritual qualities, these have yet to be found, though we do know that the heart does produce at least one hormone that stimulates other organs.

Figure 11. *The circulatory system*

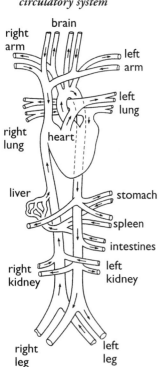

> ## THE CIRCULATORY SYSTEM
> Shown here is the circulatory system as we know it today, with the branching arteries that carry venous blood pumped by the right ventricle to the lungs and the veins, which return oxygenated blood to the left auricle and ventricle, which in turn pumps arterial blood throughout the body. Through a network of veins, blood flows back to the right auricle and ventricle and is pumped to the lungs.
>
> Aristotle came close to understanding the circulation of the blood when he recognized the difference between venous and arterial blood. Galen came closer when he realized that blood could flow in only one direction through the heart valves, and hypothesized that Aristotle's two systems were connected through the heart. Michael Servetus had the bold courage to challenge Galen's theory and was executed for his beliefs, but left the base on which William Harvey would describe the circulation accurately and in detail. Some years after Harvey's death, Marcello Malpighi saw the capillaries that linked arteries and veins, and he completed our understanding of the circuit.

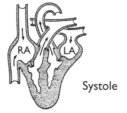

Systole

Diastole

Small granules in the muscle fibers of the atria secrete the hormone atrionatriuretic peptide (ANP), which has a powerful effect on salt and water balance. Because ANP increases the output of urine—and of sodium—it's believed to play an important role in the spectrum of mountain sicknesses.

In an average person, leading a placid, undisturbed, and inactive life for seventy-five years, the heart will beat some 2400 million times and pump about 40 million gallons of blood. Of course in our real lives, with excitement, exertion, and stress, these figures are likely to be more than half again higher. That's a lot of work for a small, self-driven, living organ.

After the Royal Society was formed in the seventeenth century, experiments with the heart and blood vessels began to flourish. Stephen Hales, a clergyman better known for his pioneering studies of plant respiration, inserted a thin tube into the carotid artery of a horse and measured blood pressure for the first time; he may have done so in a man as well. He described the capacity of the heart as a pump and, from this and the pulse rate, accurately calculated how much blood was pumped per minute—the first measurement of the cardiac output. Hales also made a remarkably accurate count of the size and number of the lung alveoli.

Once again we see how the dreams, the inspiration, and the tedious work of many dedicated people have brought us step by step to the level of understanding we have today. Using the simplest tools, without the fantastic capabilities we now have, well-known scientists—and many more now forgotten—laid the base on which our knowledge rests and developed the hard facts that we now take for granted. Sometimes they were wrong, but even their mistakes led others to the correct paths. Honor the forgotten, for they too made science what it is today. Their work showed how respiration and circulation coordinate to create the system that makes life possible for us and all animals.

The heart is absolutely indispensable. Humans can live for weeks, or months, even for years, with little brain activity, and for days or weeks with deficient kidney, digestive, and hormonal functions. But let the heart stop pumping blood for a mere five or six minutes, and first the brain and then other organs are irreversibly damaged and quickly die. An active and effective heart, or a mechanical substitute, must pump blood day in and day out without interruption for us to survive. And when lack of oxygen or lack of blood threaten the supply of nutrients or oxygen to the tissues, the heart increases its output to take care of the demand.

Automatic Control of the Heart

The basic rate and rhythm of the heart is dictated by a small strip of tissue called the *sino-atrial node,* located in the wall of the *right atrium.* Amazingly, the S-A node can stimulate the heart to beat at its own intrinsic rate, even if cut off from all outside stimuli, as long as it receives an adequate inflow of blood carrying oxygen and nutrients, and as long as wastes like carbon dioxide are carried away. In fact the properly nourished and oxygenated heart, removed from the body, may beat for a surprisingly long time, stimulated by the S-A node.

Absent external stimuli, this phenomenal little electric generator, the S-A node, steadily sends tiny electrical impulses that make the heart muscle contract or allow it to relax, unless other "instructions" arrive via the nervous system or in the blood.

External Control of the Heart

The *autonomic nervous system* is the part of the brain and peripheral nerves that automatically controls the functions we do not willfully control—among them the heart and blood pressure and the muscles that control breathing. Signals are transmitted from the brain through two subdivisions, the parasympathetic and sympathetic nervous systems; broadly speaking, they are antagonists. The sympathetic system transmits alarm impulses, while the parasympathetic sends relaxing signals. Messages appropriate to the circumstances come from the brain to the heart and blood vessels along both systems. Thus the sympathetic system directs the heart to speed up, to pump more blood, and the blood vessels to constrict so that the arterial pressure rises. The parasympathetic system sends the opposite signals. Both circulatory and respiratory responses to hypoxia are governed by the balance between them.

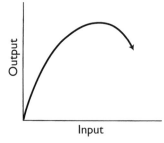

Figure 12. *Starling's law of the heart*

> ### STARLING'S LAW OF THE HEART
> Many brilliant men have studied the heart and circulation since William Harvey's day, and new findings are still frequently described. Wonderful techniques and instruments have been developed since Harvey's simple mathematics and Stephen Hales's measurements of blood pressure. One fundamental "law" was defined in 1918 by Ernest Starling, a brilliant physiologist with wide interests. He and his colleagues showed that the heart could expel more and more blood as it received more and more. But at a certain level (depending in part on the health of the heart), output would falter, and the heart would fail if the inflow continued to increase. Today this seems obvious and it applies to many other physiological, political, and economic affairs as well—under the name "Law of Diminishing Returns."

From the higher centers in the brain, nervous impulses go to the heart, prompted by excitement, anger, pain, or fear—what we might call the love, fight, or flight responses. Receptors in the skin that are sensitive to temperature will signal the brain to send orders to open skin capillaries and cause sweating or to change the heart rate or output. Other centers in the brain may send instructions to glands of internal secretion like the adrenals to release the powerful stimulant epinephrine and its analogs, which control blood pressure, for example. Some of these messengers affect the heart, and may override its basic rhythm as determined by the S-A node.

There's also an advance warning system: Veteran race horses greatly increase both rate and output of the heart in anticipation, many seconds before the start of a race. We humans also do this as we anticipate a difficult or dangerous task, and increase cardiac output (and breathing) before the need actually arises. This is an epinephrine-effected response, common to many animals.

If these effects on the heart and circulation seem familiar, they are indeed like those also signaled by the brain to the lungs and muscles that affect respiration. In Chapter 3, Moving Air: Respiration, I describe how receptors in the carotid bodies in the neck, reacting to need, stimulate breathing. They can also influence how much blood the heart pumps. On arrival at altitude, responsive to hypoxia, the carotid bodies direct the heart to beat faster and more forcefully, putting out more blood per stroke and per minute. This increased cardiac output continues for a week or so before being replaced by the other adjustments (see Chapter 12, Acclimatization).

So essential is a sustained flow of blood that redundant control centers are located in several other places; these can supplement or even take over in case others fail. Some of these small collections of cells are able to sense and can affect blood pressure, heart rate, depth and rate of respiration, and even oxygen transport. They too may be disturbed by hypoxia, but discussion of their functions is beyond the scope of this book.

Starling's Law of the Heart

The heart must pump out what it receives: If blood volume is decreased by hemorrhage or dehydration, for example, the cardiac output will decrease. But if too much blood enters the heart for too long, output will increase only so far before it begins to fall. This is the "law of the heart" developed by British physiologist Ernest Starling almost a century ago. It is an example of the general law of diminishing returns that applies to many other processes too.

There are other subtle influences on the heart. Anticipating strenuous exertion or conflict, sympathetic nervous system impulses increase the heart rate even before the biochemical changes from working muscles are received. Parasympathetic impulses affect the stomach and intestines, which in turn, through changes in the blood, affect the heart. After a heavy meal the rate and output may increase, but after a light meal the rate may slow; in either situation sleep becomes tempting. During sleep the parasympathetic impulses dominate. A great many similar feedback loops affect us every day.

Once again we see how the wisdom of the body anticipates need—for blood or oxygen—and responds before the need is evident: an amazing and beautiful system.

The Effect of Altitude

In addition to stimulating respiration in response to hypoxia, the carotid bodies will stimulate the heart to beat faster and a bit harder above 5,000 feet. The work of climbing increases the rate and strength of the heartbeat still more, and at higher elevations may push the heart close to its capacity to respond. This might limit work by older people, whose *maximum achievable heart rate* (MAHR) can be crudely defined as 200 minus half one's age. However, studies at extreme altitude show that in healthy adults it is the lungs rather than the heart that limit work capacity. Maximal breathing capacity also decreases with age, though not predictably. But even at extreme altitude, in most people, other systems falter and fail before the heart.

Cardiac output, both at rest and during exertion, increases as we ascend, but then, after a short stay at moderate altitude, the output decreases to sea level values or even lower. At extreme altitude, toward the summit of Everest for example, cardiac output falls sharply as altitude increases. These decreases in output do not signal congestive heart failure, but more likely are due to a smaller circulating plasma volume. Though the *right ventricle* works harder at altitude due to the increased pulmonary artery pressure, the *left ventricle* actually works less.

Coronary Arteries

Heart muscle receives its nourishment and oxygen through the coronary arteries, and blood flow increases when the heart is called on for more work. Once cardiac rate and output return to or even below sea level values, coronary blood flow also falls. Does this mean that persons with some coronary artery obstruction will tolerate altitude well—or poorly? Not exactly, but it does suggest that such persons may tolerate altitude better than one might expect.

Because coronary artery disease tends to be more common in older persons, we should ask if the heart affects the tolerance of the elderly for altitude. First, let me urge that anyone with coronary artery disease should talk seriously with a knowledgeable doctor before planning a climb or strenuous activity, even at moderate altitude. Going to stay in a mountain resort may be safe and good for some, but going much higher might cause problems. Of a group of ninety-seven elderly men and women sojourning at 8,250 feet, 20 percent had pre-existing coronary artery disease but all tolerated the altitude well for at least the five days we followed them. Their blood pressure rose during the first day, but then returned to their sea level values for the next four days. Those with pre-existing hypertension responded similarly but at a higher level. Those with angina at home were no worse at altitude. Several played tennis every day.

This was a small and perhaps biased sample at a modest altitude, but another larger study of persons climbing and walking in the Alps showed that *fewer* men and women had heart attacks at altitude during their walk or climb than would have been expected in a similar group at sea level.

Until the twentieth century, measurements on arterial blood were limited to animals, or obtained by slashing an artery; neither method was satisfactory for studies of the dynamics of respiration and circulation. During an epidemic of pneumonia in 1916, William Stadie wished to see whether the amount of oxygen in blood might predict the outcome in serious cases. Through a small cut in the skin, he inserted a needle a little smaller than a thin pencil into an artery, drew blood, and measured the oxygen content. Ten years later, Joseph Barcroft used this same type of needle to draw arterial blood at the same time he obtained alveolar air, and showed that the lungs did not secrete oxygen as some claimed. Arterial punctures are commonplace today, but the needles are much smaller and do less damage to the artery.

CARDIAC CATHETERS

In the mid–nineteenth century, two French physiologists, Auguste Chauveau and Jules Marey, devised a double-chambered tube (catheter) that they passed through a vein into the right side of the heart to measure the cardiac output of horses (see Figure 13, top). Another giant step was taken in 1929 when a young German surgeon, Werner Forssmann, pushed a thin flexible catheter (much like the one Stephen Hales had used on a horse 200 years before) through his veins into his own heart, monitoring the process on a fluoroscope. For this Forssman shared the Nobel prize with Andre Cournand and Dickinson Richards, who later perfected the instrument (see Figure 13, bottom) and technique and were able to measure not only the dynamics within the heart, but the flow and pressure within the pulmonary artery and the small vessels of the lung. This permitted intimate understanding of how the heart functioned normally or when damaged in some way. And of course it clarified the effects of hypoxia on the circulation of the lung, so immensely important in altitude sickness, and equally so in many illnesses that cause lack of oxygen.

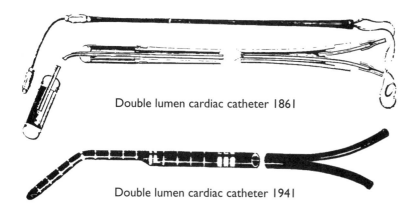

Figure 13. *Cardiac catheters*

Double lumen cardiac catheter 1861

Double lumen cardiac catheter 1941

Cardiac Catheterization

In 1940 I had a brief encounter, which did me no credit, with another advance. I was finishing my residency training when two more-senior doctors asked if they might do an experiment on one of my patients. Appalled by what they told me, I indignantly refused, saying I couldn't see any use whatever to what they wanted to do, and they went elsewhere. What they proposed was cardiac catheterization (see Figure 13). (Both of them—Andre Cournand and Dick Richards, later became my good friends. Their pioneering work has enabled others to watch the working of the heart as it had never been seen before.)

The Blood

The essential role of the heart is to move blood throughout the body, and it does so through a network of blood vessels, starting with large-bore (half-inch), thick-walled muscular arteries, which leave the heart to divide and branch into ever smaller arteries and arterioles. These lead into the pre-capillary vessels, which are especially important because, unlike the capillaries, they have thin muscular walls and are able to contract or relax.

Endothelial Cells and Nitric Oxide

The lining (endothelium) of these small pre-capillary vessels can release minute amounts of a powerful agent that was first appreciated only ten or twelve years ago and was labeled *endothelium-derived relaxing factor* (EDRF). It was soon identified as a simple chemical substance, nitric oxide (NO), which is formed in the inner lining of blood vessels. Though the principal action of NO is to relax blood vessels, it has important effects on many other physiological functions. NO may be a simple chemical, but the processes by which it causes its effects are complex.

Minute amounts of NO are produced by the action of a specific enzyme (NO synthase) in all endothelial cells in every mammalian organ at a steady basal rate. Various substances *increase* NO release, which relaxes blood vessels, allowing smaller ones to dilate. NO also slows or halts the stickiness and clumping of platelets, and thereby helps to decrease the tendency for clot formation in blood vessels.

Endothelial cells also release a family of substances called *endothelins,* one of which constricts blood vessels in direct opposition to NO. The balance between the two (and probably including other substances as well) governs blood flow and pressure. This balance is particularly important in determining pulmonary artery pressure.

Certain other physiological substances *inhibit* NO synthesis and release, and thus increase vascular tone and blood pressure, increase clot formation, and also increase the leakiness of capillary blood vessels. These are all important in adjusting to hypoxia through an intricately balanced system.

Most recently, NO has been found to play an even more important role—helping hemoglobin to "dictate" how much, and where, oxygen is delivered to tissues. It does so because the binding of oxygen to heme ions also promotes the binding of NO to hemoglobin. When hemoglobin releases oxygen in the capillaries, it changes the shape of the red cell and this in turn releases NO in pre-capillary arterioles and even in capillaries. The released NO relaxes the blood vessels, and when molecules of oxygen are released by hemoglobin, NO is captured back to the red cell, the vessels constrict, and the blood moving into the veins returns to the heart and on to the lungs for another load of oxygen. It is truly wonderful that hemoglobin not only provides oxygen but also "senses" the oxygen need and alters capillary flow to provide what's needed where and when.

As for its role in altitude illnesses, NO appears to be a central player in at least one of these—high altitude pulmonary edema, discussed in Chapters 6, AMS: Acute Mountain Sickness, and 8, HAPE: High Altitude Pulmonary Edema.

Red Blood Cells and Hemoglobin

Oxygen is carried in blood, not in solution but loosely attached to a protein, *hemoglobin,* which gives blood its reddish color and is the key player in oxygen transport. Throughout recorded history, blood has been associated with life, even more so than air has been, perhaps because it is so highly visible and so easily spilled. As noted in Gilbert's *Oxygen and Living Processes* (1991), in the fifth century B.C., Empedocles wrote that "the blood is the life," and Aristotle believed that the soul depended on the composition of the blood. Their contemporary, Anaxagoras, was more specific: "The blood is formed by a multitude of droplets, united among them," a remarkable statement that seems to anticipate observations made by a Dutch lens-maker 2,000 years later.

In 1674 Anthony von Leeuwenhoeck read his landmark paper to the Royal Society in London, and delighted the members who looked through his little microscopes:

> I have divers times endeavored to see and to know what parts the blood consists of and at length I have observed, taking some blood out of my hand, that it consists of small round globules driven through a cristalline humidity of water; yet whether all bloods be such I doubte.

Leeuwenhoeck was not the first to use a magnifying glass; single lenses had been known for centuries. But he was the first to combine lenses to make what we know as the compound microscope, which could magnify up to 300 times. He was fascinated by everything small, and estimated the size of the "little animals" he watched (varieties of protozoa), as he did every other object, by comparing it with a grain of sand. He came astonishingly close to the 7.5 micra which we know today is the diameter of the normal, average red blood cell.

The "globules" he saw are not actually round but flattened discs, shaped like a doughnut whose center has not been completely punched out, and they are flexible, distorting into narrower shapes as they pass through tiny vessels. The red cells are packed with a reddish stuff called hemoglobin that has a very special talent: It can combine easily but loosely with oxygen when the partial pressure is high during passage through the lungs, and can release oxygen easily to the cells where partial pressure of oxygen is low.

Air and Hemoglobin

Ten years before Leeuwenhoeck saw his little cells, Richard Lower, one of the remarkable group of men in the young Royal Society, noticed that blood changed from dark red to a brighter carmine when it was agitated with air. His contemporary, Robert Hooke, soon showed the Royal Society that an experimental animal could be kept alive when the chest was widely opened, so long as air was rhythmically blown into the lungs with a bellows. Lower, seizing on this, observed that blood also changed from dark to bright red while passing through well-aerated lungs. By this time the expansion of the lungs had been explained, but of course oxygen had not yet been identified, so no closer connection between breathing air and the change in blood was possible at that time.

In 1747 Menghini burned blood and showed that its ash was attracted by a magnet, which a century later led Justus von Liebig to speculate that blood contained some form of iron that carried oxygen, not in simple solution, but bound to a compound within the red cells. Lothar Meyer soon showed this to be true, and in 1865 Felix Hoppe-Seyler crystallized this substance and showed it to his friend Paul Bert.

Bert, considered the father of altitude physiology, also did much of the basic work in the last thirty years of the nineteenth century to establish the relationship between oxygen and hemoglobin. He was remarkably versatile: a lawyer, a plastic surgeon, and a physiologist until, deeply saddened by the death of two of his young colleagues in a balloon flight he accepted appointment as Governor General of Indo-China where he died at age fifty-three.

He had studied under the great Claude Bernard, became interested in blood, oxygen, and high altitude, and wrote the seminal book on high-altitude medicine, *Barometric Pressure*. A wealthy patron, Denis Jourdanet, had several decompression chambers built for Bert, in which Bert had himself taken to simulated altitudes a lot higher than Hooke had gone 150 years earlier. Bert described his symptoms at altitude, showed that they were prevented by breathing oxygen, and advised its use by balloonists for the high flights that had again become popular. Three of these balloonists were in his laboratory and soon would demonstrate how terribly important this advice was.

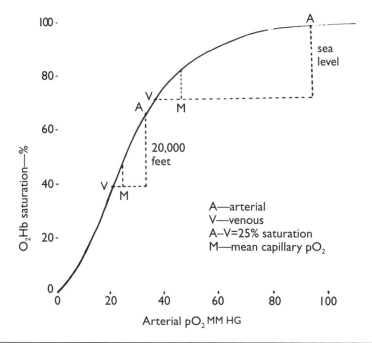

A—arterial
V—venous
A–V=25% saturation
M—mean capillary pO_2

Figure 14.
*Oxy-hemoglobin
dissociation curve*

TRANSPORT OF OXYGEN BY HEMOGLOBIN

In man and most animals, oxygen is carried not in simple solution but in combination with a "respiratory pigment." There are many different kinds of such pigments, but most mammals use one in which molecular iron—hemoglobin—(in loose combination with other materials) grasps oxygen molecules when exposed to a high partial pressure of the gas, releasing them when the partial pressure falls. The relationship between oxygen pressure and the percentage of hemoglobin combined with it can be plotted in this oxy-hemoglobin dissociation curve.

The Oxygen-Hemoglobin Dissociation Curve

Paul Bert must also be remembered for his careful studies of how hemoglobin combines with oxygen. Using instruments he designed and ordered made for him, Bert exposed measured amounts of blood to different partial pressures of oxygen. He then used a vacuum pump to extract the oxygen that had combined with blood, and was able to plot the relationship between oxygen pressure and the percentage of hemoglobin combined with it. From this he was able to draw the first oxy-hemoglobin dissociation curves (see Figure 14).

When Bert drew the rough curves describing this relationship, he was not able to measure some of the other influences (such as temperature, carbon dioxide, and acidity) that affect the shape of the curve. Consequently he could not fully appreciate the beauty of the special S-shape of the normal curve for human hemoglobin. We have made enormous strides since his innovative work and can better realize how admirably adapted to its task is hemoglobin.

When blood is exposed to a high partial pressure of oxygen, most of it is immediately saturated, its iron molecules picking up molecules of oxygen. This happens in the lungs. When oxygen-rich blood reaches the tissues where oxygen pressure is low, the iron molecules quickly release oxygen, which diffuses into cells, and the depleted blood returns to heart and lungs for another load. The S-shape of the dissociation curve in Figure 14 dictates how quickly and completely oxygen is loaded and unloaded, and thus affects how we and other animals acquire the essential oxygen and tolerate its lack.

Blood's Oxygen Content and Carrying Capacity

Blood carries oxygen almost entirely in loose combination with hemoglobin; very little is in physical solution. Each gram of hemoglobin will bind or carry 1.34 milliliters (ml) of oxygen. Because there are or should be about 15 grams of hemoglobin in each hundred ml of our blood, it follows that each 100 ml can carry fifteen times 1.34, or about 20 ml of oxygen, when hemoglobin is fully saturated. We call this the *oxygen carrying capacity* of blood, normally described as 20 volumes percent. Changes in blood acidity, temperature, and content of carbon dioxide change the carrying capacity and thus alter its *oxygen content*.

When less oxygen is available, blood is less saturated. Though the carrying capacity is unchanged, the actual content or amount of oxygen carried does change, being lower when oxygen pressure is lower. Capacity and content are the same only when enough oxygen is available to fully saturate the hemoglobin. Both capacity and content increase when hemoglobin is increased, and if hemoglobin increases in parallel with a decrease in available oxygen, we may have a near-normal oxygen content even at altitude. So it is not surprising that an increase in circulating hemoglobin should be one of the ways in which man and some animals accommodate to lower oxygen in the ambient air (discussed in Chapter 12, Acclimatization).

Blood Acidity

The shape of the oxy-hemoglobin dissociation curve (see Figure 14) is affected by carbon dioxide (CO_2) and by the acidity of blood. The former is determined by respiration, the latter by metabolism. The acidity or alkalinity of blood (like any solution) depends on the amount of hydrogen ion (H^+) or hydroxyl ion (OH^-) in solution. The degree of acidity is indicated by the symbol pH, which is the negative logarithm of the concentration of hydrogen ions. A neutral solution (when both H^+ and OH^- ions are exactly balanced) has a pH of 7.0: The lower the pH, the more acid the solution and vice versa.

Our metabolism produces many acidic substances like lactic acid, fatty acids, nucleic and uric acids, and of course carbon dioxide. These could threaten the stability of blood and the "internal environment" on which, as Claude Bernard said, our free and active life depends. When one realizes how many acids and how few alkaline substances enter the blood, the small range in the pH is all the more remarkable. It depends on the stabilizing effect of several important buffers that can "absorb" H^+ or OH^- ions without much change in pH. There are six major buffer pairs in blood, three containing hemoglobin. But of these, the most immediately effective is the carbonate-bicarbonate pair, which is as important in altitude physiology as it is in normal everyday life because of the speed with which it can be altered by exhaling carbon dioxide or by excreting bicarbonate.

In Chapter 3, Moving Air: Respiration, I describe how carbon dioxide diffuses through capillary walls much faster than does oxygen. Most of the carbon dioxide is carried in blood in solution or as bicarbonate, a compound produced by a reaction catalyzed by the enzyme called carbonic anhydrase. There is a high concentration of this enzyme in red cells, lungs, and kidneys—places where a shift in acidity can be speedily accomplished by changing the exhalation of carbon dioxide or loss of bicarbonate in the urine. The carbonate-bicarbonate buffer pair is one of the more mobile buffers in the blood, a characteristic that can be affected by a useful medication (Diamox), discussed in Chapter 10, Prevention.

Human Hemoglobin

We humans have three different forms of hemoglobin at different times in our lives. The embryo's blood contains a primitive form (P-hemoglobin) that soon changes to the F or fetal form, which has an affinity for oxygen much stronger than does adult or A-hemoglobin. This enables the unborn infant to pull oxygen more easily from its mother's blood passing through the placenta, and thus helps the fetus to survive and grow in an oxygen environment comparable to that on top of Mount Everest. It's really a useful extra means of acclimatizing to hypoxia. F-hemoglobin changes to the A or adult form soon after birth. Some experimental procedures have been able to convert abnormal human hemoglobins to the F form, which someday may help many individuals who are chronically short of oxygen from illness.

Hundreds of different or mutant hemoglobins occur in about 0.5 percent of all humans. The development of more sophisticated methods for analyzing the respiratory pigments has enabled identification of many subgroups of these abnormal hemoglobins, but very few are important in altitude physiology.

Sickle Cells

One of these that is important is S-hemoglobin, the homozygous geno-type, which causes chronic anemia in about 0.3 percent to 1 percent of Americans (mostly those with black or Mediterranean ancestry). An addi-tional 8 percent to 10 percent have what is called the "sickle trait" (heterozy-gous genotype), but are not anemic. The sickling trait, the most common abnormal hemoglobin, usually causes no problem, though some forms cause chronic anemia. But when persons with the sickle trait go to altitude, or become hypoxic from whatever cause, the cells are distorted and tension in the hemoglobin molecule make it stiff, so that the misshapen red cells may stick like a burr in smaller blood vessels and cause serious problems (see Figure 15).

SICKLE RED BLOOD CELLS

Approximately 10 percent of the population in the United States has a form of hemoglobin whose configuration is abnormal. The most common has a molecular configuration that under certain conditions can exert strong stresses within the red cell and distort some into sickle or half-moon shapes instead of the normal flat disc (as shown in Figure 15).

Figure 15. *Sickle red blood cells*

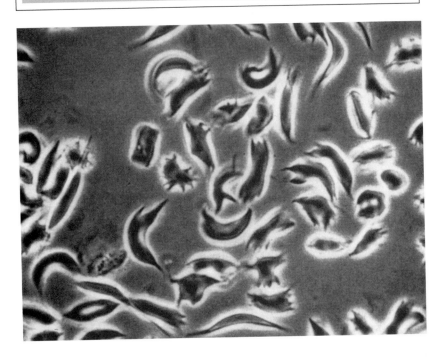

The sickle trait causes no problems—usually—and is often unsuspected, but it may become important at altitude. When sickle cells are hypoxic, the molecular stresses increase, causing red cells to form bizarre shapes that are less flexible and tend to stick like burrs in the narrow capillaries. Consequently, any cause of decreased oxygen such as altitude or lung disease can cause problems due to obstruction of small blood vessels in the spleen and kidney, less often elsewhere, by these misshapen sickled red cells. The sickle cells revert to normal with oxygen or descent from high altitude, though the damage to spleen and sometimes other places is not reversed but heals slowly. Interestingly, only alveolar hypoxia causes sickling; carbon monoxide hypoxia apparently does not.

Fortunately it is a rare problem—but one that can be serious if not recognized. Sometimes the damage caused by these obstructions causes a confusing clinical picture that has led to mistaken or delayed diagnosis. Some simple laboratory tests will solve the puzzle. About thirty years ago, when the complications of sickling were not widely recognized, the following case was reported:

> *A young white mechanic took a long bus ride from sea level to 7,000 feet and within two hours of arrival developed nausea and severe pain in the upper left quadrant of his abdomen. During the next three days he grew worse, and only after special studies was his blood found to contain sickle cells. The cause of his abdominal pain was an abnormally enlarged spleen, which was removed and found to have several infarcts (areas where blood vessels were obstructed, causing death of the affected areas). The tentative diagnosis of sickle cell disease was proven. He was given supplementary oxygen and slowly improved.*
>
> *This young man's father, on hearing of his son's illness, drove up from sea level and within three hours of arrival developed somewhat similar symptoms. Special tests confirmed the diagnosis of sickle cell disease and his spleen too was removed and found, like his son's, to be congested with sickle cell thrombi. He quickly improved with oxygen and descent, and surgery was not done. He stoutly denied mixed ancestry but later acknowledged that "miscegenation in his progenitors was likely."*

Another group, perhaps 1 percent of the population, has some mutant form of hemoglobin that combines differently with oxygen. Some forms may pick up oxygen avidly in the lungs, and release it only when partial pressure is very low. Other forms acquire oxygen slowly but release it more readily. So far these other mutant hemoglobins are rare medical curiosities with little medical importance; they don't form thrombi or *emboli* (blood clots) and don't cause such problems.

Other Respiratory Pigments

Throughout the animal kingdom, there are thousands of different "respiratory pigments," as hemoglobin is called, with different affinities for oxygen. For example, most invertebrates use a substance that strongly attracts and holds oxygen, while in other species the attraction is rather weak. Tadpole hemoglobin attracts and holds oxygen very tightly, but as tadpoles become adult frogs, this attraction weakens. The blood of animals living at high altitude—or in oxygen-poor environments, as do many marine animals—has a stronger affinity for oxygen than does human blood. When the pigment is carried in solution, as some animals' blood does rather than in cells, the "blood" tends to be thick and to move more sluggishly than when the pigment is contained in cells. There's persuasive evidence that choices between solution and cells were dictated long ago (or perhaps determined) by the lifestyles of all animals. Some marine animals in the deepest oceans rely on other pigments to carry other gases to support energy production.

The animal variations are of interest to those interested in altitude and hypoxia because they may someday show us other pathways to manage hypoxic illnesses.

Blood's Multiple Functions

Of course blood has many other functions besides its most important one of transporting oxygen and carbon dioxide. It carries all sorts of nutrients to feed all living tissues. It can pick up water and carry it where needed, and it can also release water through the skin in sweat. Waste materials (of which carbon dioxide is only one, but a very important one) are carried to kidneys or lungs or even the skin for discharge. Poisonous products are taken to the liver for detoxification. And so on . . .

Blood is also the highway over which scores of hormones and enzymes are moved. And blood contains hundreds of special materials with many important tasks, such as those that protect us against infections and that staunch bleeding from wounds without clotting in the blood vessels.

As mentioned earlier, Greco-Roman philosopher-scientists believed that blood "cools the innate heat" of the body—and they were quite right! We might call blood an air conditioner: When we are too hot, the heat-regulating center diverts blood from core to skin, where it may cool by convection, and by increasing water loss in sweat will increase heat loss further by evaporation. Cold diverts blood away from skin to organs that must be kept warm if the body is to survive. The circulating blood is indispensable for keeping the body at an even temperature, which rarely varies by more than a degree; this is somewhat more precise than many home furnaces! Even in feverish illness, the flowing blood distributes heat to the skin where it can be carried off.

The brain directs the conservation of water by shutting down urine formation and sweating when too much water has been lost from the blood; conversely, if we try to overload with water, blood facilitates its efficient discard in urine.

Oxygen transport is such a major function of blood that it's easy to forget these other functions. They may not be so urgently important, but without white blood cells to fight infection, without platelets to help stop bleeding, and without distribution of hormones and other necessities throughout the body, we would not survive very long.

Cells
THE ULTIMATE USERS

MOVING AIR AND MOVING BLOOD HAVE ONLY TWO PURPOSES, IF WE MAY speak teleologically: to nourish and to protect living cells. We breathe to give cells oxygen and remove carbon dioxide. The heart pumps blood to carry food and oxygen to the cells and take away wastes and carbon dioxide. To protect cells in a constant environment, blood also guards the body's temperature and humidity. If either respiration or circulation fails to provide oxygen and fuel or to control water balance and temperature for more than a short while, life ends and cells break up. Of these, a steady supply of oxygen is most urgent: Without it, death is minutes away.

Cells are the blocks from which a living organism is built, but unlike bricks they are busily functioning units that live and die and replace themselves. There are thousands of varieties of cells with different skills, every one of them originating from the union of two single cells, the sperm and the ovum carrying the genetic messages that define every aspect of the individual. As adults we are made of 75 to 100 trillion cells of many different types and functions. With few exceptions they all have similar parts.

Each cell is a tiny, flexible bag of fluid containing a great number of bits and chemicals, each of which has a special function in the living organism. Many cells are able to move about a little and to change their shape, but that's constrained by small fibers within the structure. Of the scores of small elements in a cell, I'll mention only a few, although most or all are essential and may be affected by oxygen lack.

Though cells with different specialties are somewhat different internally, all (except red blood cells and bone) consist of a rich soup contained in a thin skin. The soup contains hundreds of different items floating in a watery fluid called *cytoplasm.* Scores of items called organelles are highly organized and each is contained within its own membrane; each has a specific and essential job. Floating free in the cytoplasm are many other minute particles that have specific functions, as well as bits of fat and glycogen, all laced with fibers and tubules that make up what is called the reticulum. Dissolved in cytoplasm are ions such as sodium, potassium, calcium, and small amounts of others that can pass through special channels in the delicate membrane that walls the cell.

Many of these ions are constantly being moved between the intra-cellular and the extra-cellular fluid by an invisible pump that can actively transport selected ions from an area of low concentration to one where it is higher. The pump consumes a great deal of oxygen and therefore is vulnerable to hypoxia. Other molecules, such as oxygen and carbon dioxide, pass in and out freely by passive transport, controlled by Dalton's law of diffusions. It's important to remember that Dalton's law of diffusions applies to *molecules,* whether they be of gas, liquid, or solid. But active or facilitated diffusion requires energy.

The mitochondria are well-organized structures and might be called "factories," wherein many enzymes convert food to energy by the complex Krebs cycle (discussed later in this chapter), without which life would cease. In it the ATP-DPT-ATP reactions provide the energy that enables every activity, from the pumping heart to the moving muscles to the secretion of hormones and formation of urine—and scores more. The cycle depends on oxygen and, not surprisingly, mitochondria are affected by hypoxia.

The *nucleus* is the "control center" of the cell—and thus the body—because it contains almost all of the deoxynucleic acid (DNA) that carries the genetic instructions from our ancestors. The genes determine all or most growth and development, and dictate the individuality of the human each person becomes. They might be called the blueprint from which each individual is made.

As the exciting exploration of the genetic code widens, we find more and more inherited forces that define what we will be. Some genes are believed to affect how we respond to lack of oxygen, or to cold or heat, as well as other environmental, physical, or emotional stress. If the mitochondria provide the energy, the nucleus determines how it is used.

How Cells Use Food

Also in the cytoplasm are molecules of fuel waiting to be "burned" by the body. These have been actively helped through the cell membrane by more elaborate processes that are dependent on "helper" molecules within the cell walls. Active transport requires oxygen.

Most of the food we eat is digested in the intestinal tract and broken down into simpler compounds like carbohydrates, fatty acids, and amino acids, the majority of which pass easily through the intestinal walls into blood, which transports them to the tissues. There they pass into the *interstitial fluid* and into each cell. All must be assisted through the *cell membranes* because they are too large to pass without help from carrier molecules in the cell wall. Once inside, complex carbohydrates and fatty and amino acids are broken down into glucose molecules. Each contains a large amount of energy originally derived from the sun and waiting to release heat and power.

Everything done by the elements within the cells depends on oxygen and, therefore, is somewhat affected by hypoxia, whatever its cause. High altitude strikes at the heart of life.

The Cell Membrane

Every cell is enclosed in a thin membrane, which has special characteristics. Different kinds of cells have different types of membrane; some allow passage only of certain molecules, either by assisted or passive transport. Other membranes allow movement across them by many different molecules. The integrity of the cell membrane is essential for its proper function.

Because it determines what stays in and what stays out, the cell wall's structure is as important as are its contents. It is a very thin, virtually "fluid" membrane with microlayers, each being one or two molecules thick. From the outside inward, it consists of sugarlike compounds (*muco-polysaccharides*) and several kinds of protein floating on closely packed fatty substances (lipids). Only a few small molecules (oxygen and carbon dioxide, for example) can pass through the cell membrane by simple diffusion. Many others must be pumped in or out (active transport), and then only through specific channels. Precisely how the lipid molecules of the cell wall are lined up determines where these channels are. Sodium molecules in the cell wall

Figure 16A. *A typical cell.* (From *Textbook of Human Physiology,* by Arthur C. Guyton. W.B. Saunders Company, 1991. Reproduced with permission.)

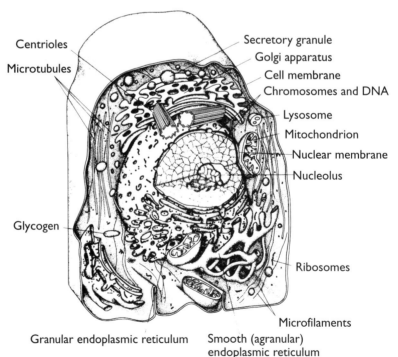

Centrioles

Microtubules

Secretory granule

Golgi apparatus

Cell membrane

Chromosomes and DNA

Lysosome

Mitochondrion

Nuclear membrane

Nucleolus

Glycogen

Ribosomes

Microfilaments

Granular endoplasmic reticulum

Smooth (agranular) endoplasmic reticulum

are responsible for the assisted or facilitated transport of fuel, handing certain substances across the wall, so to speak. Other "facilitators" reside in the cell wall.

Membrane structure and transport are crucial to life, and powerfully affect how well or poorly we tolerate an alien environment such as oxygen lack, or heat or cold or toxic substances. It is an extraordinarily complicated subject.

But hypoxia affects the mitochondria and their function, as well as the membrane that encases the cell, and other membranes that contain every other structure floating in the cytoplasm. The membrane permeability is altered by several toxic substances and also by hypoxia.

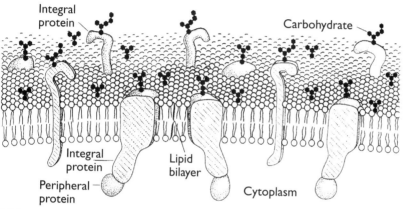

Figure 16B. *Detail of a typical cell.* (From *Textbook of Human Physiology.* Reproduced with permission.)

A TYPICAL CELL

Cells are held together in various structures that define the various parts of the body: spleen, liver, heart, and bone, for example. Each is built of its unique type of cells, supported by several forms of fibrous structure, all bathed in a common liquid, the extra-cellular fluid by which their surroundings are kept stable within narrow limits. We are made of much more water than solid stuffs, and the constancy of our cells' environment and function is totally dependent on the extra-cellular fluid.

The cytoplasm and its contents (organelles, mitochondria, nucleus) are contained within a thin, tough *membrane,* which is a liquid consisting of a double layer of *lipids* (fatty substances) and scattered protein linked to carbohydrate (glycoside) molecules. These glyco-proteins are a sort of channel through which water-soluble substances passively diffuse in and out of cells, selectively.

This cell membrane is as essential to life as are other parts of the cell, because its integrity determines what substances enter or leave the cytoplasm.

The Mitochondria

Active membrane transport is energy-intensive and requires a good bit of oxygen. After they have assisted food molecules through the membrane, sodium molecules must be pushed back out of the cell (allowing potassium to enter), which requires oxygen. This is when the cell is particularly vulnerable, and one reason why some people hypothesized that hypoxia impairs the potassium/sodium pump and thus alters cell functions. But pump failure is no longer considered the cause of the signs and symptoms of mountain sicknesses, or in fact of hypoxia from other causes, so we must ask in what other ways hypoxia affects cell functions.

The cell's work is done in many mitochondria, which have thin walls structured like those of the cell. Each contains many enzymes that recognize and act upon specific fuel particles that have entered the cell. Each mitochondrion is deeply furrowed or convoluted, giving it a very large surface area compared to its volume. We can picture each as a set of shelves in a chemical laboratory, each shelf crowded with different enzymes ready to work. Enzymes are not consumed by the work, but as facilitators they require oxygen, "burning" foodstuffs to produce carbon dioxide and water, and other products, and releasing energy.

Burning Food for Energy

Two centuries ago, the discovery of oxygen was followed by demonstrations that most materials would burn in the presence of oxygen. Burning released heat and light, sometimes a great deal of heat very rapidly. Over the years, scientists recognized that food was burned by the body much as a candle burns—as long as there is a good supply of oxygen. The nagging question became, how can this happen without torching the body?

Answers were slowly found in the first half of the nineteenth century when Justus Liebig developed equations to support the concept that sugars are "burned" gradually and slowly, step by step, in the tissues (i.e., the cells), not in the blood, to produce carbon dioxide, water, and a little heat. Louis Pasteur was studying the fermentation of sugary grape juice into alcohol and suggested that there might be some resemblance between this and what happened to sugars in the body. At the end of the century, Hans and Edward Buchner isolated the substance in yeast that turns sugar into alcohol; from this phenomenon (which had been known since Noah!) came the name *enzyme*, meaning "in yeast."

Liebig's concept was refined and tested and, finally, in the 1920s Hans Krebs described an elaborate biochemical process involving citric acid; this process is usually known as the Krebs cycle in his honor. This cycle burns fuel and thus provides the energy of life.

The Krebs or Citric Acid Cycle

The Krebs cycle begins when glucose is enzymatically converted to adenosine molecules (AMP is adenosine monophosphate, ADP is adenosine diphosphate, and ATP is adenosine triphosphate). These conversions also release energy. Then, in turn, ATP is converted to ADP. The amount and speed of energy released is controlled by multiple feedback mechanisms including ADP and AMP, which prevent release of more energy than is actually needed.

The Krebs cycle allows the "burning" of fats, proteins, and carbohydrates, producing heat and energy, to take place in small stages so that both heat and energy are produced in small amounts and are not destructive. As long as glucose and oxygen are available, and carbon dioxide and excess water are removed, the Krebs cycle produces everything we need to live and act. It is a complicated cycle but beautifully effective.

Conversion of glucose requires oxygen, but without oxygen two sources of sudden, brief bursts of emergency energy are available. They are called anaerobic because they do not demand oxygen immediately, but may run up an oxygen debt, which must be soon repaid.

The Phosphagen Cycle and the Anaerobic Cycle

The first, or phosphagen, cycle can very rapidly produce a large amount of energy for a few seconds, almost enough to run a 100-yard dash, but the cycle, like the runner, is then exhausted. The second, or anaerobic, path uses muscle glycogen (a kind of sugar) and forms pyruvic acid, which is converted to lactic acid. This is only an emergency pathway, after which the lactic acid must be changed back to ATP via pyruvic acid when oxygen is again available. If the lactic acid is not soon changed back, sensitive tissues die from acidosis.

This anaerobic cycle produces much less energy than the Krebs cycle, and we humans can do anaerobic work using either cycle for only a very short time. So far no way has been found that will allow us to work completely without oxygen for more than a few minutes. Hibernators and diving mammals can do much better than this by "going anaerobic."

The Krebs cycle is dependent on oxygen. It consists of a series of biochemical reactions, each stage leading to the next and releasing heat and energy. The heat is carried away by the blood, keeping us warm without burning us up. The released energy does the body's work, whether it is contracting a muscle fiber, thinking, making and releasing a hormone, or initiating digestion. The speed of these processes is controlled by different enzymes and by the availability of fuel. When we starve, the tissues begin to consume themselves; as the fuel supply dwindles, heat and energy decrease and, finally, we die.

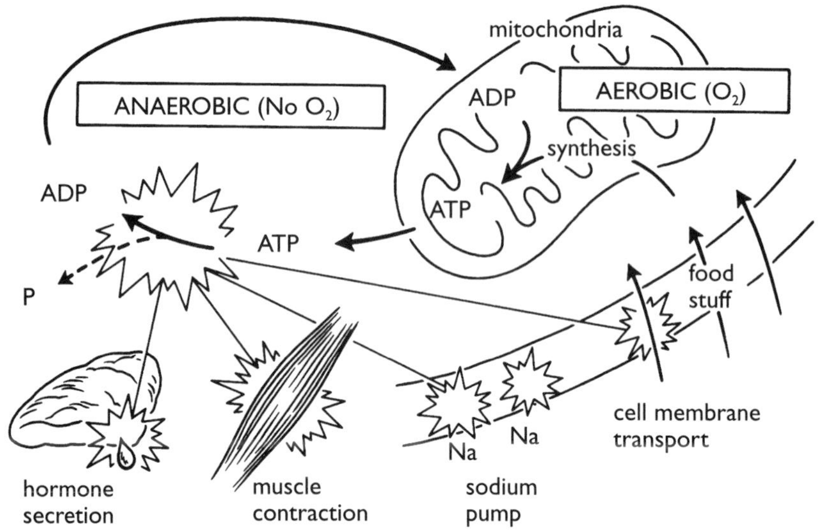

Figure 17. *The Krebs cycle and phosphagen cycle*

THE KREBS CYCLE AND PHOSPHAGEN CYCLE

The aerobic Krebs or Citric Acid Cycle (shown on the right side of Figure 17) is a series of steps in which fuel is burned to create heat and energy. The released energy does the body's work—such as contracting a muscle fiber or making and releasing a hormone. The cycle is controlled by a number of feedback loops to prevent overheating or the release of too much energy. The process takes place within the cell, where the mitochondrial enzymes convert "foods" into adenosine triphosphate (ATP), which is then broken down into adenosine diphosphate (ADP) elsewhere, releasing energy. ADP must then be changed back to ATP so that the cycle may continue, and this process requires oxygen. The whole process is wonderfully fine-tuned to meet the needs of the active, living organism, and the many stages are surprisingly well understood, despite their complexity.

A separate process, what might be called a "fail-safe," enables rapid release of energy for a few moments in the anaerobic phosphagen cycle, which is activated by a demand for energy that cannot be met rapidly or completely enough by the Krebs cycle. In the phosphagen cycle, ATP is converted to ADP and phosphoric acid, a process that produces the energy released in metabolism. The oxygen debt acquired by the phosphagen cycle must be soon repaid.

Something similar happens when we are deprived of adequate oxygen: Heat and energy generation decrease and, over time, if oxygen is not provided, we collapse, grow cold, and die, even though food may be there waiting to be used. The phosphagen and anaerobic cycles will not sustain us for long. This is one of the dangers in extreme high-altitude climbing.

Essentially what the process of acclimatization does is to help the cell to get along on a smaller oxygen budget. A well-acclimatized person need not go anaerobic, but should this happen at very high altitude, recovery depends entirely on restoring the oxygen supply and takes longer than at sea level.

Intensive searches have been made for a respiratory enzyme that could facilitate the use of oxygen within the cells. Many have been tried, among them the *cytochrome family*, but this is a complex and rapidly changing field that can't be discussed here. We can say with confidence that many enzymes within the cell activate metabolism. Possibly, just possibly, another may be found that will improve tolerance for hypoxia, and which might be given for that purpose to patients chronically hypoxic from disease.

Already exploration of the human genome has shown some specific sequence(s) that affect acquisition and utilization of oxygen—which makes for some exciting progress ahead.

Acclimatization in the Cells?

How else do cells acclimatize or adjust to lack of oxygen? Possibly by forming more mitochondria in essential cells, though this has not been conclusively proven. We have learned that, after a person spends prolonged residence at altitude, mitochondria do enlarge. There is a suggestion, too, that they move closer to the cell wall, perhaps to be closer to the incoming oxygen.

In fact most of acclimatization happens outside the cells, as I discuss in Chapter 3, Moving Air: Respiration, and Chapter 12, Acclimatization. As we picture it today, the process of acclimatization to high altitude occurs mainly in ventilation, circulation, and oxygen transport. These changes set in motion the others that make possible their continuation.

PART III

Mountain Sicknesses

AMS
ACUTE MOUNTAIN SICKNESS

OUR FOREBEARS WOVE MANY MYTHS AND LEGENDS ABOUT THE FOUR "elements"—air, earth, fire, and water. Of these, they knew that only invisible, impalpable air was essential to life, but why this was so remained a mystery for many centuries.

What we know today about the air in which we live has been learned slowly and gradually, but recognition of how this relates to the experiences on mountains is much more recent. Mountains sometimes have been worshipped as the home of gods, often feared for the havoc that might come from them, and for long years seldom visited. Two thousand years ago, Chinese Genral Du Quin advised his emperor not to send envoys to Kashmir because "travellers have to climb over Mount Greater Headache, Mount Lesser Headache, and the Fever hills. . . . " This may have discouraged travelers, but 1,500 years later another traveler (as noted by Fa-Hsien) described a more daunting obstacle:

> The lakes in the Snow Mountains are inhabited by poisonous dragons that breathe out poisonous clouds when enraged. . . .
>
> Travelers are often attacked by fierce dragons so that they should neither wear red garments, nor carry gourds with them, nor shout loudly. . . .

We haven't heard much about mountain dragons recently, but such beliefs persisted for a long time. Around 1600 an Italian naturalist published four beautiful volumes with drawings of 250 varieties of dragons, and in 1712 a distinguished professor recorded sworn statements of people who had been attacked by dragons, illustrating them with careful drawings. Dragons may have added to the reasons why only a few people ventured into the mountains to hunt for food or gold or as missionaries to make converts. In olden days a few intrepid explorers and some invaders crossed high mountains and suffered great hardship from cold and altitude, but dragons today are limited to deep waters.

In the fourteenth and fifteenth centuries, the Mongol Hordes rampaged across Central Asia and high Tibet, and into Europe, crossing deserts and high mountain passes. Mirza Muhammad Haider, one of the Mongol chieftains, described in perceptive detail the hazards of altitude on the high Central Asian plateau:

Another peculiarity of Tibet is the *dam-giri* which the Moghuls call Yas and which is common to the whole country, though less prevalent in the region of forts and villages. The symptoms are a feeling of severe sickness (*nakhushi*) and in every case one's breath so seizes him that he becomes exhausted, just as if he had run up a steep hill with a heavy burden on his back. On account of the oppression it causes it is difficult to sleep. Should, however, sleep overtake one, the eyes are hardly closed before one is awake with a start caused by the oppression of the lungs and chest. . . .

When overcome by this malady the patient becomes senseless, begins to talk nonsense, and sometimes the power of speech is lost, while the palms of the hands and the soles of the feet become swollen. Often, when this last symptom occurs, the patient dies between dawn and breakfast time; at other times he lingers on for several days. . . .

This malady only attacks strangers; the people of Tibet know nothing of it, nor do their doctors know why it attacks strangers. Nobody has ever been able to cure it. The colder the air, the more severe is the form of the malady.

Haider's account is notable in several respects: He gave us an early description of several important signs and symptoms of mountain sickness, he noted that it also affects horses, and he clearly recognized that something protected lifelong altitude residents—which may be the first unequivocal mention of acclimatization.

Jesuit Missionary Father Alonzo Ovalde, traveling in the Andes near the end of the sixteenth century, described what others might expect to experience (as recounted in Pinkerton's *A General Collection of the Best and Most Interesting Voyages and Discoveries in all Parts of the World*, 1813):

When we come to ascend the highest point of the mountain, we feel an aire so piercing and subtile that it is with much difficulty we can breathe, which obliges us to fetch our breath quick and strong and to open our mouths wider than ordinary, applying to them likewise our handkerchiefs to protect our mouth and break the extreme coldness of the air and to make it more proportionable to the temperature which the heart requires, not to be suffocated; this I have experienced every time I have passed this mighty mountain.

Father Ovalde's more frequently quoted colleague, Father Jose Acosta, was more dramatic:

. . . I felt such a deadly pain I was ready to hurl myself from the horse onto the ground . . . and almost immediately there followed so much retching and vomiting that I thought I would lose my soul, because after what I ate and the phlegm, there followed bile and more bile both yellow and green so that I brought up blood from the violence I felt in my stomach. . . . I therefore persuade myselfe that the element of the aire there is so subtile and delicate as it is not proportionable with the breathing of man.

Horace-Benedict de Saussure, a broadly educated philosopher-scientist, experienced great weakness during the second ascent of Mont Blanc (15,771 feet) in 1787. Later, impressed by his sensations on the summit, he recorded his pulse, respirations, temperature, and symptoms on that and other mountains, and wrote perceptively:

> . . . the sort of weariness which proceeds from the rarity of the air is absolutely insurmountable; when it is at its height, the most imminent peril will not make you move a step faster. . . . Since the air [on the summit of Mont Blanc] had hardly more than half of its usual density, compensation had to be made for the lack of density by the frequency of inspirations. That is the cause of the fatigue that one experiences at great heights. For while the respiration is accelerating, so also is the circulation.

De Saussure may or may not have related his fatigue to the discovery of oxygen ten years earlier, but he clearly recognized that decreased air density was involved, as did Friedrich von Tschudi, who wrote a dramatic account of his nasty experience while exploring the high Andes in 1838–1842:

> My panting mule slackened his pace, and seemed unwilling to mount a rather steep ascent which we had now arrived at. To relieve him I dismounted, and began walking at a rapid pace. But I soon felt the influence of the rarefied air, and I experienced an oppressive sensation which I had never known before. I stood still for a few moments to recover myself, and then tried to advance. My heart throbbed audibly; my breathing was short and interrupted. A world's weight seemed to lie upon my chest; my lips swelled and burst; the capillaries of my eyes gave way, and blood flowed from them. In a few moments my senses began to leave me. I could neither see, hear, nor feel distinctly. A gray mist floated before my eyes, and I felt myself involved in that struggle between life and death which, a short time before, I fancied I could discern on the face of nature. Had all the riches of earth, or the glories of heaven, awaited me a few hundred feet higher, I could not have stretched out my hand toward them. In that half senseless state I lay stretched on the ground until I felt sufficiently recovered to remount my mule.

A century later, more and more adventurous men and women were climbing high mountains and, not surprisingly, describing their different sensations. Once the nature of the atmosphere had been described, the causes of mountain sickness could be more closely examined. By the end of the nineteenth century it was generally agreed that lack of oxygen due to decreased atmospheric pressure caused most of the other illness experienced on mountains.

Early Research into the Causes of Mountain Sickness

Two hundred years after Acosta and Ovalde, after the importance of oxygen for life had been recognized, some perceptive individuals put such mountain experiences together with Perier's demonstration that air weighed less at altitude (see "The Barometer" in Chapter 1, The Air About Us), and agreed that the thinner air on mountains might cause mountain sickness. Thomas Beddoes recognized this in 1818 when he wrote:

> Now in ascending these rugged heights the muscular exertion must expend a great deal of oxygene which the rarefied atmosphere will supply but scantily. . . . The experiments of Mr. Saussure, Pini, and Reboul, concur in shewing that, independent of its rarefaction, the atmosphere of very elevated mountains contains a far smaller proportion of oxygene than that of lower regions, especially than that of the high vallies of the Alps.

Twenty years later a famous traveler, Alexander von Humboldt (whose account is described in Pinkerton's *General Collection*), after comparing his symptoms on the high Andes to seasickness, expressed the same idea as we might today:

> . . . the air seems as rich in oxygen in these high regions as in the inferior regions; but [since] in this rarefied air the barometric pressure was less than half the level to which we are normally exposed in the plains, a lower quantity of oxygen was taken up by the blood at each breath.

He was very nearly right! However, in the first half of the nineteenth century only a few persons thought that lack of oxygen was the major cause of mountain sickness. Distinguished doctors offered a variety of explanations, many of them fanciful, but some worth quoting. In 1853 Stanhope Speer, an English physician, after climbing Mont Blanc, wrote a book listing a score of symptoms and summarized his thoughts about the causes, though he avoided direct mention of the role of oxygen:

> These symptoms [of mountain sickness] may be referred to a threefold source, viz, a gradually increasing congestion of the deeper portions of the circulatory apparatus, increased venosity of the blood, and loss of equilibrium between the pressure of the external air and that of the gases existing within the intestines. . . . the causes of

mountain sickness are themselves the result of a change from a given atmospheric pressure and temperature, to one in which both are greatly and suddenly diminished.

His contemporary, Conrad Meyer-Ahrens, listed even more symptoms and more explanations in 1898:

Others [symptoms] are observed, although less frequently, such as vomiting of blood; oozing of blood from the mucous membrane of the lips and skin (due merely to the dessication of these membranes); blunting of sensory perceptions and the intelligence, impatience, irritability. . . .

When one sees the appearance of mountain sickness correspond to varying altitudes, he asks himself what [causes them]. In my opinion the principal role belongs to the decrease of the absolute quantity of oxygen in the rarefied air, the rapidity of evaporation and the intense action of light, direct or reflected from the snow; the direct action of the decrease of pressure should be placed in the second rank . . . to which are added others due to the action of light on the cerebral functions, an action which affects the preparation of the blood liquid.

In view of what we know today, it's especially interesting to note that Meyer-Ahrens, a distinguished medical practitioner, included, as an effect of altitude, the blunting of intelligence and of sensory impressions.

Figure 18. *Dr. Janssen ascending Mont Blanc*

It is also interesting to read the variety of effects that different individuals suffered and described, and the different causes ascribed by early mountaineers. For example, 150 years ago quite a few doctors considered the excessive weakness at altitude due to "dislocation of the coxo-femoral articulation

STUDYING HOW EXERTION
AFFECTS MOUNTAIN SICKNESS

In 1891 a Swiss railway company planned to build a railway to the summit of the Jungfrau (13,600 feet), which affords a spectacular view of the Matterhorn. Dr. H. Kronecker, an experienced physician-mountaineer, was hired to determine whether tourists might suffer from altitude sickness during the ascent. He first made a series of studies in a decompression chamber, taking two persons at a time to a pressure equivalent to 13,000 feet in fifteen to twenty-five minutes and then "descending" in twenty minutes, which was the time estimated for the round-trip railroad journey. He examined pulse and blood pressure and ability to exercise, finding that this simulated altitude and rate of ascent would cause symptoms in some of the thirty persons studied, and the effects would be aggravated by exertion. He studied reports from many of the mountain railroads in North and South America, and examined accounts by many mountaineers who had—or had not—suffered from mountain sickness. Kronecker began his work doubting that mountain sickness would be a problem, but his travels and his research studies convinced him that the altitude of 13,600 feet might indeed cause problems for passengers on the proposed railway.

So he recruited seven persons (ages ten to seventy) and persuaded them to be carried up the mountain, as they would be in a train. He thought this little experiment would suggest what effect the absence of strenuous exertion would have on passengers. Sixty men took turns hauling the sled and passengers from 5,500 feet to 12,000 feet. The porters worked in shifts but were exhausted by the effort, and several were too sick to continue. But the "passengers" felt no discomfort, though most noted increased pulse rates and respiration. Kronecker added: "The most important and striking symptom was the disastrous result of even the least muscular exertion." (The illustration in Figure 18 shows a similar experiment made by astronomer Janssen on Mont Blanc, as he was preparing to build an observatory near the summit; Janssen had the same experience as Kronecker.)

This satisfied Kronecker and the railroad company that the trip would be safe and feasible, providing passengers did not exert themselves at all. As it turned out, the railroad was built only to the Jungfraujoch (11,300 feet) and has been popular ever since—although many visitors do become ill after walking around at the upper station.

(hip joint) from the decreased atmospheric pressure." There's an abundance of tales from the Golden Age of Alpine climbing (1854–1885) when failure to describe one's symptoms might cast doubt on whether one had reached a summit. Some effects, like bleeding from the eyes or nose that so many experienced in those days, simply don't happen or are rare today.

Lack of Oxygen Determined to Be the Cause

Before the nineteenth century ended, serious research in mountain sickness had begun. Paul Bert was the leader in this research, and is rightly regarded as the major historical figure in altitude physiology (see Chapter 4, Moving Blood: Circulation). His pioneering studies of how hemoglobin carries oxygen, and his first curves showing the relationship of the partial pressure of oxygen to arterial saturation, were certainly as important as his best-known work in decompression chambers and with gas mixtures. These studies proved that lack of oxygen was the principal if not the only cause of mountain sickness, which could be prevented—and remedied—by breathing supplementary oxygen.

Figure 19A. *Workers starting construction of the Margherita hut, 15,025 feet*

THE MARGHERITA HUT

Queen Margherita of Italy was an enthusiastic mountain climber, and generously supported Angelo Mosso's research in mountain sickness. On August 18, 1893, the queen and entourage, including her little dog, climbed to the summit of Monte Rosa to dedicate a special altitude research laboratory. Mosso did most of his studies on the summit of Monte Rosa (15,025 feet) or in the Sella laboratory 4,000 feet lower on the mountain, whereas Paul Bert had done no mountain studies. Mosso exercised soldiers who served as his subjects, on the summit and at the base, to compare their work capacity as well as to measure respiratory exchanges. Although he disagreed with Bert in some respects, Mosso's studies of work, the use of carbon dioxide to prevent mountain sickness, and particularly his studies of the brain at altitude in his decompression chamber were complementary to Bert's and equally important.

Angelo Mosso, a distinguished Italian physiologist and ardent mountaineer, thought otherwise. With the enthusiastic support of Queen Margherita, he established a small laboratory, precariously perched on the summit of Monte Rosa (15,025 feet). Near the foot of the mountain he built a larger laboratory, including a small decompression chamber. Mosso studied Bert's book, but cited his own studies to contradict Bert:

Figure 19B.
Architect's drawing of the Margherita hut

> Mountain sickness has been thought a simple asphyxia due to lack of oxygen, whereas in reality, it is a very complex phenomenon, as the arterial blood loses a considerable part of its carbonic acid when the barometric pressure diminishes, and even before the effects due to lack of oxygen appear the phenomena produced by the diminution of carbonic acid in the blood have already manifested themselves.

He coined the word *acapnia* to describe this condition of "diminution of carbonic acid," which he believed was the major cause of mountain sickness. He buttressed his case by showing that breathing air to which a small percentage of carbon dioxide had been added enabled his subjects to tolerate very high altitude with few symptoms. (This beneficial effect may have been due to the greatly increased breathing caused by the increased carbon dioxide in the chamber air.) Mosso also made some daring experiments by taking up in his decompression chamber a man whose brain was partly exposed as the result of an accident, enabling Mosso to observe how the brain became congested at altitude.

TWO DECOMPRESSION CHAMBERS

Paul Bert's best known studies are those done in a decompression chamber built in 1870 to his specifications and funded by his friend, Dr. Denis Jourdanet. After many experiments with animals in a smaller chamber, in 1877 he wrote:

> Evidently I could not limit myself to experiments made on animals, however convincing, when I was using practical precepts intended for mountain travellers and aeronauts.
>
> I resolved to begin by experimenting on myself. I had already undergone in my large sheet-iron cylinders, rather considerable decompression to the point of experiencing certain discomforts. I then thought of trying the test again, so as to remove the discomfort by breathing superoxygenated air. I placed beside me a large rubber bag, containing air whose oxygen content was in proportion to the degree of decompression.

Bert made more experiments and effectively proved that breathing his "superoxygenated air" would prevent or relieve the "discomforts" that, as we know, were similar to mountain sickness. Thus he was able to state that lack of oxygen, and not decreased pressure alone, caused mountain sickness. I believe that this was the first use of a decompression chamber for human studies since Hooke's "barrel" 200 years before!

Angelo Mosso had a similar chamber built around 1890. This was smaller but had a window and access for instrumentation. He studied soldiers during exercise on Monte Rosa, Italy, and in his chamber. He also studied a man whose skull was incomplete after an accident; this enabled Mosso to observe changes in a portion of the brain during decompression.

Figure 20. *Paul Bert's decompression chamber*

Mosso's acapnia theory had few supporters. Paul Bert and Denis Jourdanet, building on the work of others, had conclusively shown that lack of oxygen was the primary cause of mountain sickness. Acapnia does occur at high altitude, but it is not the cause of mountain sickness, but instead a consequence of efforts to adjust to hypoxia.

High-altitude problems are certainly triggered by hypoxia, but what actually happens in the body to cause the signs and symptoms that range from unpleasant to fatal? Some other exposures, notably to heat, cause symptoms that are surprisingly similar to mountain sickness, as William Bean described in 1961:

There is a sense of overwhelming oppression which rapidly takes the spirit out of men. . . . Trifling work is fatiguing and more burdensome work rapidly leads to exhaustion. A throbbing headache may develop and reach cruel intensity. Dizziness occurs, accentuated in the standing position. Dyspnea may be a problem. . . . Nausea, vomiting and loss of appetite are commonplace. Lack of coordination reduces the efficiency. . . . Apathy may be interrupted by bursts of irritability. Judgment and morale decline. . . . Unwillingness to continue work or the onset of physical disability may rapidly disorganize a well-disciplined and efficient unit.

This suggests that the response to hypoxia is not specific but resembles those that can result from other stimuli too. We know also that not everything that causes lack of oxygen (for example, anemia or certain lung disorders) results in all the symptoms experienced on mountains. One recent study suggests that the combination of lack of oxygen and lack of

Figure 21. *Angelo Masso's decompression chamber*

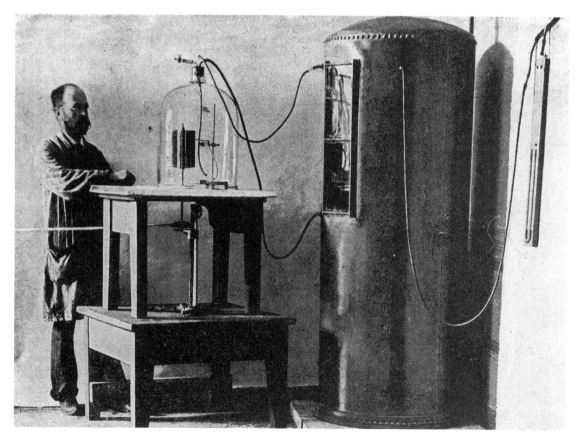

atmospheric pressure causes more symptoms than either lack of oxygen or decreased pressure alone. The question becomes more vexing as we learn more and more about our body's workings. Though we peel off layer after layer of information trying to uncover a core of "truth," we haven't reached it. We have, however, begun to see a common pathway along which the brain responds to hypoxia.

After Paul Bert's decisive work, the next big step in mountain medicine was taken by Thomas Ravenhill, physician for a mining company in Bolivia. He described three forms of mountain sickness he saw in persons coming up to 12,789 feet from sea level—a fifty-six-hour train trip—normal puna (the local name), cardiac puna, and nervous puna. These correspond to the classifications of acute mountain sickness (AMS), high altitude pulmonary edema (HAPE), and high altitude cerebral edema (HACE) that we use today.

What Is Mountain Sickness?

As mountain sicknesses have been studied more intensively, it has become evident that they form a spectrum of altitude-related problems in which now one, now another, dominates, and they are not separate discrete illnesses. Some form of mountain sickness is likely to affect anyone who goes rapidly above 8,000 feet, but lack of oxygen will affect different individuals differently.

For convenience we describe the signs and symptoms by familiar names and use acronyms as shorthand. The best known and most common has long been called Acute Mountain Sickness (AMS), or less often Benign Acute Mountain Sickness (BAMS), or in former times *puna, soroche, damgiri, yas,* and still others. Today we believe that AMS has some neurological elements, and overlaps to a varying degree with a second form, High Altitude Cerebral Edema (HACE). The current trend is to consider some hypoxic effect on the brain as provoking many or most of the signs and symptoms of AMS.

For that reason we could use the term AMS/HACE to describe the common form of mountain sickness, but to avoid confusion, here I stick with AMS for simple acute mountain sickness, and use HACE when the neurological symptoms dominate the picture and pose a greater threat. In this chapter I describe AMS, and I examine HACE separately and more completely in Chapter 7. However, it's important to remember that although AMS and HACE each has its own footprint, they run together!

Less closely related to these two is High Altitude Pulmonary Edema (HAPE), discussed in Chapter 8.

As more and more people go to the mountains, some bizarre and atypical illnesses are being reported on high mountains; these are included in this chapter, although some of them may not be unequivocally due to hypoxia. More older individuals and more people with some illness or disability are going where few of them dared go before, and they pose many questions difficult to answer. The question of who should not go to high altitudes is discussed in Chapter 11, Treatment (in Part IV, Prevention, Treatment, and the Mountaineer's World).

Acute Mountain Sickness (AMS)

At one end of the altitude illness spectrum is Acute Mountain Sickness. It is usually mild and lasts only a day or two, but it can be very unpleasant. A patient told me this typical story several years ago:

> My husband and I have gone skiing in Colorado for many years. We usually fly from the East Coast to Denver and drive up to the resort at 9,000 feet. By dinner time I have a splitting headache and feel slightly nauseated; I can't eat, and go off to bed, knowing that I'll toss and turn most of the night, unable to sleep. Usually the headache is a little better next morning, and by the second or third day I'm able to ski with pleasure for the next week.

Each time she went to altitude she was miserable for a day or two, but her symptoms never progressed or were complicated by the more serious problems in the spectrum. Over the years we have worked out a strategy that almost eliminates her symptoms.

Symptoms and Signs

We speak of *symptoms* to describe what a person experiences or feels, as compared to *signs*, which can be observed by others. Some persons who go to the mountains complain only of headache, while insomnia plagues others. Nausea and, often, vomiting is particularly unpleasant. Shortness of breath is not very bothersome unless AMS is complicated by HAPE. For many people, fatigue and weakness is the worst problem.

It's not unusual for someone to faint soon after arrival at moderate altitude, usually after a meal and a few drinks; though it is alarming, the victim recovers almost immediately. Of course, such an episode could possibly be due to something more serious, but it's important to remember that simple fainting isn't unusual.

Some individuals suffer a whole catastrophe of symptoms. Today we record specific observations. Table 1 shows the frequency of each of the common symptoms complained of by those who had AMS among the 3,158 visitors Honigman surveyed in 1993 at several resorts in the Colorado Rocky Mountains.

SYMPTOMS OF ACUTE MOUNTAIN SICKNESS

Table 1.

Symptom	Percent
Mild Headache	54%
Severe Headache	8%
Easy Fatigue	28%
Shortness of Breath	21%
Dizziness	21%
Loss of Appetite	11%
Sleep Disturbance	10%
Vomiting	3%

Incidence

Not everyone venturing onto the mountains suffers as much as those quoted earlier in this chapter, but roughly one out of every five persons going rapidly from low to moderate altitude (8,000–9,000 feet) will feel unpleasant effects. Most recover in thirty-six to forty-eight hours.

Speed of ascent and altitude reached make the difference between being sick or well, but this isn't always true: Some individuals are often sick, but others never. Some are sick on one day, but not on another in similar circumstances. It's been said for years that simple AMS is more common in some regions than in others, and that metallic ores, plants, radiation, or earth's magnetism play a role. These ideas seem far-fetched, but—who knows?—there are still many things we don't know or understand.

Table 2 shows the percentage of visitors who develop "typical" mild AMS at different elevations as reported by different observers.

INCIDENCE OF ACUTE MOUNTAIN SICKNESS

Table 2.

Author (Date)	Location	Altitude (in feet)	Percent with AMS
Montgomery (1989)	Colorado	6,765	20
		6,900	25
		8,900	40
Houston (1985)	Colorado	8,500	12
		9,500	17
Dean (1990)	Colorado	9,800	42
Maggiorini (1989)	Alps	6,700	9
		10,000	13
		12,000	34
		15,000	54
Hackett (1976)	Nepal	14,000	42
Honigman (1993)	Colorado	6–7,000	18
		7–9,000	22
		>9,000	27

Note that most of the authors in Table 2 were describing the mild form of AMS, without indicating whether other symptoms were present.

Montgomery's subjects were doctors attending medical meetings. Dean's subjects were 100 epidemiologists attending a scientific meeting. Maggiorini collected survey data from many thousands of climbers and walkers. Hackett's subjects were trekkers in Nepal.

Honigman reported data collected with a detailed questionnaire answered by 3,158 persons attending a variety of conferences during a two-year period at resorts 6,300–9,700 feet high. Some caution is needed in interpreting his numbers because most of those surveyed were males averaging forty-three years of age attending forty-five different conferences, and thus were not typical recreational visitors. The diagnosis of AMS was based on specific criteria agreed to at the Lake Louise Hypoxia Symposium in 1991 (see Figure 22, below). The significant data in Honigman's study are shown in Table 3.

FURTHER DATA IN HONIGMAN'S STUDY

	Total People	With AMS	
Gender	68% male	24%	Table 3.
	32% female	28%	
Previous AMS	47%	35%	
Live near sea level	88%	27%	

Other data in this survey showed little difference between those who had a few alcoholic drinks after arrival and those who did not, between previous smokers and nonsmokers, or between those who were overweight and those who were not. A small number gave a history of heart or lung disease or hypertension, but these conditions made no significant difference in the incidence of AMS. It is interesting that a third of all who said they had previously experienced altitude illness also had AMS on this occasion.

It was somewhat surprising to me that there is not a great deal of difference between sexes in resistance or susceptibility to most mountain sicknesses. It was less surprising to find that age made differences that are almost linear. Gender and age, and physical fitness, are discussed in Chapter 15.

Differences in Studies of AMS

The differences in incidence between different studies are striking and, although no statistical listing of specific symptoms in the Alps has been reported, many observers believe that symptoms really are fewer and milder at comparable altitudes there than in the United States. Most Alpine resorts are farther south than most of those in the United States, and therefore slightly lower "physiologically," as explained below.

The most likely explanation for the differences reported in different geographical areas lies in how the data were collected, how mountain sickness was defined, and, more important, the profile of ascent. A half-dozen lists of questions or other criteria for defining AMS and quantifying its severity have been used, with marginal agreement between them. To reconcile these differences, the Lake Louise Consensus (developed at the 1993 Lake Louise Hypoxia Symposium) defines the criteria for diagnosis, and as more workers apply these, the apparent differences may decrease.

Figure 22. *Lake Louise Consensus Report*

1. Headache	0 No headache 1 Mild headache 2 Moderate headache 3 Severe headache, incapacitating
2. Gastrointestinal symptoms	0 No gastrointestinal symptoms 1 Poor appetite or nausea 2 Moderate nausea or vomiting 3 Severe nausea and vomiting, incapactitating
3. Fatigue and/or weakness	0 Not tired or weak 1 Mild fatigue/weakness 2 Moderate fatigue/weakness 3 Severe fatigue/weakness, incapacitating
4. Dizziness/ lightheadedness	0 Not dizzy 1 Mild dizziness 2 Moderate dizziness 3 Severe dizziness, incapacitating
5. Difficulty sleeping	0 Slept as well as usual 1 Did not sleep as well as usual 2 Woke many times, poor night's sleep 3 Could not sleep at all
6. Change in mental status	0 Not tired or weak 1 Lethargy/lassitude 2 Disoriented/confused 3 Stuport/semiconsciousness 4 Coma
7. Ataxia	0 No ataxia 1 Maneuvers to maintain balance 2 Steps off line 3 Falls down 4 Can't stand
8. Peripheral edema	1 No peripheral edema 1 Peripheral edema at one location 2 Peripheral edema at two or more locations

Functional score. The functional consequences of the AMS Self-reported score should be further evaluated by one option question asked after the AMS Self-report questionnaire. Alternatively, this question may be asked by the examiner if Clinical Assessment is performed.

Overall, if you had any symptoms, how did they affect your activity?
0   No reduction in activity
1   Mild reduction in activity
2   Moderate reduction in activity
3   Severe reduction in activity (e.g., bedrest)

LAKE LOUISE CONSENSUS ON AMS

In 1993 a group of scientists working with altitude sicknesses proposed a grading system in an attempt to make reporting more uniform. According to this consensus, in an individual who has rapidly ascended to an altitude of higher than 6,000 feet, the presence and severity of each symptom is scored and the total score gives a grade by which studies by different workers in different places can be compared. It has the advantage of being simpler than several other systems in use, and after a few years has become standard in most altitude research facilities.

Of course, changes in weather and temperature affect the barometric pressure—and thus the oxygen available in the air. The higher that one is, the greater will be the effect of even small weather-related changes. In bowl-shaped snow valleys, such as are found on many great peaks, the reflected hot sun has a weakening effect, as so well described in effects from heat, which can be confused with AMS.

In addition, due to the flattening of the earth's atmosphere over the polar regions, the air blanket over the earth exerts less pressure in the high latitudes than nearer the equator: Alaska's Denali (Mount McKinley, 20,300 feet at 64 degrees north latitude) is actually more than 2,000 feet higher *physiologically* than Africa's Mount Kilimanjaro (19,340 feet near the equator).

These and other factors not well recognized will probably explain the differences found in even well-controlled studies. But individual characteristics are also important. Some people (like my patient mentioned earlier in this chapter, and many others) are often sick, while others are rarely or never affected. Recent studies have revealed a genetic factor that affects how the body processes oxygen; perhaps someday we may be able to identify a specific gene responsible for mountain sicknesses or resistance to it. Possibly this will be important not only for mountain lovers but for many more who develop illnesses that interfere with oxygen delivery.

Uncommon Mountain Sicknesses
Chronic Mountain Sickness

In 1927 Carlos Monge Senior described a new illness that he called "Erythremia Syndrome of High Altitude," which is now known as Chronic Mountain Sickness (CMS) or Monge's disease in his honor. His patient was a thirty-eight-year-old man who had come up from sea level and had worked at 14,200 feet for one year. He complained of multiple aches and pains, easy fatigue, insomnia, and mental confusion; his blood showed half again the normal red cell and hemoglobin content. All his symptoms disappeared after a time at sea level, but returned when he went back to altitude.

Over the next seventy years, many similar cases have been described and it is now a well-recognized though uncommon disease. Males who were born or have lived continuously above 12,000 feet for many months or years are affected four times as often as females. Cases have been reported among Tibetans and Nepalese, and their disease is similar to that of people in the Andes, though perhaps less common. Typically the victim is so cyanotic that his skin looks purple, with flushed cheeks and blue nails. He complains of fatigue, shortness of breath, and muscle and joint pains, and sometimes pain in the chest. Red cells are greatly increased and the hemoglobin may be as high as 22 grams (normally 14 grams), with hematocrit from 60 percent to 80 percent (normally 50 percent). The right side of the heart is enlarged and pulmonary artery pressure is high, often very high. The *hypoxic ventilatory response* (HVR) is blunted, as it is in most long-term altitude residents, which is not unusual. Death from right heart failure is likely unless the patient goes to sea level, where he or she recovers slowly, but the problem recurs on return to altitude.

A few typical cases have been described at 10,000 feet, but a few at 7,500 and 6,500 feet are questionable. Without the four diagnostic criteria (cyanosis, arterial desaturation, pulmonary hypertension, and blunted ventilatory response), excessive red cell production (*polycythemia*) may be only an over-exuberant response to altitude, or due to undiagnosed lung or other disease.

Monge later described a subacute form, midway between AMS and CMS, occurring in persons who have recently moved to altitude and have been unable to adjust. It's a rare problem, but is also due to inability to acclimatize, and the person usually gives up and returns to sea level.

Brisket Disease in Cattle

Though there's no animal model of AMS/HACE or HAPE, there is much to be learned from the effect of altitude on certain strains of cattle. When these particular breeds, native to low altitude, are taken above 8,000 feet, many develop a form of altitude illness called "brisket" disease, because they accumulate fluid in loose tissues under the neck (the brisket), in the liver, and in the chest cavity. This edema is due to heart failure—the right side of the heart is unable to pump adequate blood to the lungs against the high pulmonary artery pressure, and dilates and then fails. Brisket disease is quite a different kind of maladjustment to altitude than is HAPE, and it is fatal unless the animal is taken down to low altitude. These strains of cattle have a genetic predisposition to brisket disease, which might have some interesting implications for humans.

When I lived in Colorado a rancher called me about two valuable young bulls he had just brought up to 8200 feet: both had developed brisket disease; did I know anything about this? Actually I had attended a meeting on the subject organized by Hans Hecht, so I said happily that I would cure his bulls. At the ranch his cowhands threw one of the patients; I shaved his legs, but my electrocardiogram was a flat line. A cowhand said wryly, "Doc, I think yo' patient's daid." The struggle had caused cardiac arrest! I decided to treat the other without an EKG and that one recovered! But for a long time afterwards, when I suggested doing an EKG on a patient, the response was: "I don't know, Doc. I heard what happened to Werk Cook's bull."

Subacute Infantile Mountain Sickness

In the last few years, two other types of mountain sickness have also been identified as "subacute." The first was described in 1989 and called Subacute Infantile Mountain Sickness. The only victims so far reported have been infants of Chinese parentage taken to Tibet, or born in Tibet at altitude, who developed characteristic right-sided heart failure within a few months after birth. Later some children two or three years old were found with a similar condition. These infants often died unless taken to sea level, and autopsy showed increased muscularization of pulmonary arterioles, as well as right ventricular dilatation and hypertrophy attributed to severe pulmonary hypertension. Kept at altitude, children were not responsive to heart medication but sometimes recovered—slowly—when taken to sea level.

This childhood heart failure is due to excessive increase in pulmonary artery pressure, causing dilatation and failure of the right ventricle. It's analogous to brisket disease in cattle, which I describe above, rather than to Monge's disease.

Subacute Adult Mountain Sickness

Soon after this, reports surfaced of a similar condition that appeared in adult soldiers after months of living in combat zones in the high Himalayas, even though they had ascended slowly enough and apparently had acclimatized well. Clinically the patients developed massive edema of the legs, swelling of the liver, fluid in the chest cavity, and dilatation of the heart, especially of the right ventricle. However, pulmonary resistance was not exaggerated, and resting pulmonary artery pressure was only slightly above normal. Significantly, however, this rose very high during exertion. Because these soldiers had to work very hard for many hours in adverse conditions, it is probable that the *episodic* pulmonary hypertension led to right heart failure. When taken to low altitude, they lost fluid rapidly, and their hearts returned slowly to normal. Neither they nor the infants with Subacute Infantile Mountain Sickness showed an increased hematocrit. It seems likely that this Subacute Adult Mountain Sickness is a variant of the infantile form, and both are comparable to brisket disease in cattle.

Several features are normally seen in all persons living at altitude:

increased hemoglobin, which is excessive in Chronic Mountain Sickness; increased pulmonary artery pressure, the prime culprit in Subacute Infantile Mountain Sickness and Subacute Adult Mountain Sickness; and a blunted ventilatory drive, which is present but less striking in the subacute forms.

Digestive System Problems

The gastro-intestinal tract is often under siege in the mountains. The approach march to a mountain in developing countries can expose climbers to many parasites lurking for the unwary, and a bad spell of **dysentery** can spoil a climb. More relevant is the fact that dysentery disrupts fluid and electrolyte balance, wastes salt, and leads to *hypovolemia* (low blood volume, or shock) and *hyponatremia* (low blood sodium), which can be at best exhausting and at worst seriously disabling. Maintaining a normal water/salt balance is very important not only for comfort, but also to minimize altitude illnesses.

Peptic ulcers are not rare among native altitude residents, and have occasionally been reported among expedition members. There haven't been enough reports to judge either incidence or seriousness, but this might be a problem for some with such a history or predisposition.

Malabsorption has been blamed for the weight loss experienced by most climbers who go above 20,000 feet for an extended time, but the evidence is not persuasive. Expedition food is not always appetizing, nutritious, or plentiful, and when appetites are finicky anyway, climbers don't eat enough to make up for the great energy they expend. Even under the comparatively peaceful and comfortable conditions in the chamber during Operation Everest (see Chapter 13), all eight men lost weight—and this was directly related to their low caloric intake. It is possible that **vitamin deficiencies** may occur during several weeks on an inadequate diet, and this is perhaps the only reason for supplementary vitamins and minerals. But here too there's not a lot of persuasive data.

Bill Tilman, an expedition mountaineer icon, said that the mountaineer's worst problems were **hemorrhoids** and bedsores, but these don't appear on any list of altitude illnesses. Hemorrhoids can indeed be a problem, and a medical kit should make provision for this often neglected ailment.

Respiratory Tract Problems

Sore throat and cough affects just about everyone who has climbed very high anywhere in the world. They're blamed on overbreathing of huge volumes of cold, very dry air, usually through the mouth. The mouth is not quite as efficient at humidifying inhaled air as is the nose, and it's reasonable to expect a dry, painful throat to result. But during Operation Everest II (see Chapter 13), most of the subjects had very sore throats above 23,000 feet, even though the chamber air was warmer than 72 degrees and very damp (about 100 percent humidity). We took throat cultures and gave different medications, with no benefit, and finally concluded that this **painful throat** might be a direct effect of hypoxia.

"**Climbers hack**" is a different matter, caused by the drying effect in the airways, from overbreathing cold, dry air. The incessant cough can crack a rib, as it did for Japanese climber Sumiyo on Everest in 1996. Howard Somervell was forced to turn back near the summit of Everest in 1924 because of such a cough—which finally dislodged a large mucous plug from his airway. It's interesting to note that this same cough occurs in mountain resorts during severe weather, and also in the polar regions—so it's not so much an altitude problem as a problem of cold, dry air.

Respiratory infections do not seem to be increased in the mountains. Once an expedition has left villages behind, once the infections that may have been brought along with the party have subsided, and unless new people join, respiratory infections are unusual. However, there have been a number of cases of **pneumonia** in troops and among members of high mountain trips, and these can be very severe and dangerous.

Blood Problems

Bleeding and clotting are affected by hypoxia, but to a lesser degree than by dehydration. We don't see or hear of the frequent nosebleeds, "bleeding from the eyes," and bleeding gums so frequently described in climbing accounts in the last century, but why this is so isn't clear. **Blood clots** are frequent at high altitude due to hemoconcentration and the proliferation of red blood cells. However, several studies of fibrinolysis and the clotting mechanism at altitude haven't yet clarified the situation.

Both bleeding and clotting are discussed in Chapter 7, HACE: High Altitude Cerebral Edema, because either may be the cause of **stroke.** We have heard a good deal about strokes on high mountain expeditions and, because the population at risk is not in the stroke-risk age group, it seems likely that bleeding and clotting changes at altitude do increase this risk. Women taking contraceptive pills have been reported as more susceptible to **high altitude thrombosis,** but more recent data tend to downplay this risk.

Most experienced climbers believe that **infection** is frequent, and at altitude even minor abrasions or cuts are **slow-healing.** The anecdotal evidence is persuasive, but studies of the immune system are not consistent evidence that immunity is reduced. Whatever the cause, even small wounds should be treated more carefully than at sea level.

High Altitude Retinal Hemorrhages (HARH)

In 1968 during the Mount Logan High Altitude Physiology Study, a young climber became unconscious soon after being flown to the 17,500-foot laboratory. He was airlifted to a hospital, where he recovered rapidly from what was considered to be a severe form of altitude sickness. The internist noticed a number of hemorrhages in the retina of each eye, and tests for diabetes, kidney disease, leukemia, or other possible causes did not explain them. I was unsure of what this meant, but a few weeks later one of the scientists, also flown to the high laboratory, was also found to have a few scattered retinal hemorrhages. This seemed more than coincidence, so we added retinal studies to the Logan protocols, and over the next few years found that many of the mountaineers had similar hemorrhages.

We published several reports about these high altitude retinal hemorrhages, calling them HARH. Then in 1969 General Inder Singh of the Indian Army Medical Corps wrote two articles about altitude sickness among Indian troops flown or driven rapidly from low to high altitude during the Sino-Indian border conflict of 1962. Among other things, he noted engorgement of the retinal veins, swelling of the optic nerve head (*papilledema)*, and "vitreous hemorrhages" in several of the sickest soldiers, but he may have confused "vitreous" with "retinal." Singh's men were very sick and the eye pathology was attributed to edema of the brain (which he found in two brain biopsies).

By contrast, many of the individuals we saw on Mount Logan with HARH were not very sick and would not have been aware of the retinal hemorrhages had we not examined their eyes. We did not see hemorrhages in the vitreous, but only in the retina, behind the retinal limiting membrane, to be exact.

During the next few years on Mount Logan we took hundreds of photographs, examined retinal capillary leakage by fluorescein injection with strobe photography, and tried to correlate these hemorrhages with other symptoms, time at altitude, exertion, and other influences.

We found that half of the thirty-nine subjects most completely studied at 17,500 feet showed HARH. Our data showed that strenuous exertion did increase the likelihood of retinal hemorrhages but probably was not itself the cause. We did not find any relationship between number of hemorrhages and symptoms of AMS.

Some had only a few small hemorrhages while others had large and frightening pools of blood. Papilledema was rare, though the optic disc was engorged in several persons. Both retinal veins and arteries were distended and tortuous, and blood flow was significantly greater and faster than at sea level.

The leakage occurred from the smaller vessels but we could not be sure whether from the arterial or venous end of the capillaries. We saw "cotton wool spots," which indicate lack of blood flow (*retinal ischemia)* in a small area, in one of the thirty-nine persons. Fluorescein injection showed leakage in 40 percent of the individuals we studied, strongly suggesting that the capillaries were more permeable or more subject to tearing than normal. In our series only one or two people noticed any effect on vision, but one individual with a hemorrhage in the area of central vision (the *macula*) did describe a small blind spot. Many hemorrhages disappeared during the weeks at altitude, and others were gone at the end of the altitude stay. As has been true with other cases since then, the central blind spot in the individual with a macular hemorrhage took several years to clear.

RETINAL HEMORRHAGES

From 1967 to 1979, the Arctic Institute of North America sponsored an altitude research laboratory at 17,500 feet on Mount Logan, Canada's highest peak. It was there, in 1968, that retinal hemorrhages due to high altitude were first noted and described over the next few years. We supplemented inspection of the retina through an ophthalmoscope with retinal photographs, finding many different sizes—from single, small, flame-shaped hemorrhages to many or large blobs of blood. In addition, the veins and arteries, and occasionally the optic nerve itself, were dilated or swollen. We described these High Altitude Retinal Hemorrhages (HARH) in a number of papers, and many others have since added to our observations.

Other Studies

Since then many doctors have looked for HARH on mountain expeditions and a few times during decompression chamber work. The reported incidence has ranged from 15 percent to 90 percent, and HARH have been observed at as low as 11,000 feet and as high as 25,000 feet. Many confounding circumstances such as exertion, speed of ascent, hydration, experience of observer, and so on make it difficult to determine incidence more closely.

Almost all agree that HARH do not affect future vision, with the exception of those that occur in or near the macula. These need special mention. In correspondence with me, ophthalmologist-mountaineer Mike Wiedman writes:

> *Peripheral HARH and retinal hypoxia do not permanently affect visual function. But macular hemorrhage threatens permanent partial visual loss. By the very nature of its random occurrence, macular hemorrhage can reoccur with repeated hypoxic exposure.*

Wiedman suggests that simply by chance alone, a macular bleed could occur again and add to the damage. He has seen many victims of macular hemorrhages, few of whom recovered full vision; in my own case a blind spot the size and shape of this letter **o** has persisted for forty years. Wiedman feels that those who have had macular hemorrhages should be wary of going to altitude again, though this depends somewhat on the completeness with which macular vision recovers. He also believes that all HARH are accompanied by small hemorrhages in the brain. A few conservative doctors agree and advise that if someone has had HARH, he or she would be unwise to go very high again—advice that few mountaineers are likely to accept or heed. But if a macular hemorrhage appears, descent would be prudent—just in case the damage might increase.

Capillary Leakage

The question of capillary permeability has been debated, not only in HARH but in the whole spectrum of AMS/HACE and HAPE. Leakage from the small vessels of most of the body can happen through gaps in the lining of the blood vessels. But the endothelial cells lining the retinal capillaries resemble those in the brain and lungs, rather than those in the rest of the body, and have tight junctions between them. It's possible that the increased blood flow and dilatation may have in a few places opened these tight junctions and allowed leakage. It's probable that nitric oxide (NO) (which I discuss in Chapter 4, Moving Blood: Circulation) is involved in the retinal circulation.

In contrast to the capillaries in the brain, those in the retina are not supported by the hairlike *glia* that surround and protect those in the brain from overdistention, and they may be more susceptible to leakage due to the increased blood flow. There's one report of examination of the eye of a doctor who died of HACE, which showed that the retinal hemorrhages came from small veins.

Do Hemorrhages Occur Elsewhere in the Body?

These leaks in the retinal blood vessels raise some intriguing questions. First and foremost is whether they occur elsewhere in the body at altitude. Since the eye is often called the window of the brain, we must wonder, as Wiedman asks: "If small vessel hemorrhages occur in the retina, can the brain be far behind?" It's a distressing thought, but we can't answer with any assurance. Patients who die of altitude illness often show small (and large) hemorrhages in the brain, but these are extreme cases. Patients at the HACE end of the AMS/HACE spectrum show signs of malfunction in certain areas of the brain, but these disappear—usually—when the person recovers. A few studies suggest that there are small long-lasting mental changes after prolonged stay at very high altitudes. But today hundreds of thousands of persons have spent long periods at very high altitudes, and there's little firm evidence consistent with lasting brain damage.

Splinter hemorrhages have been described beneath the fingernails at high altitude, but these might well have been caused by the trauma of climbing or by cold. Traces of blood have been found in urine of people after ascent to moderate elevations, but this is not common, or at least has not often been mentioned along with other occasional changes in kidney function. One wonders whether the many reports of bleeding from the eyes, gums, and nose often mentioned by Victorian-age mountaineers could be somehow related to increased capillary fragility.

Clinical Importance

It's worth repeating that most HARH are not important clinically, that they cause little change in vision at the time or later, always except for those in the macula, and that they disappear without treatment. Accounts of blindness as well as blurred and double vision are almost surely due to other causes, some of which are discussed in Chapter 7, HACE: High Altitude Cerebral Edema. The importance of HARH is what they might be telling us about what happens elsewhere in the body. Although other ophthalmologists and climbers disagree, Mike Wiedman says:

> I've been sermonizing for twenty years and five Everest expeditions about HARH being a prognosticator of cerebral hemorrhages. . . . I would advise climbers that there is a probability of concurrent brain damage when HARH are seen. The brain hemorrhage may be of uncertain extent but easy odds are that it is there. . . . If mountaineers wish to go on with such full disclosure, that's their prerogative.

That might be one way to reduce congestion on the world's highest mountains, and it might also dampen enthusiasm for going anywhere above 15,000 feet! Right now it's appropriate to warn climbers about the lasting effects of macular hemorrhage, but we don't know enough to connect HARH firmly with brain hemorrhage or damage.

Other Causes of Retinal Hemorrhages

It's important to remember that retinal hemorrhages (RH) do occur in many other conditions besides hypoxia of high altitude. These others are what I thought of when I first saw what turned out to be HARH in 1968, and their possibility should be kept in mind even when altitude seems the obvious cause.

Severe carbon monoxide poisoning can cause RH, perhaps because it causes tissue hypoxia rather than through a direct impact on the small blood vessels. But RH are seldom present in chronic obstructive pulmonary disease (COPD) even though hypoxia often causes other signs and symptoms. RH aren't seen in cyanotic congenital heart disease, or even in congestive heart failure, despite hypoxia, unless caused by a complicating illness like hypertension or diabetes.

Many illnesses of blood vessels or of blood itself result in RH, and in fact

RH are sometimes the first evidence of a condition like leukemia or severe anemia, or high blood pressure, or even diabetes. Damage to the retina by RH and/or exudate is a tragic product of diabetes, even though the individual is not hypoxic. Hypertension can also damage vision by RH, but seldom as extensively as does diabetes.

Overwhelming injury causing Adult Respiratory Distress Syndrome (ARDS) or severe infection or toxic shock can also cause RH, perhaps due to hypoxia or from changes in the mechanism of blood clotting and/or vascular permeability. In these conditions we also see the competing influences of endothelin and nitric oxide.

Other Eye Problems

In 1939, as World War II was beginning, Ross McFarland, a pioneer in aviation medicine, published several important articles showing that visual acuity in dim light (**night vision**) decreases rather markedly above 5,000 feet, and is reduced by more than half a few thousand feet higher. This is due to changes in visual purple (the retinal pigment in rods), which needs a good supply of oxygen.

A forty-five-year-old engineer (who did his doctoral research in arterial blood flow) began to have episodes of flickering and often dimmed vision during strenuous exertion, most often on a mountain. He had no headache and, for a time, no other symptoms. He was an active climber and the episodes became more frequent and more serious, at times making him almost completely blind and slurring his speech. On one climb he became partially paralyzed. Since these alarming symptoms invariably disappeared when he went down, he did not seek advice until the episode of paralysis scared him! A complete workup showed nothing whatever to explain the episodes, and he had no neurological signs. He recalled that as a youth he had had occasional episodes of flickering vision (scintillating scotomata, in medispeak) and had been told he had a form of migraine. These brief episodes ended and he had none for twenty years. After his neurological workup revealed nothing abnormal, and considering the old diagnosis of migraine without headache, he was told to take one aspirin a day; he resumed climbing and had no further episodes. After several years he stopped the daily aspirin and almost at once the vision problems recurred whenever he exerted strenuously as in climbing.

I've been corresponding with this man for eight years and have met and talked with him twice. In my mind there's no doubt that he has what is called **anencephalgic migraine,** like what Dr. Walter Alvarez described in several hundred cases. I've received from other climbers half a dozen reports similar enough to suggest the same diagnosis; at least two have taken and benefitted from preventive aspirin. Does migraine affect or predispose a person to altitude illness? I cannot answer this, but migraine is thought to be due in part to excessive constriction or dilatation of the smaller arteries in the brain and by changes in oxygen or carbon dioxide in the blood. Perhaps more significantly, persons with a migraine tendency who go to altitude may not be able to distinguish migraine from severe AMS. One of my correspondents, a research scientist, suffers badly from both but cannot tell which is which!

This case is probably different from another episode of sudden complete or almost complete blindness on a high mountain. This occurs at sea level too and is named **amaurosis fugax,** attributed to brief (ten-minute) reduction in blood flow to the retina, or perhaps to the *occipital* (visual) part of the brain. It probably is not accurately blamed on altitude but might be called altitude amaurosis since it disappears with descent. I was recently told (by an ophthalmologist) about an unusual case:

> *A woman developed transient blurred vision in one eye only at 20,000 feet in the Himalayas. She stopped climbing for an hour or so and everything returned to normal. She began climbing again and within a half hour or so, the blurring in the same eye returned, and disappeared when she halted. She repeated this a third time, and then decided to go down. There were no aftereffects; she's a very perceptive observer and her story is fully credible. But what was it?*

Occasionally climbers at high altitude notice **double vision**—which can be rather disconcerting while making difficult moves. This is most likely due to fatigue plus hypoxia, bringing out a slight imbalance of the small muscles that move the eyes. Most of us have some imbalance anyway, but this normally does not affect vision because the brain is easily able to fuse the two images. But stress, like fatigue and hypoxia, weakens this central fusing ability, much as alcohol does, causing one to see double!

The popularity of **radial keratotomy,** done to improve near-sightedness, has led to reports of blurred vision at altitude that have been blamed on the operation. The logic runs that the tiny incisions over the cornea weaken it enough that decreased pressure on the micro-bubbles of air in the anterior chamber fluid causes minute stretch of the cornea and a change in refraction. It's much in the public mind as I write because during the tragedy on Mount Everest in 1996, one of those who nearly died was a pathologist who had become "almost completely blind" after a harrowing night of exposure. This was attributed to his radial keratotomy, but it seems more extreme than that due to a "slight refractive error" and more likely due to snow-blindness.

Geoff Tabin, a distinguished mountaineering-ophthalmologist, writing for the *American Alpine Journal,* explains:

> The tiny cuts made like spokes radiating from the center of the cornea weaken the cornea, and altitude hypoxia causes slight swelling around the edges of the cuts, further flattening the cornea. . . . This in turn causes a slight refractive error . . . which in an older climber, (together with) the change toward farsightedness, causes blurry vision.

Other climbers have had no difficulty after radial keratotomy, and the newer techniques will eliminate this problem because the cuts are made quite differently.

Is **glaucoma** affected by altitude? There is not enough evidence to make a confident statement. The few studies that have been done show little or no change in the intra-ocular pressure in the normal eye. However, the optic nerve is very sensitive to changes in its oxygen supply (either due to altitude or anemia) and if glaucoma may already have affected the nerve, this damage may be aggravated by high altitude. This suggests that persons with glaucoma should be carefully monitored before and after a climb, and perhaps consider enjoying lower mountains!

The good news is that Diamox is a very powerful agent for decreasing inter-ocular pressure. Indeed, it is regularly used for glaucoma. It will be just as effective at altitude, and will decrease symptoms of AMS as an added benefit. The bottom line? High altitude will not cause glaucoma but may increase slightly any pre-existing damage due to glaucoma. Diamox will protect against this small risk and should be taken. There is also the possibility that extensive retinal hemorrhage in the glaucomatous eye could cause a retinal detachment; perhaps this is some cause for concern, but in all the eye reports published in the last two decades, I don't believe there has been one describing retinal detachment.

There's been some talk about damage to the cornea if **contact lenses** are worn for a long period at very high altitude. The cornea receives its only oxygen supply from outside air, which would be excluded by most contact lenses except the gas-permeable soft lenses. One problem with contact lenses (worn by many climbers) is dehydration, which inhibits tear production so that the cornea under the lens dries and may be damaged. The other problem is the difficulty of cleaning contacts in very cold weather, and thus the risk, if they're not cleaned for many days, of corneal infection and even ulcer.

Snow blindness is more frequent the higher you go, but it's not so much an altitude problem as one related to any snow-covered landscape. It's a painful form of *conjunctivitis* (inflammation of the outer "skinlike" covering of the eyeball) due to too much ultraviolet light. Most often it happens when a person doesn't wear appropriate protective glasses on a bright sunny day while on snow, but it is a real risk in fog or under thin clouds, which allow UV light to be reflected off the snow. And UV light is more intense the higher you go. I can't stress too strongly the importance of good sunglasses, with side shields, on a high snowy mountain or indeed on any snow-covered landscape. Snow blindness is not limited to altitude.

△ △ △

SO FAR AS I KNOW, NO ONE HAS LOOKED for some of these problems among the large population who are hypoxic at sea level due to chronic illness; this would be an interesting and possibly very productive study.

Undoubtedly, with the ever-increasing crowds going to moderate and high altitude, we will hear of more unusual problems that don't fit the usual classifications. Many of these anecdotal reports are worth considering, but will need careful study before accepting them as due to high altitude alone.

HACE
HIGH ALTITUDE CEREBRAL EDEMA

ACUTE MOUNTAIN SICKNESS USUALLY IMPROVES IN A FEW DAYS, BUT WHEN the symptoms worsen and show indications that the brain is affected, we consider that the condition has shifted along the mountain sickness spectrum to High Altitude Cerebral Edema (HACE). In simpler terms, HACE means swelling of the brain. This is more serious and potentially fatal unless adequately and soon treated.

Either mathematician René Descartes or philosopher Francis Bacon said, 300 years ago: "The only thing that man cannot completely understand is the very thing man uses to understand the world around him—the mind." We have come a long way since then, but the complexities of understanding the human brain loom even larger as we approach them more closely. The next section outlines very roughly how parts of the brain function and where those functions might be vulnerable to hypoxia.

Basic Mechanisms of Hypoxia and the Brain

In the Proceedings of the 1995 Hypoxia Symposium, neurologist Roger Simon capsulized the effects of hypoxia on the brain of unacclimatized individuals abruptly exposed to low oxygen: "At sea level when the [inhaled] pO_2 is decreased to 75 percent of normal, complex task performance is altered; at 65 percent, short-term memory is impaired; at 50 percent, judgment is altered; unconsciousness occurs with the pO_2 between 30 percent and 40 percent of normal." These percentages correspond approximately to 8,000, 12,000, 18,000, and 28,000 feet, respectively. The responses of well-acclimatized individuals would of course be substantially different.

But *how* does low oxygen cause these effects? What chemical or electrical processes do we know to be altered? In this chapter I want to paint a picture in broad brush strokes of how the brain and nervous system work, and from this suggest where and how we believe the impact of hypoxia is most likely felt. But the system is complicated and the details of how hypoxia affects the system are far from understood.

Suppose, for example, you put your hand on a hot stove. Instantly the chemicals in a heat-sensitive nerve ending (*receptor*) in your skin initiate an electrical signal that races along a nerve or nerves leading to the brain (this might take a thousandth of a second). In the brain, the nerve ends in a gap (*synapse*) where the signal is converted instantly to another chemical (*neurotransmitter*), which spreads to one or many nerve endings. At each, the chemical neurotransmitter is converted into electrical impulses that flow out along other nerves to other destinations. Almost instantly these reach other neurotransmitters, for example, in muscles of your arm, ordering them to immediately withdraw your hand! All this has taken a tiny fraction of a second.

Meanwhile, at the synapses the chemical neurotransmitter spreads to other receptor sites, setting off a cascade of second messages that command other responses like shifts of sodium or potassium ions through cell membranes, or changing blood flow, or to the respiratory center to increase breathing—and hundreds more. Some messages go to the parts of the brain responsible for memory, where the sensation and responses are stored for the future: "Don't touch a hot stove!" Or, unlike Mark Twain's cat, "It may be safe to touch a cold stove."

Much of what we know today about the central nervous system involves the manufacture of these chemical messengers in the synapses and the release and effect of each across the synapse onto its specific site on a nerve ending, much like a key going into a lock. We know that some specific illnesses, for example, Parkinson's disease or schizophrenia, are due at least in part to changes in these chemical neurotransmitters. We know too that many medications, and substances that are often abused like alcohol, heroin, and others, also affect these chemicals.

Such messages are sent millions of times a day, and we are unaware of the vast majority of them. For example, those that travel the autonomic nervous system to control all the essential functions are automatic and beyond our conscious control: breathing, digesting, sweating, or shivering, and thousands more like focusing our eyes, balancing when we stand or sit, talking, typing, and many, many others.

All are quite similar: A receptor in a nerve ending chemically picks up a signal, the signal travels by minute electrical impulses along a nerve to a gap or synapse, where other chemicals transmit the signal to one or many other nerves, which in turn send electrical signals to the brain and elsewhere. Signals responding to the incoming messages are initiated by chemicals and flow out along other nerves, where actions are initiated by other chemicals. It is incredibly fast.

This rough sketch suggests where we think the brain and nervous system are vulnerable to hypoxia, as to many other hazards like infection, heat, cold, poisons, or deficiencies of necessary building blocks. Despite many protective loops, such a highly complex bio-electrical system remains vulnerable.

We know that hypoxia affects these chemical substances, but probably not the nerves themselves. From this we can hypothesize that distorted messages or those sent to the wrong address, or not sent at all, will cause or aggravate the many signs and symptoms we associate with HACE and, yes, the other altitude illnesses too. This does not mean that the other possible causes are not operative, but it may explain how they are invoked.

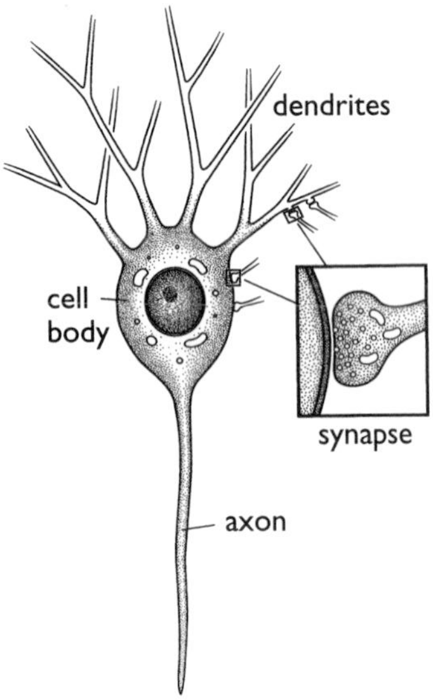

Figure 23. *Nerve cells and receptors*

BRAIN NERVE CELL, AXON, AND SYNAPSES

The basic brain nerve cell consists of a large cell (including parts similar to those in other cells), a long tail or *axon,* and a few or many hairlike branches or *dendrites* that extend to other brain cells. When the cell is stimulated, the axon carries a minute electric current to the end of the axon that terminates in a gap (*synapse*), where chemical messengers are released; these flow across the gap, connecting with and stimulating specific receptors, and return to their origin for re-use. The next nerve, carrying another minute current, may go to another synapse or to a similar gap, where the current stimulates release of another messenger that activates response, perhaps in a muscle, a blood vessel, a gland, or other organ. Meanwhile, similar impulses are reaching the brain cell through its dendrites, and leaving the brain cell to connect with other brain cells. This intricate, extremely complex nerve network carries all brain activities. Now and then, by illness, injury, medication, or disuse, a few dendrites from the brain cells are "pruned" and the connected functions inactivated.

One theory of how hypoxia affects the brain is that the chemical messengers in the synapses are altered by lack of oxygen, thus affecting specific responses. There are dozens of messenger chemicals in each of these synapses. We understand the chemistry of many and are able to change them by medication or by altering environment.

We are confident that acute mountain sickness is caused to some degree by malfunction of parts of the brain and/or nerves, which is why it is helpful to think of AMS and HACE as a continuum. However, we need to distinguish between the unpleasant but minor discomfort of AMS and what happens when the brain becomes more deeply involved. Someday we may change terminology and speak of the early stage as "cerebral hypoxia," reserving the name HACE for cases where the brain effects are more prominent. It might even be more accurate to call the more severe brain component of mountain sickness "high altitude encephalopathy" or HAE because, although the brain does swell with edema in serious cases, we can't yet show that it is edema that causes milder and early evidence of brain hypoxia.

It's also important to remember that *acute* hypoxia, which happens when the inhaled oxygen is rapidly and severely reduced or cut off completely (*asphyxia*) for one reason or another, causes very different events from the less severe cutoff at altitude or from most hypoxic illnesses.

Symptoms and Signs

One of the early signs of HACE is *ataxia,* shown by difficulty with walking, inability to do a simple heel-to-toe test or to put one's finger to the nose, and sometimes inability to control arm or hand motions. This is probably due to malfunction of an area of the brain called the *cerebellum.*

Persons with HACE do have headache but sometimes this is no worse than that experienced at the AMS end of the spectrum. Other problems common in AMS may occur in HACE, but the neurological problems dominate the picture, and it is those that threaten life.

Often there are retinal hemorrhages (see Chapter 6, AMS: Acute Mountain Sickness), but these also occur in AMS and in healthy people with no symptoms at altitude, so they aren't helpful in diagnosing HACE. Vision is usually not affected by HACE, but examination of the eyes sometimes shows that the optic disc, or nerve head, is swollen and even bulges into the back of the eye. This is called *papilledema* and is rare but ominous evidence that the pressure within the rigid skull is considerably increased, quite likely due to edema. Identifying papilledema requires an experienced observer.

Blood pressure is higher than expected and, if much higher or if increasing, the situation is serious. The pulse rate is usually higher than expected at that altitude, but if it slows markedly, this may be a sign of dangerous pressure within the skull.

On a mountain, without specialized advice or equipment, the early indicator is ataxia—stumbling while walking or trouble balancing with the eyes closed. Mental confusion, vague fears, or delusions are not always obvious because the patient may deny or conceal them quite artfully, so it takes some time and sensitivity to pick up all the cues. But once HACE is suspected, it's time to act decisively. Descent is the best and most helpful treatment, but often impractical immediately. (Other treatments are described in Chapter 11.)

An interesting example of what lack of oxygen can do to humans was described in 1920. It is particularly fascinating because it happened to two distinguished scientists with special knowledge of hypoxia, physiologist J. S. Haldane and mountaineer-chemist Alexander Kellas. And it took place in a decompression chamber where outside observers at sea level could see and record everything that happened.

> . . . it was our intention to remain for an hour at about the
> lowest pressure possible without impairment of our powers of

observation. . . . AMK and JSH went first into the chamber and the pressure was rapidly reduced to 445 mm (about 14,000 feet) and kept there for a short time for observation. . . . The pressure was then reduced to 320 mm (22,000 feet). . . . JSH had great difficulty in making observations or even counting the pulse, and especially calculating the pulse from a twenty-seconds observation, or remembering at what point on the second hand the observation had begun. Writing was also very shaky. . . . He then handed the note-book to AMK who was extremely blue but felt all right and could still write quite normally. . . . [The pressure was lowered to 300 mm (about 23,500 feet).]

To all his questions about changing the pressure, JSH replied with apparent deliberation "keep it at 320." Persons outside the window were somewhat impatient and anxious and put up messages on the window, but AMK only smiled and referred to JSH, who invariably gave the same answer. . . . After one and a half hours JSH consented to an increase of pressure to 340 mm. He then began to regain his faculties and took up a mirror to look at his lips, though some little time elapsed before he realized he was looking at the back and not at the front of the mirror, and consented to coming down. [Later] he had no recollection of the long stay at 320 mm nor of anything else after he handed the note-book to AMK. . . . AMK was much less affected. He could remember everything, and his handwriting had remained quite steady although his face was extremely blue and presented an alarming appearance to persons who saw him through the window.

This account was written by one of the persons who from sea level watched the whole experiment through a porthole. It is an extraordinary record of serious effects on the brain. Fortunately for them and for science, both subjects recovered completely. Others have not fared so well.

My first experience with what I might today call cerebral hypoxia was at 23,000 feet in 1936, many years before various expressions of mountain illnesses had been widely recognized:

We had spent several weeks approaching our mountain and relaying camps to within reach of the summit. Most of us were well and strong. The man most experienced in the Alps, who had never been at high altitude before, was convinced that he was the fittest of the party (even though at fifty-four he was the oldest) and best able to reach the 25,600-foot summit. In fact he was severely hypoxic, cyanotic, and quite irrational in his arguments. Several days later when we descended, he still contended that he was the fittest. Not until a few days after we reached low altitude did he resemble his usual self, but he held his conviction for many years.

Some climbers have pleasant hallucinations. Often the victim believes he has a companion walking or talking with him, as several climbers high on Everest have described. Although this kind of confusion was blamed on altitude, it took some time to develop the concept that it was caused by physiological changes due to hypoxia of the brain. Here are other examples from my files:

A strong young climber was soloing an easy route at 12,500 feet when he felt, as he put it, "disembodied," as if he were watching himself from a distance. He said aloud, "I hope that fellow is being very careful." He was able to put aside this hallucination by concentrating on it, but when he turned his mind back to climbing, the delusion again seemed real.

Those who survived a particularly tragic climb of over 23,000 feet said they had seen bulldozers and palm trees on the snowcapped summit and that strangers had tried to steal their flashlights. These hallucinations remained very vivid and real for days even after they had reached base camp.

A physician who was an experienced climber wrote me a long letter describing his experience at 14,000 feet. He heard voices talking to him and saw people walking nearby. He recognized these as hallucinations and had sense enough to turn back. Several years later on a different, slightly higher peak he began having more severe hallucinations, which he either denied or did not recognize. He became violent and had to be restrained in order to be evacuated. A tape recording made during the episodes shows how deranged he was, but even after hearing this, when recovered, he denied the episode.

Such experiences were serious and others have ended badly, but we have little data that show the actual changes in the neurotransmitters in the brain and nerve synapses. In hospitalized cases, affected areas have been visualized by X ray, computerized tomography (CT) scans, or magnetic resonance imaging (MRI), and some have clearly shown abnormalities such as fluid in certain pockets of the brain, while in other cases some areas show generalized edema. Fatal cases that have been autopsied show edema and old and new hemorrhages, some of which are very small and others large. But milder cases leave no identifying footprints, at least none that we can see today.

Though the effects of altitude on the brain may be subtle at first, the impact may be devastating. One need not go very high to get into bad trouble, often aggravated by failure to appreciate just what is happening. I described the following case in 1978 in *Backpacker* magazine, when the concept of HACE was just evolving:

Bill drove from New York to 8,400 feet in Wyoming and a day later set off on a cross-country ski trip that he had done before. Each day the party struggled through deep snow, climbing only a few hundred feet; each day Bill's headache grew worse and he had more difficulty keeping up and fell a lot. On the fifth day (at 10,500 feet) he was near collapse, and next morning when rescue arrived he was deeply unconscious and rigid. In hospital an X ray showed pulmonary edema and a neurological examination was abnormal. He improved slowly, regaining consciousness in forty-eight hours, though still mumbling and irrational; after four days he was almost well. He recalls "seeing Marilyn Monroe, live and in color, on the hospital walls" until the day he left the hospital.

That party did not go to very high altitude, but they had to work quite hard. Bill almost died because he and his companions simply didn't realize how seriously one can be affected even at relatively low altitude and a slow rate of climb. We know today that strenuous exertion aggravates problems like Bill's, but HACE wasn't well known then. If the party had turned back a few days earlier, he would have recovered quickly, but a day later he probably would have died.

Occasionally HACE can come on rather swiftly. In the following case, described in a local newspaper, the victim may have had some warning, but if so he did not seek help:

A thirty-eight-year-old man went to bed asking not to be disturbed, soon after driving to 12,000 feet from sea level. Twenty-four hours later when he did not appear for meals, his room was entered and he was found in a deep coma, with rigid arms and legs, weak pulse, dilated pupils, and evidence of pulmonary edema as well. Though hospitalized and intensively treated, he died; autopsy showed cerebral and pulmonary edema that were attributed to high altitude.

Such serious loss of judgment or perception is believed due to failure in the *frontal lobes,* that part of the brain responsible for such higher thinking. At first the effect is mild confusion or uncertainty, which may not be easily recognized, and in fact is often denied. A little confusion, muttered words, and clumsy finger actions may worsen to real hallucinations and ataxia. Denial, plus ignorance, have almost killed other individuals. More seriously affected victims sink into coma and, if not immediately treated, will die.

A young woman planned to climb Ixtaxuhuatl in Mexico, and because on her only previous climb, on Mount Rainier, she had AMS, she planned to take time to acclimatize at 8,000 feet before driving to 12,800 feet. She was quite tired that afternoon, felt slightly nauseated, and went to bed.

Around midnight she woke, called out, and began having continuous involuntary muscle movements that her companions called "seizures." Medication and a pressurized bag (see Chapter 11, Treatment) eased these only slightly, and during evacuation to hospital in Mexico City she continued the "wriggling" motions. Though she remained in a coma for several days and today has little or no memory of the period, she has recovered completely.

This woman was lucky: Her friends were knowledgeable and responded immediately with what treatment was available while awaiting evacuation. What is not typical in this case is the persistence of her coma even after reaching a lower altitude, but Mexico City (7,340 feet) may not have been low enough to reverse all the changes. One abnormality in her blood chemistry may have been significant: an abnormally low serum sodium. I suspect that she may have had a rare condition called Syndrome of Inappropriate Anti-diuretic Hormone (SIADH). I know of two similar cases where coma lasted for some time after descent, and in one the sodium was also dangerously low.

Stroke: Blood Clots and Cerebral Hemorrhage

Stroke, or *cerebro-vascular accident* (CVA), is caused either by a blood clot (*thrombus*) in a crucial vessel, or a hemorrhage in one or perhaps several areas. A thrombus may form when the blood, already thick due to the increased number of red blood cells, becomes even thicker from dehydration. In the brain, very small hemorrhages or clots are occasionally silent and effects aren't very obvious.

Symptoms of severe HACE have been confused with or complicated by one of several kinds of damage to the blood vessels. Because it is difficult to tell whether such an event is due to hemorrhage or a blood clot except with special tests, and because both can produce similar signs and symptoms, both are popularly called "stroke."

Minor, brief, and transient neurological signs are called *transient ischemic attacks* (TIA) and may happen at any time anywhere; they may be advance warning of a larger stroke. They may have caused brief symptoms on a mountain. Some of these might be considered part of the HACE complex, while those more lasting may be due to hemorrhage or clot formation, which can occur at any altitude at any time.

Interesting possibilities are suggested by my records for two patients whose "strokes" were probably due to altitude, and could be considered part of HACE:

A healthy sixty-year-old businessman went on a tour that flew to La Paz, a thirty-minute flight from sea level to 14,000 feet. On leaving the plane he behaved and talked erratically but made no complaints. His uncharac-teristic behavior persisted during the next day, but he denied any symp-toms. He was drowsy, slept a lot, and seemed to have trouble with memory. After forty-eight hours the tour leader saw him and called a local doctor, who gave him some medicine for AMS. He did not improve and his wife took him back to the United States, where he was hospitalized eight days after he had become ill. A complete examination showed small symmetrical hemorrhages in the globus pallidus, small areas on each side of the brain. He did not improve and was unable to run his business, and after some months was forced to retire. He sued the tour company for failure to warn of the risks of that altitude, and won the case, but the verdict was reversed on appeal.

A fifty-six-year-old woman was driven in eight days from near sea level to 14,000 feet. There she slept deeply and next day was ataxic and soon slipped into coma. Though she had no headache, nausea, or vomiting, her companions thought she had AMS. She was still ataxic and confused when she awoke. When she became much worse, they took her down to low altitude. She seemed to recover after descent, flew home to Japan, and returned to work. She appeared apathetic and dull, however, and twenty-six days after onset, a complete workup showed small bilateral and symmetrical hemorrhages in the globus pallidus, almost identical to those in the preceding case. Her affect remained flat and after a year she stopped work when a MRI study showed no change in the lesions.

These two cases are especially interesting because damage such as each had in the small globus pallidus can affect the higher centers, much as does damage to the larger frontal lobes themselves, causing what is called a "frontal lobe syndrome." This syndrome includes impaired judgment and understanding, apathy or loss of interest in everyday things, and general slowing down of thought. Perhaps transient effects of hypoxia on the globus pallidus might explain some of the mental changes at high altitude.

A twenty-nine-year-old man flew to 9,000 feet and during the next week climbed to 14,000 feet, where he felt nauseated and lethargic but insisted on continuing. At 16,000 feet, nine days after starting his trip, he became unconscious and was evacuated with evidence of pulmonary edema and severe neurological damage. In hospital he remained unconscious for ten days and still had evidence of brain damage six weeks later.

This man's judgment and realization of danger must have been seriously impaired when he persisted in going higher even as he grew sicker.

Such cases illustrate how difficult it is to differentiate what we mean by diffuse brain swelling due to hypoxia and "typical HACE" from damage due to a stroke that may be unrelated to altitude.

It's important to remember that other causes of unconsciousness and convulsions can and do occur on mountains; just because a patient is at altitude does not automatically mean the diagnosis is HACE. I've been given several reports of similar experiences:

> *A healthy twenty-five-year-old man took thirteen days to reach 16,000 feet on a South American peak. During the next four days, on the way to 17,500 feet, he developed abdominal pain, fatigue, vomiting, fever, and diarrhea. However, he said later that at 18,500 feet: "I was still the strongest member of our group. . . . There was no warning. . . . When I woke up, nothing worked for me too well, I couldn't think well, and I couldn't talk too well. . . . " During the next two days he was helped down to 13,800 feet, where he waited for helicopter evacuation for a few days, during which his temperature went very high. He lost consciousness during the flight and remained in hospital for several months.*

Two years later he still has difficulty with walking and with using his hands. Though his mental functions are otherwise normal, he also has problems with speech. These neurological problems are unlikely to improve much and it is probable that they were due to a combination of infection and stroke.

Blood Clots in Limbs

In the legs or arms, especially in someone who has been lying in bed for days while waiting out a storm high on a mountain, blood clots cause pain and swelling. I had never heard of this problem until a personal experience in 1953:

> *We had been climbing for many weeks and were well acclimatized and fit. Probably our red blood cells had increased a great deal, making the blood thicker and somewhat more prone to clot. At 25,000 feet we were pinned in our tents for ten days by a severe storm. Our stoves did not work well, so we had difficulty melting water to drink, and we became very dehydrated and weak. One of the stronger climbers developed pain and swelling in one leg, which I recognized as thrombo-phlebitis; the second leg became involved and soon small bits of clot broke off and were carried to the lungs. He was critically ill and his only hope lay in getting down to lower altitude. During a desperate effort to carry him down, all of us fell and he was carried away by an avalanche.*

Another incident illustrates how complicated such problems can become even after getting down to a lower altitude:

> *Twenty days after starting from 4,000 feet, a small party camped at 20,000 feet, having "carried high and slept low" above their 16,500-foot base camp for ten days. One of the more experienced climbers (who had felt more tired and dizzier than the others for a day or two) fell asleep during supper, could not be roused next morning, and convulsed frequently for the next few days. He was transported to a hospital and slowly recovered except for some residual damage due to blood clots in his legs. He still recalls his hallucinations during the five days when he was unconscious, and later remembered having had vivid hallucinations and "stumbling walk" at 17,500 feet during a climb the year before. On neither occasion did he have headache or cough or signs of pulmonary edema, or in fact very much warning of impending trouble.*

Did this young expert climber have a predisposition to HACE as some do for HAPE? On both occasions the climbing plan and rate of ascent seem to have been safe, though he said later that the pace felt a bit fast for him. The "stumbling" was probably ataxia, an early warning sign. His hallucinations were particularly frightening and vivid. The blood clots in his legs might easily have gone to his lungs and been fatal.

Pathophysiology

What is happening in the body to cause a disagreeable but self-limited case of AMS to progress, sometimes rapidly, to a serious case of HACE? From what we know about neurotransmitters, it seems to me that many aspects of mountain sickness may be due to changes in these chemical messengers at the synapses. This exciting field is changing very fast and I suspect will bring us many new answers quite soon. Disruption of these chemicals is reversible when adequate oxygen is restored—unless the hypoxia has been too severe or too prolonged.

There are several other scenarios that might explain mountain sickness, each with supportive evidence, but no one of them is completely satisfactory. In fact, as is so often the case in medicine, the problem is probably due to a combination of many influences.

In addition to the changes in receptor and neurotransmitter biological chemicals that I sketched above, there are more readily observed changes in the brain. First, brain tissue may swell, either all of it or only in certain vulnerable areas. This would cause pressure to build up within the rigid skull, perhaps compressing some areas more than others, or squeezing capillaries in especially sensitive areas, reducing the flow of food and oxygen to those cells. The swelling might be due to changes in the permeability of cell membranes, causing individual cells to swell.

The capillaries may leak plasma here and there into the loose supportive tissue between the cells. Because brain capillaries are different from

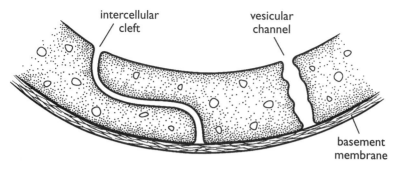

Figure 24A. *Endothelial cell of tissue and capillaries*

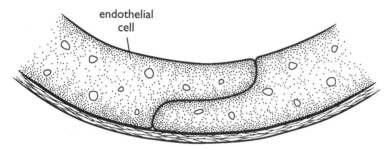

Figure 24B. *Endothelial cell of lung and brain capillaries*

ENDOTHELIAL CELLS

The endothelial cells lining tissue capillaries (shown in Figure 24A) do not have tight junctions between them and may separate when pressure and/or flow in the vessels is increased, leaving a minute gap (exaggerated here as a cleft). This can allow fluid to leak into the tissues as edema, notably in the legs, hands, and face, that is characteristic of mountain sickness, and also of exercise and other unaccustomed situations. Endothelial cells in some locations also have a potential "vesicular channel" that allows passage of certain molecules, selectively.

In contrast to those lining capillaries in the tissues, endothelial cells in the lung and brain capillaries (shown in Figure 24B) have tight junctions, and do not separate easily. Gas molecules pass through them by diffusion, and do not require "vesicular channels."

those elsewhere in the body, there is considerable debate over this, and the jury is still out. Focal edema in the cerebellum might cause ataxia or (in the limbic areas) hallucinations. Fluid accumulating in the frontal lobe would affect the higher mental processes of thought.

There has been more and more interest in high altitude retinal hemorrhages (HARH) as indicators of similar small hemorrhages in the brain. Some researchers and clinicians believe that small bleeding points in the brain cause some of the signs of HACE, and may even cause lasting damage. This is a disturbing thought for the tens of thousands of climbers who have had HARH, but thus far lacks convincing objective proof. (See Chapter 6, AMS: Acute Mountain Sickness, for a discussion of retinal hemorrhages.)

We know that the smaller arterioles moving blood throughout the brain are sensitive to even small changes in blood oxygen and carbon dioxide, narrowing during hypoxia, dilating when carbon dioxide increases (*hypercapnia*). But the ultimate blood vessels—the capillaries—do not have muscular walls, and dilate or constrict only in response to the pressure imposed on them from "upstream." Those in the brain are uniquely supported by surrounding *glial* (fibrous) "fingers," which prevent too much dilatation. Their tightly bonded lining (endothelial) cells also make them less likely to leak than are capillaries elsewhere in the body. Whether changes in small vessel blood flow cause the headache of AMS seems less certain today than we used to believe.

Other Theories

Here I mention briefly three other theoretical explanations of the ultimate cause of HACE.

The **vasogenic theory** attributes overall swelling of the brain to fluid leakage through the thin membranes that constitute the blood-brain barrier between blood and brain tissue. This could be due to opening of the tight junctions between the cells lining the capillary blood vessels, caused by dilatation and increased blood flow.

The **cytogenic theory** blames HACE on swelling of the individual cells in response to various insults, among them lack of oxygen or nutrients, or to toxins.

The **angiogenesis theory** rests on the fact that any tissue made severely hypoxic releases a protein that sharply increases capillary leakage, destroys some capillaries, and causes local edema. Thereupon a vascular endothelial growth factor stimulates the formation of new capillaries in the hypoxic tissue. This theory holds that the swelling that accompanies the destruction and rebuilding of tissue is the primary cause of HACE.

It seems reasonable to believe that each of these theories plays some part in how hypoxia affects the brain, and causes the signs and symptoms that range from the mild discomfort of AMS to dangerous HACE. Whatever the basic cause, the contents of the skull expand at least slightly when hypoxic, and the extent, if any, of this expansion causes the AMS/HACE spectrum. Some blame the altitude headache on this swelling, others blame dilatation of the small blood vessels.

By measuring the pressure of the cerebrospinal fluid by which the brain and spinal cord are surrounded, we find that pressure increases during severe mountain sickness. This can be caused by swelling of brain tissue or by hemorrhage from blood vessels, or even by dilatation and leakiness of the

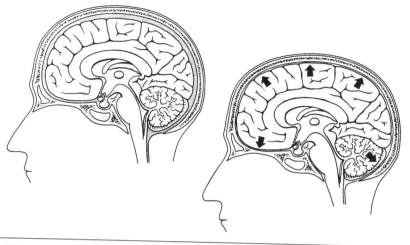

Figure 25. *The brain in its hard case—the skull*

THE BRAIN IN ITS HARD CASE—THE SKULL

Measuring the pressure of the cerebrospinal fluid (CSF) in patients with HACE has shown that the worse the symptoms, the higher the CSF pressure is likely to be. Furthermore, computerized tomography (CT) and magnetic resonance imaging (MRI) studies of patients with HACE have shown generalized swelling of the brain. In the 1970s, Peter Hackett's team on Denali airlifted a few climbers with HACE to hospital, where they took CT scans of the brain. These showed more swelling in the white than in the gray matter (which is the largest portion of the brain, and where the higher mental functions originate), as well as in a deeper layer of basal ganglia that take care of housekeeping. The white matter lies between all of these and contains over 10 billion nerve connections that service every part and every function of the body. It is especially these nerve connections (synapses) that may be affected.

If the brain accumulates only a little excess water and in only a few places like the white matter (especially the *corpus callosum*), it might unevenly compress the ventricles, or the *midbrain*. These are the areas where many of the nervous stimuli originate that trigger symptoms like nausea, vomiting, hyperventilation, rapid heart rate, elevated blood pressure, weakness, insomnia, and other manifestations.

blood vessels. One hypothesis suggests that parts of the brain may swell more than others, or that localized hemorrhage may occur in an especially sensitive area or areas such as the globus pallidum. Though we can diagnose where such a hemorrhage (stroke) occurs, we cannot always distinguish between bleeding or clot formation, nor do we know why hypoxia may cause either of these—or cause some other change.

Another response to the stress of insufficient oxygen is the release into blood (and perhaps the CSF) of large molecules called hypoxia-associated proteins. These would counterbalance those released, according to the angiogenesis theory, because they are believed to make the cells lining blood vessels *more* tolerant of oxygen lack. Since the leakiness of capillaries plays a part in many different illnesses that cause hypoxia, these proteins may be more important than we recognize today at high altitude. Similarly, specific proteins are released by heat and cold stresses.

Lasting Brain Damage

The increasing number of persons going to high mountains prompts many to ask whether some will have lasting or even permanent brain damage. It's an important question with implications for thousands of persons at sea level too. It's also hotly debated! Many who often go to the highest mountains without bottled oxygen are reluctant to believe they may become or have been permanently damaged. Others might blame their business or personal failures on altitude hypoxia. Depressions, broken relationships, even athletic defeats, aging, writers' cramp and so on could be attributed to their time at altitude.

There's not a lot of hard data and few controlled studies that scientists require to prove or disprove a hypothesis solidly. I've mentioned the neurological changes often seen in aging, perhaps attributable to decreased blood flow and oxygenation to the brain. There are, unfortunately many persons who remain brain damaged after asphyxia, cardiac arrest, or any accident or illness that shuts off oxygen or blood to the brain for more than four or five minutes. These are extreme examples. I've described a few individuals who show lasting neurological signs after severe sickness on a very high mountain. Others who may have had small strokes show residual changes, like the two individuals with globus pallidum damage described above. A few climbers who returned from Everest without mishap show small lasting effects manifested by slowed finger tapping. Recently CT scans done on two veterans of many Himalayan climbs suggest that their brains may have shrunk very slightly, though no changes in performance remain.

The question remains unanswered. My bottom line? I suspect that there may be some lasting damage for a few mountaineers who go repeatedly to great altitude without supplementary oxygen. Is this likely enough to make one hesitate? Considering the many other risks in everyday life, remembering the great rewards of mountaineering, I would accept this risk.

△ △ △

THE BRAIN USES 15 PERCENT OF THE OXYGEN consumed by the body, but weighs (in an average adult) only 2 percent of the total, so it's not surprising that it is vulnerable to hypoxia despite its many protective and redundant circuits. Like other living tissues, the brain can swell with edema; its vessels may bleed or leak plasma from capillaries. Perhaps even more often and equally harmful, the electrical networks and the biochemical neurotransmitters, unique to the nervous system, can be affected in thousands of places, with ripple effects throughout the body. Joseph Barcroft, who described his work in elegantly simple words, is quoted as saying: "Hypoxia halts the works and wrecks the machinery." The wonder is that we can survive serious hypoxia unscathed—if indeed we do!

HAPE
HIGH ALTITUDE PULMONARY EDEMA

LOOKING TO THE PAST, WE FIND THAT HIGH ALTITUDE PULMONARY EDEMA (HAPE), like other mountain sickness, has been around for a long time. One of the earliest descriptions was written by Buddhist missionary Fa-Hsien (A.D. 334–420), while crossing a pass some 12,000–14,000 feet high:

Fa-Hsien and the two others proceeding southwards, crossed the Little Snowy Mountains. On them the snow lies accumulated both winter and summer. On the north side of the mountains, in the shade, they suddenly encountered a cold wind which made them shiver and unable to speak. Hwuy-Ring could not go any farther. A white froth came from his mouth and he said to Fa-Hsien, "I cannot live any longer. Do you immediately go away, that we do not all die here"; and with these words he died.

The party had been traveling for many months and one would expect them to be well adjusted to altitude. The emphasis placed on cold suggests that Hwuy-Ring probably died from a combination of hypothermia and what we now recognize as HAPE, as I discuss in Chapter 16, The Mountaineer's World. The combination of cold and altitude has a double impact on the mountaineer; this is particularly important on Denali in Alaska, one of the coldest mountains, where HAPE is quite common. Even on the Alps, the unacclimatized who hurry may pay with their lives, as Angelo Mosso described in his book *Life of Man on the High Alps:*

In 1891 a member of a scientific party on Mont Blanc had to leave unexpectedly and a young physician rushed up from the valley to take his place. He continued to the summit and returned to the shelter a few hundred feet lower. A few hours later he developed a severe headache and nausea. He tossed all that night, unable to sleep, and next day began to cough profusely. His condition deteriorated, his mind wandered, and after writing a farewell letter to his brother, he sank into coma and died less than three days after arrival.

Autopsy showed what we recognize as pulmonary edema. This appears to be the first well-documented case of HAPE. One of the cases Thomas Ravenhill described in 1913 was typical of HAPE, which he considered cardiac in origin:

> An Englishman . . . arrived by train—a fifty-two-hour journey from sea level. . . . He seemed in good health on arrival, and said he felt quite well. . . . He woke next morning feeling quite well with symptoms of normal *puna*. As the day drew on he began to feel very ill indeed. . . . He became very cyanosed, had evident air hunger. . . . He seemed to present the typical picture of a failing heart. . . . He coughed with difficulty. He vomited at intervals. . . . Towards morning he recovered slightly and as there was luckily a train he went straight down. . . . I heard later that when he got to 12,000 feet he was considerably better and at 7,000 feet he was nearly well. It seemed to me that he would have died had he stayed at altitude another day.

Ravenhill was mistaken in calling this heart failure; if the patient had had a true heart problem he would not have recovered so quickly. The story is characteristic of the accumulation of fluid in the lungs, a condition we call high altitude pulmonary edema (HAPE), which is less common but more serious than AMS.

Though it has some of the features of fluid disturbance that contribute to AMS and to HACE, HAPE is different enough to place it slightly apart from them. Furthermore, since the lung is more easily examined and probed, we know quite a lot more about how HAPE develops and why, even though some of the pathology still eludes us.

HAPE is the most common of the really serious altitude illnesses. Travel has become so fast and so easy that millions of persons can and do go much too rapidly from low to dangerous altitudes, making HAPE a greater risk because it can develop so fast. It's true that mountain illnesses have stricken travelers for many centuries. But these problems didn't happen so often or to more than a few individuals when it took weeks or months to get to high mountains, or, more recently, several days to get to a resort in the Rockies and weeks to high Himalayas.

In this chapter I explain what we know today about the basic physiology and signs and symptoms of HAPE.

Basic Mechanisms of HAPE

Obviously the lung is a major player in supplying oxygen to the body. Its anatomy and physiology have been extensively studied, and fortunately both are comparatively accessible. Here respiration and circulation come together as nowhere else.

For the medical reader, what follows is a short technical summary of what we know or think we know about the physiology of HAPE. The nonscientific reader will find explanations for the unavoidable medical terms in the Glossary at the back of this book. In Chapter 3, Respiration, I describe the process of breathing, so here I repeat only a few special features of the passage of oxygen from lungs to blood.

The 300 million tiny air sacs (*alveoli*) at the ends of the branching airways have a total surface area about the same as a tennis court. So many capillaries surround them that it is as if the alveoli are exposed to a sheet of flowing blood. Movement of oxygen (and a few other molecules) takes place between this sheet and the whole alveolar space.

PASSAGE OF GASES—LUNGS TO BLOOD

Each alveolus is surrounded by capillaries that bring venous blood close to the alveolar air containing more oxygen and less carbon dioxide. As the capillary blood rushes past the alveolar wall, oxygen diffuses in and carbon dioxide out, so that arterial blood returning to the heart is in equilibrium with alveolar air, whatever it may contain. Diffusion takes place across the alveolar wall, which consists of a single layer of *epithelial* cells and their basement membrane; then through a loose interstitial space that is actually only a potential space; then across the basement membrane and the single *endothelial* cell layer lining the capillary. The alveolar epithelial cells are tightly joined to one another, as are the capillary endothelial cells, and each is bonded to its basement membrane. Despite these layers, the pulmonary membrane is very thin and imposes little resistance to gas diffusion, while tightly containing air on one side and blood on the other. After rapid ascent to altitude, the capillary endothelium leaks fluid into the interstitial space, where it is usually drained away by the lymphatics. But if the leak is excessive, serum and some red blood cells pass the alveolar wall, either by opening the tight junctions or by actually tearing the membrane. This causes HAPE.

Figure 26. *Passage of gases—lungs to blood*

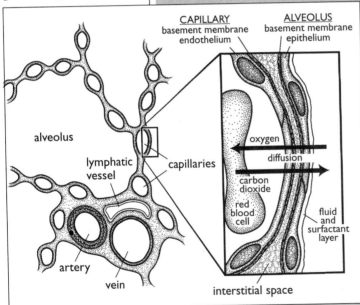

Blood enters the pulmonary artery (which carries venous blood) from the right ventricle of the heart and at the same pressure (about 25 torr) as in the heart. As the blood flows into the many branching pulmonary arterioles, this pressure falls sharply. Consequently, in the terminal arterioles as blood enters the capillaries, its pressure is about 7 torr, and normally remains at this level in the pulmonary veins carrying oxygenated blood back to the left ventricle of the heart.

The thin-walled capillaries in the lung are protected by a feedback mechanism that opens up more capillaries to accommodate more blood if pressure and flow rise too high. Unlike the blood supply to the rest of the body, that to the lungs is under local control rather than by messages from the central nervous system.

When the partial pressure of oxygen in the alveoli is low, the muscular pulmonary arterioles and precapillary vessels constrict, increasing the pulmonary artery pressure. This is just the opposite of what happens to arteries in much of the body that dilate when blood oxygen is low. As a result, at altitude, or whenever the oxygen pressure *in the alveoli* decreases from any cause, *pulmonary artery pressure* (PAP) rises.

Brownie Schoene and Peter Hackett, studying altitude sickness on Denali in the 1970s, collected fluid by bronchoscopy from deep in the lungs of climbers with HAPE, as well as from healthy ones. They found that fluid from HAPE victims was high in protein and white blood cells, indicating that HAPE was due to capillary inflammation and leakage. John West, a leader in high altitude physiology, believes that the increased pressure in them actually tears the walls of the pulmonary capillaries, allowing plasma and red blood cells to leak through.

Alveolar-arterial Barrier

Blood races through the lung capillaries in less than one second, during which it must load up with oxygen and discharge carbon dioxide. Passage of these (and a few other molecules) in either direction between alveoli and capillary takes place through diffusion. Diffusion depends mainly on the difference in molecular pressures between capillary and alveolus, and the resistance of the barrier through which they must pass.

This barrier consists of the lining of the alveoli, the interstitial space, and the wall of the capillary. Resistance may increase in any of these; the oxygen pressure difference between alveolus and capillary is normally about 5–6 torr.

The alveolus is lined with a single layer of epithelial cells and a basement membrane separating it from the interstitial space, which is not so much a real space as one that can expand when excess fluid enters.

The pulmonary capillary is lined with a single cell layer of endothelial cells and a basement membrane through both of which oxygen, carbon dioxide, water, and certain other molecules pass in either direction, through the interstitial space and into the alveoli.

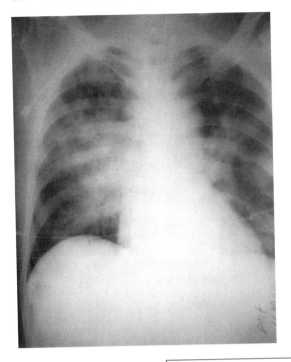

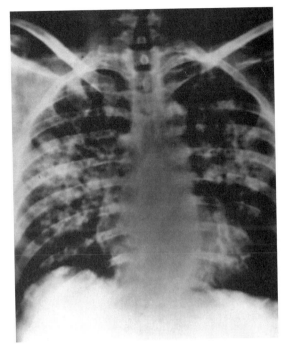

Figure 27A (left). *X ray of characteristic HAPE*

Figure 27B (right). *Computer-enhanced X ray*

X RAYS OF LUNGS WITH HAPE

The stethoscope can tell us when even a little moisture is present in the lungs. If this accumulates, as the X ray in Figure 27A shows, most of the fluid will be scattered in several places, usually more in the middle area of the lung (the right lung in Figure 27A) rather than near the *hilar* area (root of the lung). Figure 27B shows a computer-enhanced X ray of another case, showing the accumulation of fluid more clearly. The X ray is usually so characteristic that it should not be mistaken.

For those not familiar with conventional chest X rays, the well-aerated lung shows as dark gray or black, while moisture here shows white. The heart shadow and vessels leading from it, as well as the ribs, the diaphragm, and the liver, are also white.

In the patient whose computer-enhanced X ray is shown in Figure 27B, the patches of edema are more clearly defined. This patient's heart is somewhat enlarged, and the pulmonary artery (upper right of the heart) is more prominent than normal.

These two X rays are typical of moderately severe HAPE at 9,000 feet, which cleared very rapidly after descent, oxygen treatment, and rest.

Normally the higher air pressure in the alveoli keeps fluid from leaking into the alveolus, but some fluid does leak in from the capillaries. This fluid is quickly drained away by the lymphatic vessels, but if too much floods the space, the lymphatic drainage cannot keep up and fluid accumulates, slowing passage of gases and soon leaking into the alveoli. This is what happens when an abnormally high pressure in the terminal arterioles is transmitted to the capillaries.

Both alveolar and capillary walls are thin and can be torn or ruptured. Lung capillaries can also leak when subjected to certain biologically active substances. At high altitude, this leak is due to increased permeability to the substances that normally cross the membranes slowly if at all, and in small amounts. When the pressure increases, perhaps tearing the alveolar wall, or if its permeability increases, the result is HAPE.

This bare-bones explanation suggests how HAPE develops. I discuss a new element, nitric oxide, later in this chapter. The many other influences that are at play aren't essential to understanding this basic mechanism, but new insights continue to appear.

Symptoms and Signs

A person with HAPE presents a more serious picture than the individual who suffers from AMS. He or she looks sick, not just miserable.

Increasing weakness and shortness of breath are out of proportion to effort, and *cyanosis* (bluish nails and lips) is deeper than expected at that altitude. Remember that bluish nails, lips, and ears are common even in well people at altitude, and cold can cause the skin to look blue. At altitude cyanosis is due to generalized (as compared to only in skin) arterial oxygen unsaturation.

A slight cough grows worse and if the sputum is frothy or pink, or sometimes bloody, the case is more serious. Pulse rate is rapid and blood pressure may be a little high. Slight fever and a small increase in the infection-fighting white blood cells are common. More important: The patient looks really sick. Audible crackles (*rales*), gurgling, and wheezes can be heard in the lungs, often without a stethoscope and even across the room.

Sometimes there are ominous signs of the HACE portion of the spectrum: headache, confusion, and ataxia—the staggering walk of HACE. In a person who has come up too rapidly to altitude, this combination of symptoms should be considered dangerous and treated urgently because rapid deterioration is not uncommon. Until thirty years ago many such persons were diagnosed as having flu or bronchopneumonia, were inadequately treated, and often the correct diagnosis came too late.

Be alert, though: All the above signs can be due to several other causes, including infections, any of which may be as serious as HAPE and should always be considered in the diagnosis.

Remember too that by far the most frequent cause of lung edema at *any* altitude is increased venous pressure due to a failing heart that is unable to handle blood arriving from the lungs. Backed-up blood begins to flood the lungs, leaking into the alveoli, and flagrant pulmonary edema follows. This is caused by weakness of the heart muscle, specifically of the left ventricle, or to a badly leaking heart valve, and it's a common event after years of high blood pressure (systemic hypertension). But in HAPE the heart functions normally, except in the uncommon subacute or chronic mountain sicknesses described in Chapter 6, AMS: Acute Mountain Sickness.

Most of the common altitude-related problems are precipitated by going too high too fast, but there's a lot of wiggle room in defining "too high and too fast." (See Chapter 10, Prevention, and Chapter 12, Acclimatization.) With few exceptions, those who take time to ascend do not get sick from altitude. "Alpine-style" assaults on very high mountains are an important exception, and they are popular today. Here the climber spends many weeks at a base camp around 14,000 feet, each day climbing nearby slopes, higher and higher, and returning to base camp to sleep. In this way he or she acclimatizes and, choosing a day with good weather, is able to push for the summit in one long effort. Many succeed, some fail, and a few die.

It may be helpful to look at a representative case. One early report has often been quoted because it was so typical and so graphically described by the victim's companion:

Over a five-day period, W. B. climbed to 16,000 feet carrying a heavy pack. He was far more short of breath than others in the party, did not eat, and began to cough. His companion later said, "He obviously had fluid in his lungs." Despite penicillin it was harder and harder for him to breathe, his cough got more severe and frequent, and as his companion wrote in his diary, "Over the next hours his breathing became progressively more congested and labored. He sounded as though he were literally drowning in his own fluid, with an almost continuous loud bubbling sound as though he were breathing through liquid." His breathing grew much worse during the night, he became limp, and he died on the second day of illness.

This sad episode, so characteristic of HAPE, happened two years before HAPE became well known; the autopsy was reported as showing "fulminant bilateral pneumonia." Such cases continue to happen; some people still die, but many more know what to do when they are affected:

A fifty-two-year-old man flew from Pittsburgh to Denver and at once drove to 9,000 feet. Next day he consulted a doctor because of severe headache, inability to sleep, lethargy, and increasing shortness of breath. On examination he looked poorly and had scattered moisture (rales) in both lungs, but no other abnormal findings. His chest X ray was typical of HAPE; he was given oxygen for a short time with benefit, and then drove back to Denver (5,000 feet); he had recovered by the time he arrived.

This man was lucky or wise, or both, and today his is a more common scenario, like others that end more happily now that the risks of mountain sickness are better known. Even so, HAPE is still a danger, on low as well as very high mountains, and it still kills the heedless and uninformed, like this man:

A commercial pilot and his wife flew from his home to Colorado and drove to a ski area at 9,500 feet. He skied hard the next day but tired easily, and on the third day fell a lot and went home early. During the night his breathing became increasingly labored, and early in the morning his wife managed to take him to the medical clinic. In the car he stopped breathing. Though resuscitated and flown to intensive care, he died eleven days later with pulmonary and cerebral edema and subsequent pneumonia.

This is one of the deaths that would never have happened if the victim or his companion had paid attention to his condition—and to what his flight training should have taught him about altitude. In this particular instance, the victim also showed signs of HACE in the ataxia that made him fall so often and in the poor judgment that blinded him to how bad his condition had become. We frequently see evidence of brain hypoxia in patients with severe HAPE.

The diagnosis is sometimes more difficult.

A healthy, though inactive, 39-year-old man flew from Miami to Mexico City (7,500 feet) where he spent three nights before flying to Bogota (8,400 feet). He taught a class the day after arrival and telephoned his wife that evening, saying he felt fine except for a little shortness of breath. Next morning he was found dead, lying on top of his bed with his glasses on and a newspaper on the floor. He seemed relaxed and there was no evidence of a struggle. Autopsy showed pulmonary edema, and slight arteriosclerosis of a coronary artery. At issue was whether this was due to altitude or to cardiac arrest. Such a sudden death from HAPE is rare, and very uncommon as low as 8,400 feet. In addition, because he had been above 5,000–7,000 feet for seven days (including flight times), I considered HAPE slightly less likely to have caused his death than a sudden cardiac episode. Peter Hackett thought HAPE somewhat more probable.

Characteristics

Herb Hultgren reviewed medical records at a clinic in a mountain resort, and described the characteristics of 150 persons proven to have HAPE at the 9,000-foot-high area during a three-year period. This is probably the best overall picture of HAPE at moderate altitude, so I've summarized it in Table 4.

Table 4.

CHARACTERISTICS OF 150 INDIVIDUALS WITH HAPE

Mean age	34.3 years
Gender	84% males
Onset	3–4 days after arrival
HACE	14%
Temperature	99°
Fever	20% over 100°
Rales	85%
X ray positive	88%
Bilateral	52%
Right only	34%
BP >150	17%

The diagnosis of HAPE was made by the clinical picture plus either or both rales and X ray. Listening carefully to the lungs was at least as accurate for diagnosis as was X ray, but since rales often persist for days after full recovery, the X ray is helpful in demonstrating progress—not to mention differentiating HAPE from another problem like pneumonia.

HAPE is a dangerous illness, not rare, easily cured when treated early—and, above all, preventable. The more that people know about cause (in this case, altitude) and the more attention they pay to prevention, the lower will be the number of HAPE cases. Prevention of all forms of altitude illness is so important that I describe it separately in Chapter 10.

Incidence

Because it's difficult to determine the number of people at risk, we can only approximate the percentage of visitors to mountainous areas who develop HAPE. Many contributing influences like speed and method of ascent, level of exercise, individual susceptibility, and more are involved in addition to altitude. Extensive data collected from Mount Kenya, the Mount Everest region, the Indian Himalayas, Peru, Colorado, and the European Alps give the incidence of HAPE from 0.01 percent to 4.5 percent; one report from the Sino-Indian war in 1962 gave an incidence of 15 percent.

Most cases occur after twenty-four to forty-eight hours at altitude, and mainly above 10,000 feet. These large differences illustrate the difficulty of interpreting information collected in different ways by different individuals in different situations.

In a resort at 9,000 feet in Colorado, Jack Reeves made a careful study of the frequency of HAPE during winter and summer months, matching this to barometric pressure and temperature, finding a small but statistically significant difference: Of all the patients who saw a doctor for any reason in one resort area, the percentage who had HAPE was a little higher in winter than in summer, and on colder than on warmer days. This was not true of AMS: Weather made no difference. This apparent effect of cold isn't too surprising because animal and some human studies have shown that the pulmonary artery pressure increases slightly (even at sea level) while breathing cold air, or even when the face is exposed to severe cold. The increase is small but might make a difference in the cold, windy air on a very high mountain, especially to an individual whose pulmonary circulation was more vulnerable than normal.

As a very rough estimate, based on the unfiltered information collected from many areas, I believe that about 2 percent of all those who go to moderate elevation (above 8,500 feet) will develop clinical HAPE. Most are treated and recover, some descend and recover quickly, but, as many of the reports I have collected at Colorado resorts show, a few unacclimatized visitors die from HAPE each year. Many are hospitalized at least briefly. Deaths due to HAPE occur in every mountain range, and at altitudes from 8,500 to 22,500 feet.

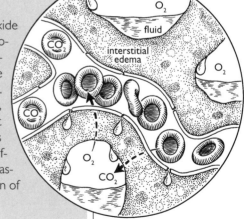

HAPE IN ALVEOLI

Alveolar air normally contains oxygen (O_2), carbon dioxide (CO_2), nitrogen, and water vapor—but no liquid. When alveolar oxygen partial pressure falls, blood pressure in the pulmonary artery rises, and this pressure is transmitted to the precapillaries, causing dilatation of the capillaries themselves. This causes serum to leak into the interstitial space, and, when this cannot be drained rapidly by the lymphatics, it leaks further into the alveoli. If excessive fluid accumulates in the interstitial space (shown on the right in Figure 28), diffusion of oxygen into the capillary is impeded, further increasing pulmonary artery pressure, and worsening oxygenation of blood and tissues.

Figure 28. *HAPE in alveoli*

Unlike AMS and HACE, there's a distinct gender difference in the incidence of HAPE: Several studies show that five or six times as many men as women develop HAPE under comparable conditions. Without much more information about attendant circumstances and the numbers of each gender at risk, it's anyone's guess why this should be true. Data defining influences like activity level, speed of ascent, and others simply aren't available much of the time. The menstrual cycle appears to have no influence on HAPE, but the data are inadequate.

There's an age gradient: Children are more vulnerable than adults, especially children resident at altitude returning after a brief stay nearer sea level. Strenuous exertion soon after arrival increases the risk. Even a mild respiratory infection like a cold or 'flu' seems to increase the likelihood of HAPE.

HAPE is an uncommon problem and most people, even the unwary who take risks by climbing too fast, never experience it. On the other hand, some are often hit. Several studies in the Alps, for example, on Monte Rosa (15,200 feet), have shown convincingly that certain persons are "HAPE-susceptible," while others are not. We call them HAPE-S, and they are at risk whenever they go to moderate altitude. Of many possibilities, no explanation has been proven.

> *Twenty years ago a young doctor-mountaineer developed HAPE at a modest altitude, recovered immediately on descent, but over the next few years had several more episodes during similar climbs. A complete and thorough study provided no explanation. Since then he has frequently noticed the warning indications of impending HAPE when he goes above 11,000–12,000 feet. He always recovers promptly after descending to lower altitude. With adequate time for acclimatization he has climbed above 20,000 feet without any evidence of HAPE. There is still no explanation for his susceptibility, and he has not routinely taken the HAPE preventive nifedipine.*

This well-informed and intelligent physician, active in altitude research, has learned to handle his problem and could probably take appropriate measures if, for some reason of weather or injury, he were unable to get down before his HAPE became severe. Others may not be so fortunate and should carry appropriate medication.

A few of these HAPE-susceptibles may have had some old lung infection or injury or multiple small emboli to the lungs, any of which might predispose them. A score of individuals have developed HAPE due to congenital absence of one pulmonary artery, and several have died before the diagnosis was made. Perhaps others with minor congenital or other abnormalities in their lungs retreat to lower altitudes when they begin to have symptoms, and remain undiagnosed.

Recent work suggests that nitric oxide deficiency may predispose an individual; this is discussed in Chapter 4, Moving Blood: Circulation.

Whatever the reason, we now recognize that there is a group of individuals highly susceptible to HAPE, for whatever reason. Nitric oxide is discussed later in this chapter.

In early 1998 a Japanese team studied eight HAPE-S patients, matched to a control group. They found that compared to controls, the susceptible group had a very significantly higher prevalence of an auto-immune disorder called a human leukocyte antigen or HLA. There are several subgroups of HLA, two of which were found in the HAPE-S subjects. This may be another important clue to the causes of HAPE and needs much further study.

HAPE is serious: At least 10 percent of all patients with HAPE will die unless promptly and appropriately treated. This number too depends on many variables, and obviously is lower in places where good medical care is immediately available and greater on high, difficult mountains where help is often inadequate or unobtainable in time.

Precipitating Factors

Many anecdotes and case reports suggest that even a mild respiratory infection like a cold or 'flu' increases the chance of HAPE, but there's no firm evidence one way or another. There's no doubt about exertion: Strenuous effort or prolonged hard work greatly increases the possibility—and the severity—of HAPE. This is almost certainly because such exertion increases pulmonary artery pressure even at sea level, and the added pressure at altitude may tip the scales.

Cyclists in a long and difficult race at 8,000–9,000 feet showed evidence of interstitial or even early alveolar pulmonary edema by X ray, but so too did a comparable group of ten cyclists racing at sea level. Several cases of pulmonary edema occur each year among thousands of runners in the grueling 97-kilometer Comrades' marathon in South Africa, which is all run at low altitude. Is this "exertional pulmonary edema" really a manifestation of excessive blood flow in portions of the lung, and unrelated to hypoxia? Though there are no exact animal models of HAPE, it is interesting and maybe significant that race horses, pushed to the limit, cough bloody sputum and develop lung edema that can—and sometimes does—kill them.

Acclimatization does protect against HAPE, but not completely: Even after weeks at moderate altitude, veteran mountaineers, working too hard high on the mountain, have succumbed. Even as I write, a second person this month has died of HAPE on Everest at an altitude higher than 20,000 feet, despite having taken weeks to get there. Very strenuous exertion in extreme conditions almost certainly can precipitate such fatalities, as it has at much lower elevations.

Re-entry HAPE

A newspaper clipping from the *Rocky Mountain News,* July 1997, described what happened to an Air Force Academy cadet at 6,500 feet in Colorado Springs:

> S. P. . . . collapsed and died after a day of hiking during cadet survival in the mountains west of the Academy. She died of cardiac arrest caused by buildup of fluid in the lungs. She had just returned from El Paso and doctors think a change in elevation may have caused the condition.

Although this sounded like a case of "re-entry HAPE," El Paso is only slightly lower than Colorado Springs, and some other cause was suspected; under suspicion was an environmental pollutant. So called "re-entry HAPE" is a curious twist that affects some acclimatized individuals who have lived at altitude for many months or even years. A small percentage of them occasionally (but not always) develop serious HAPE when they return to that altitude after a week or two near sea level. Cases have occurred after only one or two days at lower altitude. Children are more likely than adults to develop re-entry HAPE, for which no explanation has been found. It is no different in any respect from ordinary HAPE. Those who have had this problem once are more likely to have it again and should take extra precautions. Though the percentage of residents so affected is small—perhaps only 6 or 7 percent of those altitude residents who visit lower altitude—it's real, and there may be an important clue here that we are overlooking.

Some expeditions attempting high mountains use a strategy that calls for climbing high on the mountain slowly enough to acclimatize, and then returning to base camp for a period of rest before rushing back to summit. You might think this would predispose them to re-entry HAPE when they go back up to their highest camps, but it does not seem to. Perhaps months rather than weeks of residence at high altitude are needed to set the stage for re-entry HAPE.

But this isn't the whole story either: I don't know of any reports of re-entry HAPE among Tibetan natives, but I have read of cases among high altitude Andean natives.

Other Types of Pulmonary Edema

I've mentioned brisket disease of cattle (see Chapter 6, AMS: Acute Mountain Sickness), in which fluid accumulates not in the lungs as in HAPE, but throughout the body, in the liver, and in the chest cavity. This is due to failure of the right side of the heart because of high pulmonary artery pressure (PAP). Two forms of heart failure like brisket disease are occasionally seen in specific human ethnic groups or in those exposed to hard work for months at very high altitude (19,000–20,000 feet). These are Subacute Infantile Mountain Sickness, and Subacute Adult Mountain

Sickness (also described in Chapter 6). They are probably the same problem in different age groups.

Another type of pulmonary edema, called Adult Respiratory Distress Syndrome (ARDS), results from severe trauma or toxic shock. ARDS is not like HAPE either clinically or as seen by X ray and the attendant circumstances should preclude its being confused with HAPE. The prognosis is much worse. Nitric oxide and its antagonist endothelin-L are deeply involved in ARDS.

Many toxic substances cause lung edema, for example, the 1984 pesticide explosion in Bhopal, India, or chlorine gas in World War I. Indeed it is often a distressing terminal event in any cause of death. These are very different from HAPE. Any kind of lung edema will cause hypoxia; in HAPE it is the hypoxia, but only alveolar hypoxia, that provokes the edema.

These other causes of pulmonary edema have characteristic appearances by X ray or CT scan that are very different from HAPE. Any radiologist should be able to diagnose HAPE by X ray alone and in most instances can differentiate it from pneumonia. However, some atypical pneumonias from unusual organisms may look something like HAPE. Just remember that HAPE strikes healthy individuals who have rapidly arrived at altitude.

Pathophysiology

The basic cause of HAPE is pulmonary hypertension and the train of events initiated when pulmonary artery pressure (PAP) increases above tolerable limits. Oxygen lack, specifically in alveolar air, increases PAP, and exertion magnifies the increase; HAPE does not occur unless the PAP is high. In many circumstances PAP can rise very high without causing pulmonary edema.

How is HAPE different from brisket disease of cattle, and from chronic, subacute infantile, and adult mountain sicknesses? In all of these, pulmonary artery pressure is high, but heart failure rather than lung edema results. Why this is true we're unable to explain satisfactorily today. In HAPE some lung areas receive too much blood and others too little. This is normal under everyday conditions, but when excessive (as at altitude), it would mean that the oversupplied areas would flood and edema would accumulate. Blood leaving such areas will carry less oxygen than its capacity because there is less diffusion area in the alveolus. In fact this has been demonstrated by lung perfusion studies of persons with HAPE. It seems likely that this uneven perfusion is due to erratic production of nitric oxide and/or endothelin—for which, see below.

The uneven distribution of blood flow results in areas of lung that are overperfused and in effect underventilated, while other areas are underperfused but normally ventilated. This is described as $\dot{V}/Q$ *mismatch* or $\dot{V}/Q$ *inequity.* Some medical conditions can cause $\dot{V}/Q$ inequity by scattered obstructions from blood clots (thrombi) or from smaller particles (emboli) lodging in smaller vessels.

The evidence for the patchy overperfusion theory advanced by Hultgren in 1966 can be summarized today as follows:

1. Although pulmonary artery pressure at altitude is high, in HAPE neither the left nor right ventricle is found to be dilated or failing.
2. X rays show only patches of increased density indicating localized edema; this is very different from the X ray of congestive heart failure. Swelling of the liver, fluid in the abdominal or chest cavity, elevated venous pressure—all signs of a failing heart in brisket disease and chronic or subacute forms of mountain sickness—are not present in HAPE.
3. Recovery from HAPE—when treated early by descent or oxygen—is complete and usually rapid.
4. Congenital absence of a pulmonary artery causes overperfusion of the normal lung at even moderate altitude (6,000–8,000 feet) and precipitates HAPE. Similarly, a large, unilateral pulmonary embolus will cause pulmonary edema at any altitude.
5. Patchy edema, similar to HAPE, can be produced in animals by injecting tiny glass spheres to simulate emboli.

The magnitude of pulmonary artery pressure increase is not predictive of the likelihood or severity of pulmonary edema. For example, residents of Leadville, Colorado (10,000–11,000 feet) have a slightly higher PAP than a comparable population at sea level, and some of the school athletes actually increase their PAP during strenuous exercise to a level higher than the systemic blood pressure without showing edema. A high PAP is found among natives living in many mountainous areas—but the data from different studies are somewht conflicting. High altitude Tibetan natives do not have as high a pulmonary artery pressure as the Ayamara at comparable elevations in the high Andes.

When fatal cases of HAPE are autopsied, micro-thrombi as well as larger clots are found scattered throughout the lungs, but it's likely that many of these occurred after death, though others may have contributed to elevated PAP and worsened HAPE.

Biologically Active Substances

When pressure increases in the pulmonary arterioles, sheer stresses cause release of biologically active substances, some of which *stimulate* while others *oppose* platelet clumping (aggregation), which can add to the vascular obstruction and increase PAP even more. Two of the more important are nitric oxide (NO) and endothelin-L, which also have opposite effects on platelet clumping. The balance between these and other contrary forces determines blood flow in most of the smaller blood vessels of the body. Whether or not pulmonary artery pressure increases due to NO deficiency or to inactivity of the enzyme (NO-synthase) that stimulates its release, or to excess of its adversary, endothelin, may determine the appearance of HAPE. It's a neat little conflict between competing responses that influence blood flow through capillaries anywhere in the body.

This is the status in worsening HAPE, which quickly bcomes a self-reenforcing feedback loop: The worse the hypoxia, the worse becomes the transfer of oxygen, and even more fluid moves abnormally into the alveoli.

Many questions linger. Why does hypoxia (particularly altitude hypoxia) cause a greater percentage increase in PAP than in the systemic blood pressure, which sometimes does not rise at all? Do capillaries in the lung leak more easily than those in the rest of the body?—and if so, why? We know that either exercise or hypoxia (and other stresses) causes capillaries to leak into the interstitial tissues beneath skin, and perhaps some vessels in the lungs become similarly leaky under certain conditions. Strenuous exercise even at sea level can cause massive edema of extremities and face.

Another possible entry in the arena of different HAPE theories is the hypoxia-activated proteins that have been detected in the pulmonary blood in certain forms of lung edema like ARDS. Whether or not this happens in HAPE is not known today. Hypoxia-activated proteins *increase* the tolerance of endothelial cells for hypoxia and thus possibly might protect the capillaries from leaking.

Nitric Oxide—A "Universal Chemical?"

About ten years ago an important new agent was suspected of involvement in a number of vascular activities, and was labeled *endothelium derived relaxing factor* (EDRF). It was soon identified as a simple chemical substance, nitric oxide (NO), which is formed in blood vessels in the endothelial cells throughout the body. Though the principal action of NO seems to be regulation of vascular tone, more than 5,000 papers published in the last ten years describe its important action in almost every other physiological function.

NO may be a simple chemical, but its effects are complex. Minute amounts of NO are produced by a specific enzyme (NO-synthase) in all endothelial cells in every mammalian organ at a steady basal rate. Various substances increase NO release, which relaxes vascular tone, allowing small blood vessels to dilate. NO also inhibits the adhesion and clumping of platelets, and thereby helps to decrease the tendency for clot formation in blood vessels. Certain physiological substances inhibit NO synthesis and release, and thus (among other things) increase vascular tone and blood pressure, increase clot formation, and also increase the leakiness of capillary blood vessels.

Endothelial cells also release a family of substances called endothelins, at least one of which has an effect on blood vessels exactly the opposite of nitric oxide, i.e., constricting vessels by increasing their tone, and increasing platelet stickiness. The balance between these antagonists (and perhaps others too) affects blood flow through smaller vessels.

Recently NO has been reported to play yet another role in the precapillaries—essentially "dictating" how much and where oxygen is delivered to tissues! It does so because hemoglobin carries NO and releases it by changing red cell shape in precapillary arterioles and in capillaries. The released NO relaxes the blood vessels, and when molecules of oxygen are released by hemoglobin, NO is scavenged back to the red cell, the vessels constrict, and the blood, moving into the veins and carrying less oxygen, returns to the heart and on to the lungs for another load of oxygen.

As for their role in all altitude illnesses and perhaps hypoxia from many causes, NO and endothelin appear to be central players. One study of individuals with HAPE showed that inhaling small concentrations of NO (40 parts per million) decreases pulmonary artery pressure dramatically, shifts blood flow away from the flooded sections of the lungs to those less perfused, and raises arterial oxygen saturation. Several other studies show that inhaling NO (40 ppm) rapidly decreases PAP and relieves HAPE.

Furthermore, in individuals who are susceptible to HAPE, inhaled NO decreases PAP (at altitude) considerably more than it does in nonsusceptibles. This has raised a fascinating question: Can HAPE susceptibility be due to a deficiency of NO, or of the NO-synthase that releases NO in the endothelium? Or does an excess of endothelin contribute? Looking even further, because NO appears to be so influential in so many other normal and abnormal functions, might NO also play a role in AMS and HACE, and perhaps other conditions caused by hypoxia?

Nitric oxide, the various forms of synthase that release it, and the actions of NO on fluid and electrolyte shifts make it the focus of a great deal of attention and excitement today. The role of endothelins in hypoxic illnesses has not been as extensively studied, and other substances are also active.

Summarizing HAPE

Over many years of painstaking research, scientists have put together many parts of this puzzle, and in late 1997 this much is known about HAPE with a high degree of certainty:

1. HAPE occurs only when pulmonary artery pressure (PAP) is elevated and when the capillaries leak. However, PAP may be high without causing HAPE.
2. Hypoxia increases PAP by causing some of the smaller precapillaries (which have muscular coats) to constrict, thereby changing the distribution of the blood in parts of the lungs. But only lack of oxygen in the alveoli increases PAP; other types of hypoxia do not.

3. HAPE is the result, not the cause, of constricted blood vessels in the lung, increasing pulmonary artery pressure.

4. Vasoconstriction and vasodilation are due to substances, among them nitric oxide and endothelins, released from the cells lining blood vessels. Other direct stimuli also alter PAP.

5. Some individuals who move from sea level to moderate altitude develop higher pulmonary blood pressure than do others. This is quickly restored to normal if they return to sea level in a few months, before the muscular coats of the small blood vessels hypertrophy.

6. Some longtime high altitude natives (Ayamara) have elevated PAP; other ethnic groups (Tibetans) do not. PAP increases with exertion in both groups. HAPE does occur, but only seldomly, in high altitude natives going to even higher elevations.

7. Some residents at high altitude who descend to low altitude for a short time (one to ten days) are subject to HAPE when they return to altitude.

8. Some individuals are more susceptible to HAPE and these HAPE-S persons may have a genetic defect called *human autoimmune leukocyte antigen* (HLA) contributing to this susceptibility.

Obviously there is still a great deal to discover about HAPE, as there is about all altitude illnesses. What makes the quest so fascinating are the flashes of insight that altitude hypoxia gives into the many causes of oxygen lack at sea level. This, almost more than mountaineering, was what led me to write this book.

△

CHAPTER 9

Hypoxia in Everyday Life

WHY SHOULD ALTITUDE SICKNESS CONCERN ANYONE EXCEPT CLIMBERS AND trekkers and other mountain visitors? Not very many people ever go above 4,000–5,000 feet unless they live in the mountains, so who is listening? Well, the fact is that almost all of us may and often do experience hypoxia at some time during our daily lives even though we often don't realize it. Many millions cope with serious hypoxia from illness, for months or years. In this chapter I discuss some of these other causes of oxygen lack and explain why they are in fact so important to many sea level dwellers.

Fortunately our oxygen transport and utilization system (see Chapter 3, Moving Air: Respiration) makes mild hypoxia almost unnoticeable. In fact many people become slightly hypoxic during sleep—even at sea level. There are many environmental, respiratory, circulatory, and tissue conditions that do cause clinically important signs and symptoms—and even death—from hypoxia. It's convenient to classify these as shown in Table 5.

	EXAMPLES OF HYPOXIA			
Table 5.	**Environmental**	**Circulatory**	**Ventilatory**	**Histotoxic**
	High altitude	Airway obstruction	Heart failure	Cyanide poisoning
	Air pollution	Alveolar defect	Anemia	Tissue toxins

Responses to Hypoxia

We react to hypoxia from any cause in two ways. The first we might call emergency measures, the "struggle responses," which are slight or marked depending on the degree and the cause of hypoxia. These are the first efforts our body makes to restore oxygen to normal levels.

If hypoxia persists, these emergency measures evolve into what we call acclimatization, a series of adjustments that enable us to tolerate considerable oxygen lack, and to climb very high. This process of acclimatization is discussed in Chapter 12.

STRUGGLE RESPONSES   Table 6.

Increased rate and depth of breathing
Increased heart rate and output
Increased circulating red blood cells
Decreased plasma volume
Decreased blood flow to nonessential parts
Enzymatic changes permitting some anaerobic work

Environmental Hypoxia

In the preceding chapters I discuss how decreased atmospheric pressure on mountains, together with individual characteristics, cause various altitude-related sicknesses. Here I describe how some environmental changes near sea level increase the effects of hypoxia, just as infection, injury, or damage to different organs complicate chronic shortage of oxygen.

Flying

By far the most frequent cause of brief everyday hypoxia is flying. Wherever they fly, the cabins of commercial aircraft are kept at a pressure equivalent to an altitude of between 5,000 and 7,500 feet, depending to some degree on the actual altitude above the earth and the duration of the flight. You may board your plane at sea level and, in normal flight procedure, in a half hour the plane will be higher than 20,000 feet while the cabin is pressurized to 5,000 or 6,000 feet. On a long flight you may be at this altitude for twelve hours or more. During flight most people sit quietly or doze and few notice the effects of altitude, though it seems likely that it may contribute to what we call "jet lag" after long trips. For some with chronic illness, even this cabin altitude may be difficult to tolerate.

Cabin altitude varies in commercial aircraft, depending on the actual height at which the aircraft flies. The flight course is influenced by weather, which in turn affects the outside atmospheric pressure. The structure of the aircraft puts a limit on the pressure difference between the cabin and the outside air: the Concorde, flying at 70,000 feet may have a cabin altitude higher (i.e., cabin pressure lower) than other commercial flights. Very long flights also may fly high and keep cabin altitude higher than usual.

I carry a small altimeter with me on most flights and this leads to many pleasant and informative discussions with crew and now and then a passenger. I've asked six commercial pilots (four-stripers) about the following story I've heard: if overly boisterous and noisy passengers, or incessantly crying babies annoy the passengers, a pilot may "bump the cabin altitude up" a few thousand feet, putting people to sleep!

Two senior pilots said yes, they sometimes do this and it works. Two others had never heard of it. One said cabin pressure was automatically set (which is true) and cannot be changed by the crew (which is not true). The sixth said he too knew it could be and was occasionally done but was not included in any manual!

Polluted Air

Among the many causes of environmental hypoxia are gases that may contaminate the air we breathe, like carbon monoxide, propane, carbon dioxide, and nitrogen. Many gases are toxic but cause hypoxia secondarily due to alveolar damage, resulting in a type of interstitial and/or alveolar edema that is different from pulmonary edema at altitude (HAPE).

Each year in the United States some 1,500 persons die from **carbon monoxide** (CO) and 10,000 more require medical care. Even more are affected in less developed countries where means of heating or cooking are more primitive. Incomplete combustion of any substance like wood or fossil fuel will produce CO. Stoves, automobiles, space heaters, and especially combustion in confined places like shacks, parking garages, fishing shanties, and tightly woven tents cause problems from carbon monoxide hypoxia. It's probable that many people unknowingly are exposed to brief, minor carbon monoxide poisoning, which causes a few symptoms blamed on other things. But others aren't so fortunate:

> *Five members of a family died from carbon monoxide poisoning in their home, apparently after a car engine was left running in the attached garage. . . . The bodies were found scattered about the house in a Maryland suburb.*

Carbon monoxide is nontoxic but kills from hypoxia by displacing oxygen in hemoglobin. CO also interferes with muscular activity, including the heart muscle, because it combines with myoglobin as strongly as it does with hemoglobin, thus further compromising heart activity in persons who have coronary artery disease.

> *Commuters on congested highways like the Los Angeles freeways may spend an hour or more twice a day sitting in slow traffic where exhaust fumes are particularly bad. For some with early or mild coronary artery disease, this exposure is enough to cause angina.*

More than half of atmospheric CO is formed from oxidation of **methane**. This is produced in huge volumes in cattle feed lots, rice paddies, termite nests, and rotting biomass such as marshes.

Methane is inert and kills by displacing air in the lungs. Methane itself is a rare cause of hypoxia, but some unwary people have died from methane inhalation after falling into manure pits. Methane in the atmosphere is twenty times as effective as **carbon dioxide** (CO_2) in trapping infrared light and thus increasing the greenhouse effect, even though there is less than half as much methane as CO_2 in the atmosphere.

Like methane, carbon dioxide kills by suffocation, displacing air in the lungs. A sensational epidemic occurred in 1987 when a flood of CO_2, released suddenly from Lake Nyos in Cameroon, flowed down a valley and instantly suffocated 1,700 people and thousands of cattle. Smaller episodes have occurred near other African lakes. Occasional deaths have been caused by pools of CO_2 or methane in dug wells or in desert "sinks."

Propane and **natural gas** cause suffocation (*asphyxia*), and they also contain carbon monoxide. **Liquid nitrogen** used for instant freezing of many materials has been fatal when used in inadequately ventilated space. **Gaseous nitrogen**, used commercially in containers where all air must be excluded, has killed careless workers. Like nitrogen, the evaporation of solid carbon dioxide (dry ice) can be fatal for workers handling it in a poorly ventilated area.

> *Inside a refrigerated and closed truck, two men were transferring vials of frozen sperm from one container to another. The containers carried solid carbon dioxide (dry ice) and during the transfer—which took an hour— the dry ice vaporized. The carbon dioxide accumulated and when the door was opened by the driver, the two men were dead.*

Ventilatory Hypoxia

This includes any illness or damage that interferes with the flow of outside air through the airways into the lungs, or with the diffusion of oxygen from the alveoli into blood. This can happen anywhere along the way: in the respiratory control center in the medulla from polio or other brain problem, or along the nerves activating the chest muscles and diaphragm, as in several kinds of neuromuscular disease, or in the lungs. The chest can be injured and unable to move adequately. The airways can be partially obstructed by spasm or infection.

Lung Damage

Often lung tissue itself is damaged. Chronic bronchitis over time often leads to **emphysema**, in which the alveoli are first dilated, then torn and combined into larger sacs with less surface area for oxygen diffusion. As emphysema worsens, hypoxia stimulates greater effort to breathe—and when this is not enough, hypoxia is increased. Exertion becomes difficult, subtle mental changes appear slowly, and the deterioration all too frequently becomes irreversible. Usually this happens gradually so that signs and symptoms like those experienced in mountain sickness aren't apparent.

Figure 29. *Normal* (above) *and emphysematous* (below) *alveoli*

NORMAL AND EMPHYSEMATOUS ALVEOLI

The most common cause of chronic hypoxia in everyday life is chronic obstructive pulmonary disease (COPD). This develops over many months or years, usually initiated by inflammation of the bronchi (airways), which has progressed to chronic bronchitis. Repeated severe cough, increased difficulty with exhaling, and perhaps alveolar wall damage lead to stretching of alveolar walls, tearing, and gradual formation of larger cystlike air sacs from several alveoli (shown in Figure 29). Emphysema may also, less often, be congenital, or develop without obstruction. As the number of individual alveoli decreases, the surface area available for gas transfer decreases and hypoxia gradually worsens. Patients respond approximately in two different ways: by increasing ventilation ("pink puffers") or by increasing hemoglobin ("blue bloaters"). I describe these interesting responses later in this chapter.

Chronic Obstructive Pulmonary Disease (COPD)

The name says it all. COPD is something of a catchall phrase describing problems due to obstruction by increased airway resistance, inflammation of the bronchial passages, the spasm and inflammation of airways that we call asthma, and changes in the size and structure of the alveoli. It's the most common lung disorder, and a slowly worsening condition that impedes the flow of oxygen into alveoli and out into blood. Although "essential" or cystic emphysema occurs, the term COPD usually refers to the common combination of chronic bronchitis and emphysema.

About 16 million people in the United States have COPD, and each year 90,000 die from associated pneumonia, respiratory failure, or other complications such as right heart failure due to pulmonary hypertension. The incidence of COPD is said to be increasing by more than 5 percent annually. This might be caused by air pollution or by the increasing population of older individuals with the unhappy slow deterioration of aging! Whatever the reason, COPD often becomes a slow and expensive disability.

COPD is of special interest to us because of the different responses the body makes in its attempt to achieve normal oxygenation. Patients with COPD can be divided roughly but picturesquely into the "pink puffers" and the "blue bloaters," depending on the response. There's some overlap.

"Pink puffers" automatically overventilate all the time, thereby bringing more oxygen into the alveoli—but losing some carbon dioxide in the process. The resultant *alkalosis* is compensated by the kidney. This is the same way a healthy individual responds when going to moderate altitude. This will take care of such individuals unless some infection intervenes, but they may have difficulty going to the mountains, and sometimes even in flying.

By contrast, **"blue bloaters"** do not overbreathe; in fact they may actually breathe less than a normal person. Instead they increase the capacity of their blood to carry oxygen by increasing the number of red cells and amount of hemoglobin. Blood becomes slightly thicker and moves more sluggishly, so there's a tendency to clot formation. Over time the increased load, together with the increased pulmonary artery pressure, leads to enlargement of the right ventricle and failure. This "blue bloater" adjustment strategy is an exaggeration of how healthy persons respond to moderate altitude by making more hemoglobin. Their condition resembles Chronic Mountain Sickness (Monge's disease; see Chapter 6, AMS: Acute Mountain Sickness) and follows the same course. Not surprisingly, "blue bloaters" do not tolerate altitude and often cannot fly without supplemental oxygen.

It's interesting to compare a few of these problems with the normal responses of healthy persons going to altitude, summarized in Table 7.

ARTERIAL BLOOD IN CERTAIN CONDITIONS

Cause	Arterial Oxygen (in torr)	Arterial Carbon Dioxide (in torr)	Hemoglobin (gms/100 ml)	
Sea level (normal)	88	42	15	Table 7.
10,000 feet	56	33	16	
20,000 feet	41	21	16	
25,000 feet	37	13	18	
Pink puffer	70	37	15	
Blue bloater	50	51	17	
Chronic mountain sickness	47	34	20	
Congenital cardiacs	52 (33–75)	37 (33–37)		

A few patients with certain forms of congenital heart disease combine several responses and, like "pink puffers," are able to engage in near-normal activities. Some aspects of their tolerance resemble the acclimatization developed by healthy high altitude residents and long-term visitors to high altitudes.

We must be careful not to overemphasize the analogies between normal acclimatization to altitude and accomodation to chronic illness. Natural acclimatization to thin mountain air involves many small balanced changes that are rarely as extreme as the desperate measures in COPD.

Damage to Alveolar Walls

The delicate alveolar-capillary membranes may be damaged or thickened and the interstitial space obstructed (*fibrosis* or *alveolar proteinosis*). Anything that disrupts diffusion from alveoli to blood may lead to clinically important hypoxia. This thin membranous wall is described in Chapter 4, Moving Blood: Circulation.

Disturbed Breathing During Sleep

Many people tend to breathe unevenly during sleep and notice it little if at all. However, in the extreme case this may become a problem. Misnamed Ondine's Curse and often called Pickwickian syndrome (a literary misnomer), disturbed breathing during sleep can have serious effects. Normally, the breathing is automatically controlled when awake or during sleep, and several fail-safe mechanisms ensure normal ventilatory exchange. But anatomical obstruction due to weakening of the muscles of the soft palate causes **Intermittent Upper Airway Obstruction** (IUAO)—a big name for simple snoring. Some patients are partially obstructed enough during the night that arterial oxygen saturation fluctuates markedly. Sleep is disturbed by the struggle to breathe and the hapless victim is sleepy all day. This sleep disturbance has been blamed for a good many automobile accidents, and in some states legislation requires drivers who have had a few sleep-related accidents to have sleep studies done before regaining their driver's license. It's a real problem and more frequent than we realize.

In bad cases of snoring, preventive measures should be considered, to avoid eventual pulmonary hypertension and failure. Breathing low-flow oxygen may not change the breathing but prevents the fall in oxygen saturation and minimizes the long-term effects on pulmonary artery pressure.

A device called Continuous Positive Airflow Pressure (CPAP) provides a steady flow of air through a small tube in the nose to provide a slightly higher pressure in the airway; this may be enough to prevent the soft palate from obstructing the airway. A mask can also be used. Surgery to modify the nasopharynx is rarely curative. A dental device to prevent the jaw from relaxing and allowing the tongue to block the airway is quite effective.

Sleep Apnea

Less common is some malfunction of respiratory control, which causes irregular breathing with long pauses—similar to the periodic breathing common at high altitude. This is *central apnea* and its cause is not known. But whether central or peripheral, sleep apnea causes brief but repeated periods of mild arterial oxygen desaturation, which over time can cause pulmonary hypertension and even right heart failure. Victims of advanced sleep apnea, like "blue bloaters" with COPD, share some of the features of Monge's disease.

It's interesting that during the periods of sleep apnea, systemic blood pressure increases slightly and falls back to normal on wakening. But over many years the systemic blood pressure during the day gradually increases and stays high, so that years of sleep apnea may be one more, though infrequent, cause of hypertension and its problems.

Another sleep problem is important at any altitude. Recent studies have shown that when sleep is so frequently interrupted that the individual gets no period longer than a few minutes of unbroken sleep, some of the higher mental functions falter: Judgment, decision making, even reflex actions are impaired next day. Obviously this would be especially important high on a mountain where these processes are already affected. Sleep at the highest camps is seldom sound but usually interrupted every few minutes by wind, noise, discomfort, etc. It seems likely, even probable, that such sleep disruption has contributed to some of the dreadful errors sometimes made at altitude.

Clearly, disturbed sleep, and specifically sleep apnea, can become a serious medical problem of everyday hypoxia.

Sudden Infant Death Syndrome (SIDS)

The exact cause of Sudden Infant Death Syndrome (SIDS) is unknown. Until recently it was thought to be due to episodic sleep apnea in some infants and very young children, causing respiratory arrest, often after several premonitory "near misses." There's increasing evidence that SIDS is more often due to sleeping position: Infants who sleep on their backs are less susceptible, though this is not the whole answer. Survivors of many "near misses" have been brain damaged by these repeated episodes of apnea. However, whether SIDS is due to sleeping position, asphyxia from bedding, central respiratory failure, or some external cause, is still energetically debated.

It's claimed that more *very young children* die from SIDS (or Crib Death) every year than all who die from cancer, heart disease, pneumonia, child abuse, AIDS, and cystic fibrosis combined. Whether or not this is exaggerated, it's a particularly tragic problem because the infant is otherwise normal and—unless he or she has had repeated "near misses"—healthy. However, failure to gain weight and size normally, together with fussiness and daytime somnolence, should at least lead to a suspicion of sleep apnea.

Automatic breathing begins the moment the child is born but is uncertain and erratic at first, sometimes with sighs and even short apneic periods. This smoothes out rapidly. Infants are thought to have a blunted hypoxic ventilatory drive in the first few days or weeks, and thus some may not respond briskly or promptly to brief hypoxia. But whether this is related to SIDS is unknown.

Cystic Fibrosis

This recessive genetic defect causes accumulation of excessive thick mucous in lungs that are normal at birth. Repeated accumulation of this viscous material in small airways causes hypoxia and slowly leads to thickening of the alveolar-capillary membrane, pulmonary hypertension, and recurrent infection. With unremitting daily care, some patients may reach adulthood, but infection is a constant risk. Hypoxia stunts growth and may have other effects. This is not a rare cause of hypoxia: One out of every 2,400 white infants (but only one of every 17,000 black infants) is born with the defect; many die young from infection and hypoxia.

A few other hereditary enzyme deficiencies have been identified that lead to chronic lung problems. They are uncommon and as yet not curable except by lung transplant.

Asthma

Asthma impedes airflow by spasm and inflammation of the airways, which interferes with exhaling. Attacks are frequent, usually short-lived though recurrent, but often part of the combination of problems that lead to COPD. Asthma is a frequent cause of intermittent episodes of hypoxia with many of its symptoms.

Toxic Gases

Silo filler's disease causes hypoxia by the corrosive effect of nitric acid formed in fermented silage; it is rare thanks to farmers' education. Many other vapors cause hypoxia by their direct effect on lungs. Gas warfare in World War I killed or permanently disabled thousands; other toxic gases have occasionally been used against people since then. In 1984 many thousands died and many more were lastingly injured when a pesticide factory in Bhopal, India, exploded, releasing methyl cyanate that caused pulmonary edema, killing by respiratory hypoxia.

Submersion

Submersion is a frequent cause of death. The human brain is irreparably damaged after six or at most ten minutes of *anoxia* (complete absence of oxygen). How, then, have a number of children and adults survived, undamaged, after complete submersion for an hour or even longer?

Diving mammals often stay submerged for more than an hour, during which they can see, think, and swim actively without breathing. This is attributed to the dive response, which immediately halts breathing when a dive is started, and soon diverts blood away from nonessential to vital organs. Conflict between the need to conserve oxygen and the demands of swimming muscles is resolved by drawing oxygen from saturated myoglobin, of which diving animals have a large supply to act as a kind of storehouse. Oxygen demand is also met for a short period by changing metabolic fuels and "going anaerobic." This strategy is used by some animals that stay submerged for long months in winter. The anaerobic debt must be quickly repaid when oxygen is again available.

Humans are different. Long submersion is only survivable in water that is near freezing temperature. Central reflexes usually halt breathing at once, or else the victm will inhale water and drown. During the first ten minutes of accidental submersion, the diving response protects the brain by redirecting oxygenated blood to it and to the heart and a few similarly essential sites, and by shutting off blood to skin and extremities and soon to kidneys and liver. The heart slows markedly (reducing its demand for oxygen), and blood flow to the brain soon decreases.

After several minutes in freezing water, hypothermia due to passive heat loss further slows the demand for oxygen and decreases metabolism; the victim becomes unconscious. Children lose heat faster than adults due to their greater ratio of surface area to body mass. Thus the first defense is the dive response, the second and final is hypothermia. Survival of children is much more common than for adults.

However, some studies suggest that passive cooling may not be rapid enough even in children to protect the brain; other currently unknown factors may be operative. Not many such victims are fortunate enough to survive, but if so, most are not brain damaged.

Hyperventilation

A swimmer may hyperventilate before a sprint or a long underwater swim, hoping to increase blood oxygen content and to decrease carbon dioxide, thus reducing the urge to breathe. Subsequent breath holding has caused death from acute hypoxia when the hypoxic ventilatory response failed before the hypercapnic response was activated. Death after a long deep-breath-hold dive is often due to the rapid diffusion of oxygen *from* pulmonary capillaries *into* alveoli because of the rapid expansion of the lungs while surfacing too rapidly.

Circulatory Hypoxia

Any interference with the carriage or delivery of oxygen can be described as circulatory hypoxia. This includes anemia, *hypovolemia* (shock), abnormal hemoglobin, circulatory failure (cardiac or in obstructed blood vessels), and congenital heart or vascular disease.

Toxic Substances

Like carbon monoxide, certain chemicals combine with hemoglobin to cause hypoxia; some form methemoglobin, which does not carry oxygen and thus causes hypoxia that may be symptomatic.

Severe Anemia

Lack of blood from anemia or hemorrhage decreases the oxygen-carrying capacity and therefore oxygen content, and causes hypoxia. If chronic, some of the responses to anemia resemble those due to high altitude; if acute, the "struggle responses" appear. Lack of circulating hemoglobin is not an uncommon cause of everyday hypoxia. Interestingly, like CO poisoning, anemia does not cause pulmonary hypertension.

A young woman bled internally from a ruptured ectopic pregnancy. She had a cardiac arrest in the ambulance and was comatose and in shock, with a hematocrit of 13 percent in hospital. She remained comatose for a month, then began slow recovery. This was a severe case of circulatory hypoxia.

Shock decreases blood flow, and when the brain is deprived of both nutrients and oxygen because of decreased blood flow (due in the above case to shock plus anemia), the damage is more severe than when either circulation or oxygen alone is reduced.

Heart Failure

When the heart muscle is damaged because arteriosclerosis has reduced circulation to one or several parts of the heart muscle, it cannot pump enough oxygen-carrying blood to the body to meet demands. Rare congenital defects also jeopardize the heart as a pump. Distortion of one or more heart valves may cause reflux, or obstruction, also reducing blood supply to the body. These are common causes of lack of oxygen to cells and, depending where the lack is more pronounced, cause signs of hypoxia. Ross McFarland, a dedicated student of all forms of hypoxia, compared the effects on mental functions due to altitude with those of aging. He made a persuasive argument that most of the mental changes blamed on age were really due to narrowing of arteries to the brain, which decreased its oxygen supply.

Mutant Hemoglobins

When persons with sickle trait become hypoxic, the abnormal cells are distorted into shapes that can't take on as much oxygen as normal; this reduces the oxygen-carrying capacity of blood and decreases supply to the tissues. In addition, the distorted, burrlike cells often plug small capillaries, causing death of the tissues they supply. (Sickle cells are discussed in Chapter 4, Moving Blood: Circulation.)

Histotoxic Hypoxia

Excessive oxygen demand due, for example, to strenuous exertion, high fever, an overactive thyroid—in short, anything that increases tissue demand without an adequate compensatory increase in oxygen supply—may result in hypoxia severe enough to cause signs or symptoms. The delirium of a thyroid storm may be partly attributable to cerebral hypoxia. The defensive measures taken by the body are the "struggle" type.

On the other hand, even when the flow of oxygen is normal, cold (*hypothermia*) or low blood sugar (*hypoglycemia*) interferes with the higher brain functions and causes problems that are similar to, and synergistic with, those of hypoxia.

Poisons

A variety of poisons that interfere with the mitochondrial energy cycles cause tissue or cellular hypoxia. The best known of these is cyanide, which inhibits cells' use of oxygen. Several pesticides also inhibit essential metabolic processes. The role of these and many other man-made (and some natural) substances in disturbing molecular dynamics is being studied extensively, but is beyond the scope of this book.

△ △ △

FROM THIS BRIEF OVERVIEW IT IS OBVIOUS that lack of oxygen is not rare in everyday life. In fact, many common situations can and often do cause hypoxia. At some point the decreased oxygen partial pressure in blood, however and wherever it originates, may cause significant signs and symptoms.

It would be a mistake to stress these sea level analogies to altitude illnesses too much because so many other influences are active. Nevertheless, as Sir Joseph Barcroft suggested seventy years ago, the lessons from high altitude can teach us much about illnesses at sea level.

PART IV

Prevention, Treatment, and the Mountaineer's World

△

CHAPTER 10

Prevention

OBVIOUSLY, THE BEST WAY TO AVOID MOUNTAIN SICKNESS IS TO STAY home . . . but if you long to go to the mountains, there are several good ways to stay well. It doesn't take much.

First, of course, you must know what the problems can be, and you should know something about why they exist. Even a little understanding of air and the atmosphere, even a vague idea of how the heart and lungs do their work, is a good start. In earlier chapters I tried to give some insights by explaining how lack of oxygen affects the body and how to recognize when minor discomforts become dangerous. In this chapter I explain what you can do to avoid some of the problems, and in the next I discuss treatment.

The first and best preventive measure is to take your time—go up slowly. How slowly? Very few people will even notice the effects of altitude at 5,000 feet. We used to advise climbing only 1,000 feet a day above this—but in the real world, few people are willing or able to take that much time. We all seem to be in a hurry these days.

How Slow Is Slow Enough?

Except for those who have had and fear they will again have mountain sickness, most people can go to 7,000 feet in one day from sea level and feel little discomfort. Above that—especially starting up a big mountain—2,000 feet of elevation gain a day is a reasonable rate, unless the effort is very strenuous. Above 17,000 feet, even this is too fast for some people. A demanding climb requires more oxygen for physical and mental effort, and both of these strain your resources. However, the better your acclimatization, the higher you can climb in a day.

If you're planning to climb or ski or hike above 9,000 feet, it might be wise to spend a few days at a lower elevation first. There's quite a bit of evidence that altitude sicknesses are uncommon at 8,000 feet but more likely at 9,000 feet. Although there is no firm data, many anecdotes and personal experiences suggest that there's more physiological difference between these two altitudes than one would expect from a difference of only 1,000 feet. Why this might be so, anyone can guess! But if you do plan to stop over, stay for more than thirty-six hours: less time doesn't seem to have much effect, according to Honigman's study (see Chapter 6, AMS: Acute Mountain Sickness).

If you're going higher, say, to peaks of 14,000–15,000 feet like Mount Rainier, you will do better by halting for two nights on the way up, and setting a pace that accommodates the slowest member of the party. If you can't do this, then it's reasonable to turn to some of the preventive medications suggested later in this chapter. Almost half of those who try to summit Rainier in one or two days get sick on the way, and many are forced to turn back.

Higher mountains require more time. You can drive or fly to the foot of Denali, or to the volcanoes in Central and South America, the smaller Andes and Himalayas, and even to some high peaks in Africa. It's tempting to start climbing right away. On very popular mountains like the Mexican volcanoes and Kilimanjaro, tour conductors and guides too often rush the party higher and faster than is prudent. As a result, many get sick, some seriously, and are disappointed. Now and then someone dies from avoidable altitude illness.

I don't know of any accurate numbers showing how many climbers get sick on Kilimanjaro or the Mexican volcanoes and similar mountains where it's relatively easy to get to very high altitudes very fast. Even if we had the numbers, there would be so many variables in the different ascents that the data wouldn't mean much. But the bottom line is that many who, for one reason or another, rush such peaks fail to summit because of altitude sickness, and some die.

Denali is a special case. Being closer to the pole than other major mountains, it's physiologically several thousand feet higher than its measured altitude of 20,300 feet, a fact that few climbers make allowance for, if they even know it. So those who rush Denali are very likely to get sick, perhaps very sick, and some die. Others are so impaired by hypoxia that they make bad decisions, move awkwardly, and are likely to fall, often to their deaths. Only half of those who attempt Denali make it, and of those who fail, many are sick or injured. Denali is always cold, often as cold as any mountain anywhere; this adds hypothermia to the stress of hypoxia, making it even more dangerous. Denali is in a class with the major Himalayan giants and should be approached as such.

Why Go Slow?

Conventional wisdom advises mountaineers to "sleep low and climb high," and that's smart. Why? Because during sleep at high altitude, breathing is less efficient and often erratic, so that your arterial oxygen saturation periodically swings downward from the waking level. During sleep most people breathe less often and less deeply even at sea level, lowering the blood oxygen slightly. This means that in terms of oxygen delivery, you go up a little higher in altitude during sleep.

How does going slowly help the unacclimatized? The obvious reason is because it takes time for the body accustomed to sea level to set in play the many physiological changes needed for us to function with less oxygen. Some of these changes begin very soon after you start up, whether on foot or by plane, and are automatic. Each affects the direction and extent of other adjustments, which are also automatic but not so speedy.

Our bodies are marvelous and intricate machines with many fail-safe functions to protect us from disaster, whether from going too high too fast or from other causes of oxygen lack. In previous chapters I discuss many of these protective measures; a familiar example is the "fight or flight" reflex, which instantly puts us into overdrive in emergency situations. More subtle is Selye's "stress adaptation syndrome," a series of responses that defend us against different kinds of stress. Another is the "dive response," which closes off breathing when we are suddenly submerged.

In this book, we're interested in our immediate and delayed responses to hypoxia. When these are given time to mature, they are life-saving, but without time to develop, mountain illness is likely. And don't forget that lack of oxygen is not rare at sea level, where many of the same functions respond to the need for more oxygen, often in similar ways.

It's important to listen to your body. In circumstances in which you are endangered, your body will signal what it needs—whether that is more oxygen, water, warmth, or fuel. These needs are synergistic; that is, lack of any one of them increases the effect of the others. When your body screams "Help!" or "Stop!" you'd better pay attention.

> *A friend of mine was climbing Kilimanjaro (19,340 feet) with a distinguished group of college presidents and other leaders. Their guide had led them up gradually, but even so, some were feeling the altitude. A few thousand feet below the summit, several of the party sat down to rest while the others continued on, slowly. After a while my friend said to the others, "I feel awful. I don't know about you, but I think if we stay here we might all die. I think we should go down, now," and they did. His description in his diary of how he felt is typical of early HACE, and the group made the right decision to get down, as they all agreed later. Some mild aftereffects persisted for several weeks.*

On the other hand, if you want to climb the highest mountains or compete in exhausting sports, you can't always yield to the warnings or you'll be a loser. So you must not only pay attention to the early warnings, but you should also recognize when your reserves approach exhaustion. Then you either retreat or else . . .

In extreme conditions you can't always be prudent. But know your absolute limit and quit before it's too late. The tragedies I cite earlier, on Everest in 1996 and K2 in 1986, are examples of persons whose judgment was so blunted that they stretched themselves too far and paid with their lives. At great heights, hypoxia saps the judgment so much that one cannot always recognize the approaching limit.

On Everest in 1996, a very experienced guide started from the high camp to the summit, even though he was already very tired from months of stress, and perhaps even ill. He felt and looked poorly and moved very slowly. He climbed all day, growing weaker and slower despite his supplementary oxygen. Finally he stopped short of the top, too weak to continue, and remained with one of his exhausted clients; both died.

In these sad cases, as in many others in other years and on other mountains, climbers ignored and then did not hear the warnings screamed at them by their bodies. They passed the point of no return and died. Their judgment was blunted, their perception blurred by the combination of lack of oxygen, cold, hunger, thirst, and lack of sleep. On Everest in 1996, four others did realize their extremity, turned back below the summit, and made it down safely. In Chapter 12 I discuss acclimatization and its limits.

Is Everest that much more dangerous and difficult than the other Himalayan giants that are a few hundred feet lower? On these the available oxygen is only 1 or 2 torr more—does that make such a big difference? Probably not. Mountain tragedies attract attention and in 1996, as discussed in Chapter 16, The Mountaineer's World, a whole series of stresses cascaded, many of which could or should have been avoided. By contrast, on May 10, 1993, in perfect weather, forty persons reached the summit; during the unusually mild spring of 1991, ninety persons summited. No, altitude alone is not the major killer, but one that exacerbates all others.

Adjustment and Acclimatization

Why can't you speed up the adjustments? Isn't there some way you can hurry them along? Can't you "train up" for the summit? Good questions—to which the answer is a qualified "no." In Chapter 12, I discuss various ways of acclimatizing for the highest mountains. Different veterans choose different plans, but they all have one thing in common—time.

Remember the immediate adjustments to hypoxia known as the "struggle responses," discussed in Chapter 9, Hypoxia in Everyday Life and Chapter 12, Acclimatization: deeper breathing, greater output from the heart, more concentrated blood. Think of these as analogous to a freight train, required to deliver more goods: first more goods are brought to the station for loading, then more freight cars are added, the train moves faster, and finally the goods are unloaded faster at their destination. The demand is met.

These are temporary measures that can't be sustained for long; they keep you functioning while slower changes of acclimatization develop.

Obviously avoiding strenuous effort for the first few days after a rapid ascent to moderate altitude is sound advice because of the additional demands that heavy work places on breathing and moving blood. Wait until the adjustments have had a few days to develop into acclimatization before tearing off on a strenuous ski or climbing day.

Medication

Because many of those who go to the mountains are impatient, have little time to spare, or want to get up there quickly, use of preventive medicine is enticing. We're accustomed to taking a pill for anything and everything—why not one to speed up adjustment to altitude? Why not, indeed!

Acetazolamide (Diamox)

One medication enables a climber to breathe more often and/or deeper without paying a price. It has been proven an effective preventive over many decades, and its benefit is based on solid theory as well as experience. Think of acetazolamide, widely known as Diamox, as an artificial acclimatizer. It blocks or slows the action of carbonic anhydrase, an enzyme that regulates the conversion of carbon dioxide to bicarbonate. This allows the body to hyperventilate without paying the full price of alkalinity by enabling the kidneys to excrete more bicarbonate in urine. Carbonic anhydrase is strategically located in lungs, blood, and kidneys, where it is accessible to circulating acetazolamide.

Because it helps to normalize the pH of blood, thus modifying the impact of pH on the respiratory center, Diamox also decreases the swings in respiration that are called Cheyne-Stokes or periodic breathing (C-S, or PB) during sleep. Some periodic breathing occurs normally in many people during sleep at sea level but is exaggerated at altitude and during other causes of hypoxia. By smoothing out the fluctuations in arterial oxygen saturation, Diamox decreases the morning headache and the "wobbles" due to AMS. Currently there's a bit of argument about whether this is the reason Diamox decreases AMS, but the strong association of more normal breathing and less AMS in almost all persons taking Diamox is quite persuasive evidence.

Controlled studies matching placebo against Diamox confirm the benefit, though the mechanism may be more complicated than this brief statement suggests. Analogs of Diamox aren't any more effective.

For some, but not all, people, Diamox increases urine flow and so interrupts sleep; because of this, some climbers don't favor its use. In fact it was originally developed as a diuretic, but preventing AMS requires a small enough dose that the diuretic effect is slight. It is also used to treat glaucoma, discussed in Chapter 6, AMS: Acute Mountain Sickness.

At first the recommended dosage was 250 mg three times a day, starting several days before the ascent. This increased urination, especially at night, and caused some unpleasant symptoms. Then the recommended dosage was reduced to 125 mg twice a day; I generally recommend 125 mg once a day, at bedtime. This is effective for most people, causes few symptoms, and does not increase urine flow at night. If this does not prevent symptoms, I advise increasing the dose to 250 mg twice a day, and starting only on the day of ascent. It's important to tailor the dose to a person's experience or wishes, and over time an ideal dose can be found. Other authorities and many articles and books still suggest the larger dose. Because Diamox is an enzyme inhibitor and acts rapidly, perhaps you don't need to take it several days before starting your climb, as is sometimes advised. Delayed-action pills provide a larger dose, but by a sustained slow release, which some like. I prefer the regular form so the dose can be adjusted if needed.

Some critics of Diamox say it is better to rely on natural acclimatization rather than on pills—and there's little quarrel with this. Others don't like the numbness and tingling in the fingers or lips, and the bad taste it gives to beer and other carbonated beverages. But these symptoms are absent or slight with the smaller dose, and probably indicate that one has more than enough of the medication on board. A rare individual who is oversensitive to sunlight may develop a rash while taking Diamox (as is true of many sulfa drugs). A few individuals feel nauseated or sick while taking Diamox, but this is unusual with the smaller dose.

All things considered, "If you can't take time, take Diamox" is good advice, but if you do take Diamox, start with a small dose and drink plenty of water. There's some good—but also a great amount of bad—advice on the World Wide Web. Unfortunately not all doctors are familiar with the proper dose of this very useful medicine—or, in fact, knowledgeable about altitude in general. Not many doctors will take time to explain why these suggestions are important. You, the climber or tourist, must take the initiative to learn—and teach. One doctor told his patient to keep her windows closed in the mountains to decrease lack of oxygen! A recent book about the 1996 Everest tragedy states categorically that Diamox is not a preventive but should be used only for treatment; this is completely false.

Dexamethasone

Another currently used preventive is dexamethasone, a steroid. This is scientifically reasonable, because AMS is due in part to changes in the brain, and dexamethasone is effective in treating HACE, which today is considered one end of the AMS/HACE spectrum of altitude illness. Dexamethasone taken for a long time has been reported to cause osteoporosis and gastric bleeding, but this isn't a problem if used for a few days at altitude. The optimal dose for prevention is 2–4 mg twice a day.

A syringe loaded with dexamethasone was carried by many Everest climbers in 1996, and used by one or two in the emergency. The rationale was that it would give an added burst of energy, or decrease the hypoxic impact on the brain, but both of these are improbable because this steroid takes time to be effective, especially in the brain.

Both acetazolamide and dexamethasone require a doctor's prescription, but only Diamox has been certified by the FDA for preventing mountain sickness.

Other Medications

Nifedipine, a calcium channel blocker, relaxes the muscular coat of small arteries throughout the body and lowers blood pressure. Nifedipine also relaxes pulmonary arteries and lowers pulmonary artery pressure, which makes it a valuable *treatment* for HAPE. It has been wrongly used to *prevent* AMS—which it does not do. Some recommend nifedipine to *prevent* HAPE (which it does), but because it may also lower systemic blood pressure, it should be used only by persons who have had HAPE a few times and are considered HAPE-susceptible. These individuals are a recognized group (HAPE-S) and should be advised to take nifedipine if going above 8,000–9,000 feet. For dosage recommendations, see Chapter 11, Treatment.

Nitric oxide (NO—a gas) is a clumsy but effective treatment for HAPE, but should not be used for prevention. Nitroglycerine tablets beneath the tongue have been unwisely used for *treatment* of HAPE, and certainly cannot be recommended for prevention or treatment.

Another preventive medication, **ammonium chloride** (to acidify the blood) was carefully studied and recommended many decades ago but has not been revisited for a long time. Newer coating materials may make the tablets less irritating to the stomach and yet allow them to dissolve in the small intestine. Ammonium chloride is worth another look. Rolaids were touted by a few individuals, but have neither a scientific nor experiential justification.

Other Means of Prevention

The possible value of brief repeated exposure to simulated altitude has been well publicized recently. Popular sports clubs and some fashionable hotels in this country and in Europe offer low-oxygen "acclimatization" rooms where one can rest or exercise at a simulated high altitude in preparation for a climbing or ski trip to a mountain resort. Enticing though this sounds, it hasn't been proven to be more than an "in thing" to do.

Japanese mountaineers and those of some other nationalities have prepared for an assault on Everest by sleeping in decompression chambers at progressively higher simulated altitudes, but their climbing records don't show impressive benefits. With so many variables, it would be very difficult to arrange a statistically significant controlled study.

An ambitious French study called "Everest Turbo" ran a program to pre-acclimatize five elite mountaineers for an attempt on Everest. The procedure called for a week on Mont Blanc up to 15,000 feet, then many hours during the next four days going a little higher each day in a decompression chamber; they went up to 28,000 feet simulated altitude on the fourth day. Many tests were done every day. About a week later, after flying to Nepal, they were at 16,000 feet on Everest. Unfortunately, despite very rapid climbing, the weather turned them back at 24,000 feet.

The findings of this project suggest that continuous and then intermittent exposure to increasing altitude triggered acclimatization without the deterioration often encountered on a high mountain. A significant observation was that the subjects experienced dramatically fewer symptoms of AMS each day during the four days of intermittent exposure to increasing and very high altitudes. The study was an "experience" and not a practical effort to acclimatize.

A highly secret program to improve competitive edge by intermittent exposure to altitude was developed twenty years ago for Olympic candidates in East Germany. The Kienbaum project is described in Chapter 14, Training for Athletic Competition.

All of these intermittent exposures to progressively higher altitudes are similar to the successful tactics used in "alpine-style" climbing, which are discussed in Chapter 12, Acclimatization.

Interval Hypoxic Training

Interesting studies supported by the Russian Academy of Medical Sciences have been conducted in Moscow for the last ten years at the Clinical Research Laboratory of the Hypoxia Medical Academy (HMA). This group is testing the hypothesis that repeated brief exposures to lack of oxygen are useful for *treating* a variety of illnesses, and also in *training* for athletic performance. This concept would fit Selye's General Adaptation Syndrome (GAS), which was also mentioned independently in Russia several decades ago.

Selye argued that any stress like injury, illness, or a hostile environment would provoke a general response by the endocrine system, which would cause adaptation leading to recovery or to failure. His specific evidence fills a very large book but can be simply defined in Figure 30.

Hypoxia Medical Academy's Interval Hypoxic Training (IHT) consists of "courses" of cyclic repetition of brief normobaric hypoxic episodes and subsequent re-oxygenation. The intensity and duration of each "session" and the number of "sessions" in a "course" are customized for specific diseases and individuals. The air-oxygen mixture is exactly measured and administered by a calibrated machine, with oxygen provided through a membrane generator. A variety of illnesses are treated in different "courses" of varying length.

Results have been published in Russian in the Russian press, and in a quarterly journal in English published by the HMA. Few of the reports have appeared in peer-reviewed journals, which may explain the skepticism withwhich some American scientists regard the materials—but which few have read. Many of HMA's studies appear to have been carefully done, well controlled, and statistically significant, although exact procedures are not

SELYE'S GENERAL ADAPTATION SYNDROME

From 1936 to 1980, Dr. Hans Selye published 1,700 papers and thirty-nine books defining how organisms respond to stresses of different kinds. He concluded that response to any threat follows a general pattern of alarm, resistance, and outcome. Fortunately, in everyday life humans generally react by adjusting or accommodating, after which the physiological changes return to normal. If adjustment fails, deterioration results in either chronic illness or death.

Figure 30. *Selye's General Adaptation Syndrome*

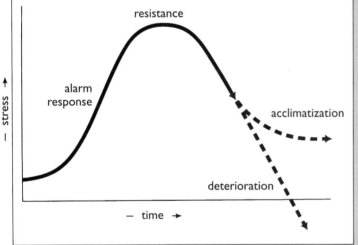

Hypoxia is a classical example of Selye's General Adaptation Syndrome (GAS). Hypoxia stimulates prompt alarm responses and resistance—"struggle" responses, described in Chapter 9, Hypoxia in Everyday Life, and Chapter 12, Acclimatization. If the altitude is not too high, or the hypoxia too severe, the body acclimatizes by slowly replacing these "struggle" responses with those that are more sustainable. These changes enable humans to live permanently as high as 17,000 feet, or to live with illnesses that cause the same degree of hypoxia at sea level. Above 17,000 feet (or equivalent), deterioration sets in.

Selye pioneered our recognition that this general reaction is responsive to many, perhaps all, stresses—emotional, environmental, and physical. It involves muscular, hematological, hormonal, mental, and central nervous system changes. Not surprisingly, it has stimulated great interest in medicine, research, industry, and in fact all walks of life!

always well described. I asked Dr. Tkatchuk, director of the Hypoxia Medical Academy, to explain why she believes the treatments are effective:

Mechanisms of IHT include both central mechanisms of neuro-humoral regulation and local regulatory mechanisms. This is the reason for the increase in efficacy of the oxygen-transporting and oxygen-utilizing systems at all levels of the organism, similar to the physiological acclimatization as a result of prolonged altitude exposure. . . .

IHT effectively decreased the response of pulmonary ventilation and heart rate to a physical load (the effect similar to that observed in altitude exposure). . . . At a load of 150 Watts, the double product (heart rate multiplied by systolic blood pressure), an indirect measure of myocardial oxygen consumption, was significantly lower (P<0.04) in the group of volunteers (sport students) after the IHT course as compared with placebo group. Similar results were obtained in patients with coronary heart disease (stable angina of effort). At a load of 50 Watts, the decrease of the double product was accompanied by the increase of physical load tolerance (P<0.05). [When the load was further increased, the benefit attributed to IHT was increased (P<0.01).] The above results suggest the outlook for the therapeutic use of IHT.

IHT might be considered for use in altitude preacclimatization. . . . The placebo controlled study was carried out . . . on young healthy volunteers . . . at the altitude of 3,000 meters (10,000 feet) in the decompression chamber. . . . [The course of IHT] was shown to retain significantly higher arterial blood oxygen saturation (P<0.05) than placebo controls.

[There was] a statistically significant 1.7-fold increase in erythropoietin level in blood . . . from the fourth IHT session, with the level remaining high during the IHT course.

Hypoxia Medical Academy has used IHT to decrease the rise in epinephrine and glucose in pregnant women before and immediately after abdominal delivery. Good results have been claimed in treatment of rheumatoid arthritis, chronic bronchitis, and asthma, and in preparation for general surgery. IHT is also used in training for competitive sports, allegedly decreasing the double product during a set level of performance.

The only element common to the wide variety of illnesses reportedly benefitted by IHT appears to be stress, which IHT is said to decrease "through neuro-humoral and local regulatory mechanisms." This is not unreasonable, in keeping with Selye's General Adaptation Syndrome. The procedure is interesting and possibly an important different approach to stress, and perhaps a helpful means of acclimatizing to high altitude. While keeping an open mind, it is nevertheless appropriate to reserve judgment until more detailed information is widely available, and until similar results are obtained by others using the same procedures.

Strategies for Work at High Altitude

Mines have been operated at 10,000–14,000 feet in the Andes for many centuries. In the last few decades, the demand for minerals has increased mining activity greatly, increasing the need to find the best way for miners to work most efficiently at high altitude. One strategy has been to transport workers from sea level to the mine, where they live and work for the next ten to fourteen days before returning home near sea level for a week. The work time lost and cost of transportation is considerable. The miners seem to lose some of their acclimatization during the homestay and are again somewhat affected by AMS after return to the mine. I would expect some of them to have re-entry HAPE, but so far this has not been reported. The mine operators' conclusion seems to be that this approach is helpful but is not the optimal approach to working at high altitude. The mining companies keep looking for tests that will predict which workers will acclimatize best, but there's no reliable predictor in sight.

Other companies have been developing different approaches because valuable minerals are now being mined at altitudes of over 20,000 feet. One program calls for miners to work there every day but go down several thousand feet to sleep, with an occasional homestay at low altitude. Daily travel time takes away from work time, and transportation is expensive. Some of the miners get mild AMS, and a few are said to have had re-entry HAPE from this yo-yo life.

A new proposal is now being tested at the minesite by providing sleeping quarters near the mine, in which during the night a steady flow of oxygen sustains an oxygen partial pressure equivalent to that at 10,000–12,000 feet. This may prove to be a more effective and efficient way of adjusting people for prolonged high altitude work.

A few resort areas at 10,000 feet have considered making similar rooms available, where tourists who are feeling the altitude can sit and read, exercise, or even sleep in a higher oxygen partial pressure. None have been made so far, possibly because of safety restrictions, but I think the idea has real merit.

In competitive athletics, one attempt to gain a competitive edge is to live at altitude and to train there in an oxygen-enriched room, which would enable training at peak intensity, while acclimatizing during the night. This may be efficient in time and money but, like other training programs, hasn't been adequately tested—and because of the many variables will be difficult to test well. I discuss this and other training strategies in Chapter 14.

Historically one of the especially interesting studies was an effort (in 1947) to acclimatize pilots by a stay on the summit of Pikes Peak in Colorado and then a brief stay in a decompression chamber on the summit. A secret strategy by East German athletes in Kienbaum is described in Chapter 14, Training for Athletic Competition.

Diet and Vitamins

Can you prevent mountain sickness and adjust more rapidly to altitude if you add vitamins, minerals, and other supplements to your diet? This depends on your usual diet—which, under some conditions, may not be adequate. For those subsisting mostly on expedition supplies for a few weeks, added vitamins may be a good idea. Dozens of diets have been recommended for big expeditions, but appetites are capricious and fade at high altitude. Absorption of food from the intestinal tract is thought (but not proven) to be impaired at very high altitude, bowel action is often a problem, and in the end the carefully planned diet usually comes down to food that the individual finds most palatable and easily digested.

If you do take vitamins, nutritionists advise a balanced formula rather than large doses of one or two. Despite a good bit of publicity, I don't know of any research that indicates vitamin E, or any other vitamin, improves tolerance for altitude. Folic acid (folate) may be shown to be important at high altitude because it sharply reduces homocysteine in the blood, a substance that increases arteriosclerotic deposits and clot formation. But as yet this hasn't been explored.

The popularity of vitamins ebbs and flows, depending on the intensity with which they are commercially promoted. Many people hunger for a panacea or an elixir of health, and are willing to pay without looking critically at the promised benefits.

Adding an iron supplement is important if iron stores in the body are low—which requires testing. Because many women do have low iron reserves and some are actually iron-deficient, added iron is reasonable for young women going to altitude for a long time. The benefits of supplements of other minerals like selenium, calcium, and trace substances have never been carefully evaluated. Here too there are shifting vogues and fashions.

We have good theoretical reason to believe that a diet that is very high in carbohydrate and contains virtually no fat or protein will decrease mountain illnesses. In practice, though, such a pure carbohydrate diet becomes too distasteful after a day or two and really is hard to accept. Recent studies of a diet that is 70 percent carbohydrate have shown no benefit in preventing mountain sicknesses.

Generally accepted is a game plan for eating frequent small high-carbohydrate snacks during the working day, and adding protein at night. A few special high-carbohydrate products have been touted, but so far no well-controlled study at altitude has been reported.

For years climbers have been urged to drink extra water, and there's pretty good basis for this. We've also recommended less alcohol, knowing that "one drink does the work of two" at altitude. This is an unproven recommendation, awaiting a good controlled study, which might be a rather attractive project. The rationale is that the effects of hypoxia and alcohol on the brain and its functions are similar—and additive. Alcohol is one of the few substances that passes rapidly through the blood-brain barrier into the brain.

Fitness

Finally, there's the vexing question about physical fitness. Does the fit and trim athlete tolerate high altitude better than the couch potato? The short answer is "not exactly." In Chapter 15, Gender, Age, and Fitness, I discuss this in a little more detail. The cheering fact is that the trained athlete and the experienced mountaineer climb more efficiently, with less exertion, and therefore use and need less oxygen than the neophyte to do the same climb.

This suggests that it is not a waste of time to train before any climb wherein you'll welcome every oxygen advantage. How rigorously isn't easy to answer. Are there specific training exercises? Logically one would expect that increasing muscle fitness of arms and legs would be most helpful. If you're a bit overweight, should you trim down, eat a bit less, toughen up, run more? That's a good idea—but in the olden days one great climber deliberately gained a dozen pounds before going to a major peak so he would have some fat to lose; I have friends who do the same today—with beer.

From all the studies that have been done in laboratories and from actual experience on mountains, only a few strategies have been proven to prevent or minimize mountain sicknesses: slow rate of ascent and use of acetazolamide. Others remain to be substantiated.

Treatment

OBVIOUSLY, THE TREATMENT FOR LACK OF OXYGEN FROM ANY CAUSE IS TO get more of it to the cells. In clinical illness or injury, it's sometimes difficult to change the basic problem, but breathing extra oxygen usually helps. In the mountains it's often simple—get down to thicker air, with a degree of urgency that depends on the problem.

Simple Acute Mountain Sickness

Most symptoms of simple AMS fade away in twenty-four to forty-eight hours and don't require any treatment except the conservative approach described in Chapter 10, Prevention. If the mild symptoms are bothersome, 125 mg or 250 mg of Diamox or 4 mg of dexamethasone every six hours will help; if one is already taking either of these, the extra dose(s) can be added. Breathing supplementary oxygen during the night will likely improve sleep if insomnia is a problem, and will make one feel better in the morning anyway. Periodic breathing, often a cause of insomnia, is relieved by low-flow oxygen and almost eliminated by a small bedtime dose of Diamox.

Nausea and/or vomiting can be helped by one of the many anti-emetic medicines available, Compazine being the old standby. As soon as vomiting stops, it's important to replace fluids, as well as in case of diarrhea, which isn't common in AMS and more likely due to something else. Once the acute vomiting is over, most victims can keep down small sips of fluid like tea, slightly salted water, or diluted juice, or Jell-O. If an intravenous solution and set is available, fluids might be given by vein. If the victim is very dehydrated, water can, with some difficulty, be given by rectum, and dexamethasone can be added to the water in an urgent case.

If the headache is quite bad, ibuprofen usually is a little more effective than aspirin; breathing supplemental oxygen for a few minutes wipes out the headache quickly—but it tends to return after a while.

High Altitude Cerebral Edema

If the headache worsens or early warnings like confusion or a stumbling walk (ataxia) appear, medical advice is important because these mean that the problem has moved toward the HACE end of the AMS/HACE spectrum. More dexamethasone by mouth may help, but it's more effective and faster if given by injection or intravenously. A careful examination is important to be sure that immediate descent isn't imperative. Of course, on a big mountain or away from medical care, that may be out of the question, and one can only carefully watch developments and treat them with one's best judgment. Discretion should dictate descent before things get out of hand. Breathing oxygen will buy time, but don't mess around with HACE: Evacuating a semiconscious patient with HACE is very serious business. Helping a semiconscious but walking patient is a lot better than trying to carry him or her a day later! The pressurizable bag is discussed later in this chapter. It's a good way to buy time when the victim is far from help and evacuation will be long and difficult. But it doesn't always work; once the diagnosis is clear, better get down!

> *During the early days of the Mount Logan project, a young paratrooper was flown from 2,500 to 17,500 feet. He was in charge of a small squad, which might explain why he did not mention his headache as it grew worse. By day's end he was obviously confused, and sixteen hours after arrival he became comatose. The radio was nonfunctional for several crucial hours, delaying rescue. During midnight evacuation by air I thought he would die. But by the time we reached low altitude, his alarming periodic breathing had become normal, and my partner and I thought it best to hold him at our base laboratory and give him large doses of dexamethasone intravenously. He regained consciousness eight hours later and made a rapid and complete recovery.*

In retrospect, several things are worth mentioning. First, in those days we took a big risk by flying people directly from 2,500 to 17,500 feet in ninety minutes. Even in 1968 there was enough experience to show the likelihood of altitude illnesses far more serious than the AMS we knew we would have. Second, lack of a way to get down except by air was also dangerous, and in this case, a temporarily inactive radio delayed evacuation for several hours, which might have been disastrous to the victim. Third, though he was given oxygen at the high laboratory, he did not improve, which is another lesson others have since learned on high mountains. Finally, it might seem a mistake that we did not fly him to a fully equipped hospital, but our rationale was that we knew more about altitude problems than anyone else in the region.

High Altitude Pulmonary Edema

If the normal and to be expected shortness of breath gets worse, or if a cough appears, perhaps with some frothy, even pink or bloody sputum, the problem is probably due to HAPE. Even an inexperienced person can often hear rattles and wheezes and crackles that don't disappear after a cough, strong evidence of HAPE. This can progress rapidly to a serious situation.

In HAPE, nifedipine (50–100 mg) by mouth usually will improve breathing and decrease the cough in less than an hour and is faster and more effective than oxygen. Nifedipine rapidly lowers pulmonary artery pressure, an essential part of HAPE. It may also lower systemic blood pressure and cause dizziness or faintness, so the smaller dose should be tried first. If the improvement wears off, as judged by worsening of cough or cyanosis or dyspnea, the dose can be repeated every hour or two—or given intravenously.

But *descent should not be delayed.* Getting down a few thousand feet almost always improves the situation, often dramatically. Strong diuretics such as Lasix (furosemide) are potentially dangerous and aren't always effective; they should not be used except in extreme circumstances.

> In 1969 while we were working on the Mount Logan study, a young climber in another party became weak and short of breath at 14,000 feet and was half-carried down to 9,000 feet, where both his lungs were found to be filled with fluid and HAPE was obvious. High-flow oxygen did not improve his rapidly worsening condition, so he was given several doses of Lasix. He did not diurese and in a few hours became shocky and then unconscious. I flew through a gathering storm in a small helicopter and brought him down. To add fuel from a reserve gas can, we landed on a moraine at 4,000 feet. The patient roused enough to leave the aircraft and pass a very large amount of urine. When we landed at 2,500 feet, he was alert and able to walk around and even joke and, though his pulmonary rales took several days to disappear, he recovered rapidly and completely.

This young man would have died had he not been brought down, and it seems likely that the diuretic had worsened his condition until descent may have enhanced its effect. Herb Hultgren has described HAPE patients who were ambulatory until loss of fluid by a diuretic caused shock due to a sharp fall in blood volume and complicated rescue.

Nitric oxide (NO) is the newest and most interesting influence in hypoxia from any cause. Though it's been recognized as a toxic vapor for a long time, only in the last ten years have the physiological effects of minute amounts been studied and appreciated. At this writing, the extent and importance of this gas can't really be grasped: It is changing many well-entrenched beliefs.

Clinical studies of NO have already shown that persons susceptible to HAPE can go to altitude and be protected by inhalation of 40 parts per million (ppm) nitric oxide (a very tiny amount) for a short time before or after arrival. NO lowers pulmonary artery pressure, which is a *sine qua non* for developing HAPE. But although effective, at this time NO is too clumsy a way to treat HAPE except in special surroundings. We're going to hear a great deal more about NO in the near future, so I try to describe some of its actions in Chapter 8, HAPE: High Altitude Pulmonary Edema.

Morphine is potentially dangerous in HAPE because it may suppress breathing even though it does relieve the pulmonary hypertension and decreases the alveolar fluid. Both strong diuretics and morphine are treatments of last resort.

A small masklike device is sometimes helpful in treatment (as in prevention) by increasing the pressure of exhalation, which increases the alveolar gas pressures slightly. This allows the wearer to inspire easily, but requires him to breathe out against a spring-loaded valve. This simple device has been quite helpful at night for patients with moderate chronic obstructive pulmonary disease (COPD), helping them to sleep, as low-flow oxygen does, but it's not clear yet whether either the mask or nighttime oxygen changes the long-term course of COPD. It does seem to benefit a few HAPE patients.

This is similar in principle and action to something called "grunt breathing," advocated by some mountaineers. This originated during WW II as an emergency breathing method for airmen who lost their oxygen supply at a dangerous altitude, and early tests appeared to show it was effective. However, further studies showed that the emergency (pressure) breathing procedure (EBP) was no better than simple overbreathing without the grunt! In my altitude training unit, we proved that deliberate, careful hyperventilation increased the arterial oxygen saturation as much or more than EBP, and maintained full consciousness while doing assigned tasks (without oxygen) for an hour during several test flights in a B-24 bomber aircraft at 25,000 feet. In fact, the extra effort of "grunt breathing" uses more oxygen than simple overbreathing. In a then-confidential report, brief training in controlled overbreathing was recommended as an emergency survival method at altitude.

A word of caution: *Any* voluntary increase in respiration must be carefully done to avoid excess, because this washes out carbon dioxide and causes anxiety, tremor, tingling in face and fingers, and soon severe muscular arm cramps and even unconsciousness from alkalosis. Try it—but be careful. Nor are these measures the best prevention or treatment, and they should not delay more effective measures (as has happened in one or two instances).

Simply exhaling against pursed lips may also increase alveolar pressure slightly, and without grunting. In fact many asthmatics have known for years that this is a good way to open airways and to breathe more easily. I don't know of any controlled studies to show how much, if any, it increases arterial oxygen saturation.

The Pressurizable Bag

There are three ways to get more oxygen into the lungs: (1) going down to thicker air, (2) breathing supplementary oxygen, and (3) increasing the atmospheric pressure around the victim. This last can be done in some sort of pressurized bag or room in which the patient is placed and the opening sealed while an air pump increases the pressure within the bag.

The best-known device in the United States is the cylindrical Gamow bag, made of tough canvas or plastic with a clear window, a tight-locking zipper, and safety tapes around the cylinder. Pressure is increased in the bag through a tube from a pump of some kind, with a pressure relief valve to prevent overpressurizing. Some form of absorbent for carbon dioxide is necessary inside the bag, because the pump cannot move enough air to get rid of the carbon dioxide exhaled by the patient as fast as it is produced. Different-sized and -shaped bags or "tents" are available, for one patient or a patient and attendant.

The sick person is placed inside the bag lying down, and communicates with helpers by voice; seldom is a small radio needed. A pulse oximeter to measure arterial oxygenation is helpful, but basically the patient's appearance and clinical condition determine the course of events. The bag is inflated and maintained at about two pounds pressure above the outside atmosphere; this "takes the patient down" several thousand feet, which is sometimes enough to relieve the problem for several hours. But if HACE or HAPE is severe, the bag gives only brief benefit; descent is mandatory.

Using the bag plus dexamethasone is slightly more beneficial than either alone, and should be tried early in severe cases, but, again, *don't delay descent.* In the mountains, there's no question that the bag has saved lives in difficult circumstances far from definitive care. In some cases the bag has enabled a victim to recover enough to totter down to safety or rescue.

In several instances it has improved the individual enough to go on climbing higher. This is not an appropriate use because symptoms are likely to return in a few hours. In one case the second attack that followed when the climber went up the next day was fatal. The bag isn't worth using where oxygen and skilled care are quickly available, as in mountain resorts.

Most models are difficult or impossible to use during a carry-out, but they do protect the critically ill patient in camp. Although some victims have been in a bag for many hours, most become restless as they improve and don't tolerate the bag for more than a few hours. It's also difficult to monitor vital signs or to give medication without releasing pressure for a brief time, which may undo some of its benefit.

The pressurizable bag is a special instrument that is valuable in limited circumstances but should never be seen as a substitute for descent to more complete treatment. Unfortunately, this is not adequately recognized;

guidelines are under consideration to make a pressurizable bag a requirement on big expeditions to high mountains (and even on treks), not so much because of need, but for fear of litigation if a bag were not available when and if needed. I think it's unfortunate that in the effort to cover all bases and protect people from every hazard, fear of lawsuits has made life so complicated—and not only in the mountains!

High Altitude Retinal Hemorrhage

High altitude retinal hemorrhages don't require—or respond to—any treatment we know today. It would be prudent to descend if the individual has a central blind spot, evidence of a hemorrhage in the macular area that might increase. In my opinion, HARH need not affect plans, but at least one ophthalmologist disagrees, believing that HARH are evidence of small hemorrhages in the brain. They don't change with descent—or any other treatment—and (except for those in the macula) they resolve spontaneously in a week or two. One case has been reported in which extensive HARH and a very high hematocrit led the doctor to remove a pint of blood from the patient; the hemorrhages gradually disappeared, but obviously there's no way to judge if bleeding made any difference.

Chronic Mountain Sickness

Chronic Mountain Sickness (CMS) is uncommon and rarely occurs below 11,000 feet even among longtime residents, though a few cases have been reported in Leadville, Colorado (10,150 feet). Untreated CMS causes congestive heart failure. Although repeated removal of a unit of the thick blood buys time for these unfortunates, the only real cure is to go down to near sea level, where recovery is slow. Thrombosis and heart failure are the major problems and must be treated as such, and immediate descent advised. Treatments used for primary polycythemia, such as immuno-suppressive drugs or hydroxyurea, seem too drastic for a problem that is readily improved by descent to thicker air.

Subacute Infant or Adult Mountain Sickness

Subacute Infant or Adult Mountain Sickness affects some infants and also some adults at elevations above 15,000–16,000 feet (see Chapter 6, AMS: Acute Mountain Sickness). This is another form of heart failure, due to an excessive or intermittent increase in pulmonary artery pressure and resultant right-sided heart congestive failure. In these two rather unusual forms of altitude sickness, descent is essential because the failing heart simply does not respond to treatment at altitude. Giving nifedipine to lower pulmonary artery pressure in addition to the conventional treatment of congestive heart failure might buy time but should not be a substitute for descent.

△ △ △

AS EXPERIENCE GROWS, WE WILL HEAR of more "altitude illnesses," but whether they are truly related to altitude or to hypoxia may often be hard to determine. "Post hoc propter hoc" reasoning is difficult to resist—all of us tend to associate some unfortunate event with some act or circumstance that preceded it. With this caveat, let us keep looking for abnormalities that are associated with—and may be caused by—hypoxia from any cause.

Acclimatization

On April 15, 1875, as Paul Bert was completing his studies proving that lack of oxygen caused mountain sickness, two of his young colleagues, Croce-Spinelli and Sivel, died during the ascent of their balloon *Zenith* to over 28,000 feet; the third balloonist, Tissandier, survived undamaged. His dramatic story is included in Bert's book, and is of special interest:

> I come now to the fatal hour when we were about to be seized by the terrible influence of the atmospheric decompression. At 7,000 meters we are all standing in the basket; Sivel, numbed for a moment, has revived; Croce-Spinelli is motionless before me. . . . At this height, however, I was writing in my notebook almost mechanically. . . . But soon I was keeping absolutely motionless, without suspecting that perhaps I had already lost use of my movements. Toward 7,500 meters the numbness one experiences is extraordinary. The body and the mind weaken little by little, gradually, unconsciously without one's knowledge. . . . I wanted to cry out "We are at 8,000 meters [above 26,000 feet]." But my tongue was paralyzed. Suddenly I closed my eyes and fell inert, entirely losing consciousness. It was about 1:30.
>
> At about 3:30 I opened my eyes again. I felt numb, weak, but my mind was active. The balloon was descending with terrifying speed. . . . My two companions were crouched in the basket, their heads covered by the travelling rugs. I assembled my strength and tried to raise them. Sivel's face was black, his eyes dull, his mouth open and full of blood. Croce's eyes were half shut and his mouth bloody.

Can Everest Be Climbed?

These were not the first deaths at high altitude, and although widely noticed, they did not end interest in climbing Mount Everest. Twenty years later, surgeon Clinton Dent speculated:

> Possibly even while these lines are being written, Mr. Conway and his mountaineering party in the Himalayas may have collected that grain of fact which proverbially outweighs the pound of theory.

To the writer the question has been for years a subject of interest from the mountaineering world as well as from the physiological point of view; on neither ground does [climbing Everest] appear an impossibility. To some extent a question of men, it is still more largely a question of money. Prejudice, perhaps, is father to the idea that the money which is always forthcoming to favor attempts to reach the North Pole may be still more advantageously employed in attempting to reach the top of Mount Everest. Selected men will have to work for a year or more with the one definite object before them. What they have to do is to ascend some 8,000 feet higher than any point that has hitherto been reached on foot. We may agree with Mr. Whymper that the effects on respiration will impose limits on the range of man, but it does not seem inconceivable that this limitation is beyond the highest point on the earth's crust. The attempt would be costly, laborious, long and possibly not free from risk. The same may be said of any extension of discovery. Let those who think that what can be done in the way of enterprise and discovery should be done consider the matter well. It is a tremendous undertaking, but a magnificent possibility.

In 1907 W. G. Fitzgerald, himself not a mountaineer, quoted observations made by those who were—Martin Conway, Fanny Bullock Workman, Douglas Freshfield, Edward Whymper, and others—and agreed with Dent. He quoted Angelo Mosso, a mountaineer and researcher in high altitude. Mosso had exercised Alpine troops at 14,000 feet, and conducted experiments in a small decompression chamber in which a man could exercise while being taken to a simulated altitude of almost 30,000 feet! In 1898 Mosso wrote:

If birds fly to a height of 29,000 feet, then man ought to be able to reach the same altitude at a slow and cautious rate of progress. I am convinced that a capable climber may attain the summit of Everest without serious sufferings.

Douglas Freshfield, one of the leading mountaineer-explorers of their time, was also cautiously optimistic:

I see no reason why the modern mountain explorer should not attain Everest's 29,028 feet. Remember how gradually the rarity of air increases between 20,000 and 30,000 feet. I am sure too that a big expedition can attack Everest.

In 1920 Alexander Kellas, a mountaineering chemist, calculated from data collected by others:

Mount Everest could be ascended by a man of excellent physical and mental constitution in first rate training, without adventitious aids if the difficulties of the mountain are not too great, and with the use of oxygen even if the mountain can be classed as difficult from the climbing point of view.

In 1953, with oxygen, and in 1975 without it, these predictions made at the start of the century were proven true.

Are Everest Summiters Different From Us?

As I write, more than eighty men and women have stood on top of Everest breathing only the high, thin air about them since Kellas wrote. Are they somehow different from Croce-Spinelli and Sivel, who died at the same altitude in the balloon *Zenith?* Do those who summit very high mountains have some secret ingredient in blood or tissue, or do they react differently to lack of oxygen? What, if anything, do they share with the thousands who are also short of oxygen from illness at sea level? Or with the millions who are born, live, and die three miles high in the Andes or Tibet?

Based on what we know today, most of the extreme climbers differ very little from the rest of us. Whether genetically or through exposure, they may have a larger ventilatory capacity or a more sensitive hypoxic ventilatory response. But this isn't completely true: several who have summited Everest *without* bottled oxygen actually have lower than normal hypoxic ventilatory responses. Furthermore, as acclimatization matures during a long stay at altitude, the HVR tends to become blunted. Persons with a brisk HVR tend to show more periodic breathing at altitude. They have learned to climb more easily, to pace themselves, and to use every bit of oxygen efficiently. After having acclimatized many times, their bodies *remember* how and do so more easily and completely. These are the only differences we recognize today.

The natives who live high in the Andes, in the highlands of Ethiopia, and on the Tibetan plateau are in fact different from sea level humans. Over hundreds of generations, they have *adapted* (in the Darwinian sense) by inherited changes that make them better able to live and work where the new arrival from lower altitudes becomes sick.

In Chapter 6, I quoted Mirza Muhammad Haider, who recognized this characteristic of altitude natives when he described mountain sicknesses at around 15,000 feet in Tibet: "This malady only attacks strangers; the people of Tibet know nothing of it, nor do their doctors know why it attacks strangers."

Accommodation and Acclimatization to High Altitude

The immediate reactions of sea level humans to abrupt oxygen lack are the "struggle responses" (see Chapter 9, Hypoxia in Everyday Life), prompted soon after exposure to hypoxia, by which the body tries to keep the oxygen flow to cells as close to normal as possible. Alexander von Muralt called these struggle responses *accommodations,* a useful and appropriate name for them. Today we add the terms *acclimatization* for changes that develop in weeks or months, and *adaptation* for those that take generations.

The distinction was the subject of a rather heated exchange about fifty years ago and that continues more moderately today. In 1925, after working for many weeks at 14,000 feet in Peru, Joseph Barcroft (who knew as much about high altitude as anyone at the time) wrote:

> The acclimatized man is not the man who has attained to bodily and mental powers as great in Cerro de Pasco as he would have in Cambridge (whether that town be situated in Massachusetts or England). Such a man does not exist. All dwellers at altitude are persons of impaired physical and mental powers. The acclimatized man is he who is least impaired, or, in other words, he who has made the least demand upon his reserve.

Carlos Monge Sr. (one of the Peruvian pioneers in altitude research) was outraged. Not having access to his paper published (in Spanish) at the time, I can only imagine what he told Barcroft then. But years later he was still angry and wrote:

> For our part, as early as 1928 we proved . . . that Professor Barcroft was himself suffering from mountain sickness without realizing it. His substantial error is easy to explain as resulting from an improper generalization on his part of what he himself felt and applying his reaction to Andean man in general. . . . Andean man must be physically distinct from sea level man, requiring much further research before one may define, let alone apply, the terms *inferior* and *superior.*

Monge was right: He recognised that Barcroft was comparing longtime residents without the health and educational benefits he had enjoyed, with himself as a visitor who had partially acclimatized. But Barcroft was also right to a degree: Even the longtime resident above 14,000 feet is not as physically or mentally able as his counterpart living at sea level.

The Blood at High Altitude

Fifty years earlier in Paris, Paul Bert's colleague Dr. Denis Jourdanet anticipated Monge. He had spent twenty years studying the people and country of Mexico. Noticing the stocky build of the highlanders, he described "the vast chest (which) makes him comfortable in the midst of this thin air," an observation echoed years later by Barcroft in the Andes.

Jourdanet's book *The Anemia of Altitudes* (1863) contains curiously confusing statements about men and women born and living in the highlands of Mexico:

The dwellers at great elevations, above 2,000 meters, are generally anemic. I made my first investigation on a young man twenty-five years old whom I knew to be suffering from gastralgias and vertigo. He fell from a horse and the consequences of this fall made bleeding unnecessary. My analytical tests . . . showed me that the proportion of corpuscles was 15/1,000. I repeated my experiments on four young women who were bled following accidents. Their pallor, their general prostration, and their nervous condition showed that they were suffering from chloro-anemia, although auscultation revealed no arterial murmur. Their blood furnished the normal number of corpuscles.

He and Paul Bert tried to explain these observations and were unconvincing, but we should bear in mind that at that time, the importance of hemoglobin had not been fully established.

Jourdanet's writings caused quite a storm among entrepreneurs who were contemplating establishment of a French empire on the high plateaus of Mexico, and French military surgeon L. Coindet was sent to investigate. He reported that the natives had the same respiratory and pulse rates as the more recently arrived French, but acknowledged that the natives could do more strenuous work and for longer than newcomers. Most of his reports dealt with convoluted discussions of carbonic acid and respiration, which were heatedly contested by many others.

Finally Bert, acknowledging he could not understand some of Coindet's arguments, turned back to his work on mountain sickness. He predicted that an increase in red corpuscles (which he showed carried oxygen) and an increase in breathing (in volume per minute if not in rate) would be important to acclimatization. A great dust had blown up, obscuring a fundamental point: the role of hemoglobin. I discuss Bert's great contributions to this subject in Chapter 4, Moving Blood: Circulation.

Studies of Acclimatization
Pikes Peak

The first studies of acclimatization on a high mountain came about almost by chance, when Yandell Henderson, a young professor from Yale, met John Haldane at a medical meeting in Vienna in 1910. Haldane rather casually said he would like to find "a nice comfortable hotel on a high mountain" where he could continue his study of how oxygen passes from lungs into blood. Henderson suggested Pikes Peak and helped make arrangements for two leading physiologists—Edward Schneider and C. G. Douglas—to join Haldane and himself in Colorado. The four spent a month on top of Pikes Peak, where they measured respiration and alveolar and arterial gases at rest and during and after exercise, and charted Cheyne-Stokes breathing. And so began a century of studies on 14,000-foot Pikes Peak.

These four men shaped generations of students and scholars, and their happy communion was probably the most lasting heritage of that summer, rather than their detailed data. In Chapter 3, Moving Air: Respiration, I describe the debate between Haldane and Barcroft over oxygen secretion, which Haldane insisted was one of the major contributors to acclimatization, even after Barcroft had effectively disproven this.

An incidental product of this first Pikes Peak project came about because the mores of the time considered it "unsuitable" for a single lady to be unchaperoned for weeks on the summit with the men. Mabel Fitzgerald was undaunted and, alone with her pack mules, she took her gas analysis equipment with her and visited mining communities throughout Colorado. After several weeks she brought back the first—and still the most complete—alveolar air samples from men and women living at different elevations.

Later Studies of High Altitude

The next major study of acclimatization was conducted in 1935 by a large international expedition led by Bruce Dill. The party spent six weeks at 14,000 feet in Peru examining the physico-chemical changes of blood in natives and in acclimatizing sojourners.

World War II halted mountain research but energized scores of studies of *acute* hypoxia, because aircraft could go higher than their crews, whose lives depended on oxygen when flying at altitudes that gave the most tactical advantage. (Acute hypoxia causes severe effects immediately, and has little in common with acute mountain sickness, in which onset is more gradual.) Even a brief interruption of the pilot's oxygen supply could cause tactical errors or even unconsciousness at combat altitude, so aircrew had to be taught to recognize the early, subtle effects of hypoxia. Before this training was adequate, many pilots perished—some unaware that their night vision at altitude was half that at sea level, others because they failed to recognize the early warnings of hypoxia. Some were too confident—"I've been to 20,000 feet many times and it never bothered me a bit" was one refrain—but some of the overconfident died.

Our task as teachers was to show them realistically what lack of oxygen would do, and we did this by setting up in the decompression chamber a model airplane with a stick and rudder like their actual aircraft controls. The pilot was asked to "fly" this little model after he had removed his oyxgen mask at 25,000 feet, but told to replace his mask immediately when he noticed anything at all wrong with his "flying." In my unit, which taught some 55,000 pilots and gunners, we asked one or two men from each group to do this demonstration, and I don't believe more than a few dozen were able to replace their mask, even when we ordered them to do so, before they fell unconscious. It was a small demonstration but showed aircrew quite convincingly how hypoxia at altitude would affect their skills.

At war's end, it would have been unfortunate if all the energy invested in altitude research were dissipated, and it was not. Many of those who would later contribute mightily to what we know about oxygen and humans became interested in altitude physiology in these military aviation training and research programs. My interests were in climbing and medicine rather than in flying, and I was able to persuade the Navy to let me organize a research study called "Operation Everest," even though this was more relevant to mountaineers than to aviators. This project and its sequel forty years later are described in Chapter 13, Operation Everest I and II. Most of my colleagues went back to their clinics and laboratories, but my special friend Dick Riley remained and shared the major part of the Everest study. As we anticipated, hypoxia would soon become less relevant to flying with the advent of pressurized aircraft, but mountaineering was about to enter a new era wherein altitude would be very important.

The Himalayas Become Popular

In 1950 the country of Nepal, closed to foreigners for centuries, opened some of its highest mountains to climbers, and the Golden Age of Himalayan climbing began. Within a few months the first 8,000-meter peak, Annapurna (26,700 feet), was climbed and others soon followed. That same fall a small party of us were granted the first permission to visit Everest from the south side, access from the north being forbidden by the Chinese occupying Tibet. In 1951 and 1952 attempts were made on Everest and other high peaks in Nepal, and finally in 1953 Everest was first climbed by Edmund Hillary and Sherpa Tenzing Norgay, using supplementary oxygen. The new generation would go on to feats we could only imagine. Everest was the supreme goal. Medical research did not lag far behind.

In 1952 prominent British physiologist Griffith Pugh led a small party to Cho Oyu primarily to gain experience with oxygen equipment for the next attempt on Everest, which he would accompany the following year. Pugh and others brought back a wealth of data from these two expeditions, some from as high as 25,000 feet. Pugh predicted that on the summit of Everest, without extra oxygen, a person would be close to his or her limit and able to do very little physical work: Staying alive would be difficult enough no matter how well acclimatized he or she might be. Since then scores of men and women have reached Everest's top by breathing only air. But, as Pugh predicted, they have been at the limits of their strength and will, and many have died.

The Silver Hut

Pugh returned to the Himalayas in 1961 as scientific leader of a project called "The Silver Hut." Some of the finest British and American mountaineers and physiologists participated. An insulated hut was erected at 19,000 feet and continuously occupied for five and a half months. Some of the men stayed as long as nine weeks without descending, though others went down for short periods of rest and recuperation. Despite good food and comfortable living conditions, all of the party lost weight, and they concluded that 19,000 feet was too high for long-term living—a conclusion supported by the fact that no high altitude natives live permanently above 17,000 feet. Among many studies, Pugh reported:

> After weeks at altitude, lack of oxygen was still driving respiration despite the lowered blood carbon dioxide, but the respiratory center had become more sensitive to carbon dioxide . . . . Newcomers were as physically fit or even fitter after a few weeks at altitude as those who had been there for months. . . . Physical work seemed to be limited by the fatigue of working, and respiratory muscles and the heart could only work at about two-thirds sea level capacity. Diffusion of oxygen from lung to blood was also a limiting factor at 19,000 feet. . . .

SILVER HUT

Prominent British physiologist Griffith Pugh went to the Himalayas in 1961 as scientific leader of a project called "The Silver Hut." A prefabricated insulated hut was erected at 19,000 feet in the Everest region, and was continuously occupied for five and a half months. Some of the people stayed as long as nine weeks without descending, though others went down for short periods.

Figure 31. *Silver hut*

Pugh implied that 19,000 or 20,000 feet was the highest altitude where further acclimatization was possible. We now recognize that at or above this altitude, deterioration outstrips acclimatization, and the longer the stay, the worse the fall-off.

Pugh's comment that the respiratory center had become more sensitive to carbon dioxide is significant too because it suggested that physical work by a fully acclimatized person might cause more shortness of breath than in the unacclimatized. This suggests that carbon dioxide accumulating during work might drive breathing as hard as or harder than hypoxia. As an aside, it is interesting to note that breathlessness with exertion is rather prominent for a few days after returning from high altitude.

This was the first thorough study of acclimatization at very high altitude, and the findings in human physiology, nutrition, and oxygen equipment were new and important; it was a major contribution to altitude medicine.

The Sino-Indian Conflict

The importance of acclimatization was dramatically highlighted a year later when Chinese armies crossed their troubled border with India high in the northwestern and southeastern Himalayas. There was fighting at as high as 18,000 feet in very difficult conditions. The Chinese were well acclimatized after living at 15,000 feet in Tibet for many months; Indian troops, on the other hand, were hastily moved to over 18,000 feet by truck or aircraft from the low Indian plains. As a result of their rapid ascent, Indian soldiers suffered more casualties from altitude illness than from enemy action, while the Chinese suffered no altitude problems other than from cold.

The experience of the Indian Army on the high frontier yielded more information than had ever before been collected about mountain sicknesses, and led to publication of many landmark papers by Singh, Menon, and others (see Bibliography).

Military men around the world should not have been startled by what happened on that high faraway frontier, because it was quite predictable: Other troops had suffered on high mountains many centuries ago.

The Arctic Institute Mount Logan Project

The Indian experience stimulated several studies of high altitude physiology, some by the military, others supported by state or private sources. From 1967 to 1979 the Arctic Institute of North America, with support from the U.S. National Institutes of Health, the Canadian Armed Forces, and others, carried on research in a summer laboratory at 17,500 feet near the summit of Mount Logan, a massive mountain in the Canadian Yukon. The first studies attempted to define exactly what caused mountain sickness and how this could be prevented. But after a few years, and some rather frightening experiences, we decided to look at the process of acclimatization in subjects who spent several weeks at the high laboratory. In addition to the high altitude retinal hemorrhages we saw on Logan, described in Chapter 6, AMS: Acute Mountain Sickness, we did many other studies, which I collected in the book *High Altitude Physiology Study.* One new study documented how Diamox eliminates periodic breathing during sleep at altitude. Another demonstrated that most of our subjects did accumulate a small amount of fluid in the pulmonary interstitial space, though showing no evidence of HAPE.

Meanwhile, Himalayan climbing increased furiously; speed climbing at dangerous altitudes became popular, and hordes of unsuspecting and inexperienced tourists, trekkers, and climbers were flown too rapidly to dangerous altitudes. Hundreds became sick and many died—not only visitors but experienced mountaineers as well.

Everest

In Nepal John Dickinson and Peter Hackett (and later David Shlim) organized the Himalayan Rescue Association, which established a clinic below Everest Base Camp, where volunteer doctors took care of the sick and collected a great deal of information about mountain sickness. Altitude physiology became even more popular and facilitated (or was used to justify) many big-mountain climbing expeditions.

A large and elaborate Italian expedition to Everest in 1973 not only managed to get seven men to the summit but also made extensive studies of work capacity and metabolism in thirty-six men during a long stay at 17,500 feet. The American Research Expedition to Everest led by John West in 1981 set up a well-equipped laboratory at 17,700 feet and a smaller one at 20,700 feet, where many exercise studies were done. Alveolar gas samples from one man were collected on the summit and matched with blood samples taken later and lower on the mountain. The findings of this major scientific effort can be briefly summarized as follows:

▲ Confirmed the Silver Hut estimate of the barometric pressure on the summit of Everest.

▲ Confirmed the Silver Hut estimate of maximum work capacity high on the mountain.

▲ Obtained alveolar gases on one subject on the summit.

▲ Calculated blood gases on the summit from blood drawn at 26,000 feet.

▲ Correlated hypoxic ventilatory response of climbers with their performance at altitude.

▲ Obtained hormonal, electrolytes in blood, and ventilatory and circulatory data higher than ever before on a mountain.

These were important observations, made in the real world and subject to all the stresses of the mountain environment.

Denali

From 1982 to 1989, a combined rescue clinic and research laboratory was established by Peter Hackett and Bill Mills at 14,000 feet on Mount McKinley (also known as Denali, The Great One), a mountain that attracts almost 1,000 mountaineers each year. It was ideally sited to study and treat the dozens who required treatment for altitude illness. The project was generously supported by the U.S. Army and the U.S. Department of Interior's National Park Service, and many climbers attempting Denali passed through the facility daily. Many of those who were well volunteered as control subjects for tests, and those who were badly affected by the altitude provided a wealth of research data. The climbers covered a wide spread of age, both sexes, different experience levels, and different rates of climb, so the large amount of information collected was representative of the population attempting a big mountain. The most important observations as reported in more than forty medical papers can be summarized as follows:

▲ Between 2 and 3 percent developed life-threatening pulmonary edema (HAPE).

▲ Fluid drawn from the lungs showed more protein and evidence of inflammation in seven HAPE victims than in the seven control subjects, indicating that HAPE is due to increased lung leakiness.

▲ The hypoxic ventilatory response (HVR) was weak and the arterial oxygen saturation low in those who developed HAPE. On the other hand, periodic breathing during sleep seemed related to a brisk HVR.

▲ Thirty percent of all who were studied had Acute Mountain Sickness (AMS), in which headache and sleep disturbance were major symptoms.

▲ Diamox relieved periodic breathing during sleep but did not increase cerebral blood flow. Diamox was shown to be helpful in *treating* as well as *preventing* AMS.

Doctors working on the Denali project rescued many sick and injured climbers and, not withstanding many interruptions, collected more important data on various aspects of altitude illness than any other before or since. Hackett was among the first to state unequivocally that AMS originates in disturbed brain functions.

Mountain laboratories are the "real world," where people are exposed to many stresses, but from such mountain studies it became clear that one could not tell whether some of the effects attributed to altitude might be due in part to cold, dehydration, exhaustion, inadequate food, and a host of other unpleasant environmental influences. We needed to study hypoxia in its pure form, in the more sheltered decompression chamber, bigger of course than the small cylinders used by Paul Bert a century earlier. An important and often overlooked advantage of chamber studies is the fact that the observers themselves are not affected by the altitude they are studying.

So in 1985 Operation Everest II, a repeat of the first one in 1946, was completed (see Chapter 13).

The Physiology of Adjustment and Acclimatization

Earlier in this chapter, I describe the immediate adjustments to hypoxia—the "struggle responses"—that bring more air deep into the lungs by stimulating deeper and/or faster breathing. At about the same time that the struggle responses begin, some of the same reflexes that stimulate breathing cause the heart to beat faster and harder, moving more blood around the body from lungs to cells and back again. The more vigorous these two adjustments are, the greater the volume of oxygen to reach the cells and the more carbon dioxide discharged from cells to blood to lungs and to outside air. But there's a price for hyperventilation—the loss of carbon dioxide that is washed out of the lungs and blood.

Because it's a gas, and easily soluble in water and blood, carbon dioxide is the principal and most effective mediator of blood acidity. In solution it forms a weak acid, and therefore when more CO_2 than usual leaves blood and diffuses into alveoli, the blood becomes more alkaline. The acidity (pH) of blood lies between 7.35 and 7.44, and normally the range is narrower. The quickest way to correct a too alkaline blood is to decrease the loss of CO_2 by breathing less, and obviously this is not desirable at altitude. Next best is by getting rid of bicarbonate in urine, a process that takes longer and also loses water. This strategy is basic to acclimatization. It's how Diamox works to speed acclimatization and minimize mountain sickness.

The Kidneys

The kidneys are very busy organs, almost as hard-working as the heart. About a fifth of the blood pumped by the heart passes through the kidneys, which filter some 180 liters a day. Of this filtrate, 99 percent is reabsorbed, and 1 or 2 liters of urine excreted. Figure 32 describes very briefly the elaborate mechanism of this small human wastewater treatment plant and suggests how important the kidneys are to acclimatization. However, in the words of Eric Swenson at the 1997 Hypoxia Symposium: "Despite much intensive field and laboratory investigation, the responses of the kidney and its role in acclimatization remain uncertain."

At least one of our two kidneys must function reasonably well in order for us to survive. Not only does the kidney regulate water balance, it must also carry away many waste products of metabolism and wear and tear of tissues. In hypoxia the kidney plays a key role in acclimatization by excreting enough bicarbonate to restore blood acidity toward normal levels.

Two of the many enzymes in the kidneys are particularly important in how we adjust to hypoxia. One is a substance that prevents excessive loss of bicarbonate in urine. The action of this enzyme is partially blocked by Diamox, the medication that is helpful in preventing mountain sickness. The other is erythropoietin (EPO), which the kidneys (and a few other organs) secrete almost immediately they sense lack of oxygen. EPO stimulates an increase in red blood cell and hemoglobin formation in the bone marrow, which is an important part of acclimatization. As acclimatization matures, the formation of both enzymes is decreased by some of the many automatic controls that make the human body so versatile and endlessly fascinating.

Low barometric pressure (*hypobaria*) alone, with normal oxygen, has no effect on the kidneys, and hypoxia with normal barometric pressure does not affect urine flow unless hypoxia is quite severe. Evidently the combination of decreased atmospheric pressure and hypoxia is what affects the kidneys. The kidneys draw from blood a lot of water to filter out and eliminate bicarbonate and other waste substances. This implied the need to drink more water in the mountains, and suggested that a copious flow of urine at altitude would minimize mountain sickness and speed acclimatization.

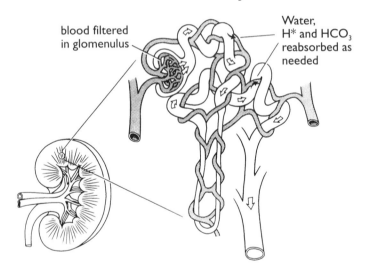

blood filtered
in glomenulus

Water,
H* and HCO₃
reabsorbed as
needed

Figure 32. *The kidneys*

THE KIDNEYS

Arterial blood is pumped through a dense network of capillaries surrounding thousands of tiny filtration capsules (*glomeruli*), where active transport removes selected substances, allowing water and other materials to continue to the next network, which surrounds tubules whose functions are specialized in different areas. The net result is that most of the water is returned to the blood while unwanted wastes are thrown out in urine.

"Drink Lots of Water"

The basis for this advice came from a report of altitude diuresis by von Wendt, who measured his urine while climbing in the Alps in 1910. The term *Hohendiuresen* ("high diuresis," in German) was coined in 1944 after the observation on the Jungfraujoch that those new arrivals above 10,000 feet who passed the most urine tolerated the altitude better than those who passed only a little. Right or wrong, this has become conventional wisdom and taken as a good sign that acclimatization is progressing satisfactorily. It led logically enough to the use of diuretics to increase urine output by medication (see Chapter 9, Hypoxia in Everyday Life). But, again quoting Eric Swenson's comments at the 1997 Hypoxia Symposium:

Despite physiological plausibility, careful examination of the older literature and now more recent studies suggest that the fancy that a lack of high altitude diuresis precedes the development of AMS and is a critical determinant in the pathophysiology of AMS is not true.

Those who do not pass excess urine have been shown to secrete excessive *anti-diuretic hormone* (ADH) and this has come to be considered, perhaps wrongly, a contributor to AMS.

Sojourners in the mountains have long been urged to drink extra water to replace that lost in exhaling moist air and in sweat. There's little question about the value of this, although it may not be true that more urine lost means less edema in tissues and perhaps elsewhere.

A word of caution: Drinking too much water can cause problems too:

A young woman called me from a mountain resort several years ago. She had been at 8,000 feet for a week and was feeling steadily worse. Her head ached and she felt bloated; indeed, she had gained ten pounds and her face, hands, and feet were badly swollen. She told me she had done just what her doctor ordered: "Drink plenty of water and take extra salt because you'll lose a lot in sweat." She had done this in spades! The surplus water and salt had caused massive edema, which disappeared rapidly when she stopped taking salt and cut down her water intake.

Even without salt, excess water can cause problems. Head injuries, and brain swelling from other causes like HACE, may cause *hyponatremia* (low blood sodium), not from excess water or too little salt, but because the body secretes an abnormally large amount of ADH. Some schizophrenic patients with an obssession to drink water will dilute their blood and lower serum sodium enough to cause collapse, coma, convulsions, and death. Sometimes marathoners drink more water than they need and do not replace lost sodium; they too risk collapse from hyponatremia. So too much water, and/or too much salt, may cause as much trouble, especially at high altitude, as too little of either.

The Kidney and Edema

Unfortunately, we don't have—or else we don't understand—enough facts to be certain of the complete role of the kidney in hypoxia. For one thing, why should some individuals secrete more anti-diuretic hormone (ADH) than others? For another, how important is the kidney in preventing (or allowing) peripheral edema? The evidence for increased leakage (permeability) of small blood vessels has been challenged—although the majority of studies show that capillaries (except in brain and lung) do leak at high altitude, and the kidney is not involved. Finally, there's some question whether anti-diuresis and edema *cause* AMS or *result* from it.

Oxygen Transport—Hemoglobin

The overriding need of the body at altitude is to restore adequate oxygen to tissues. So, together with hyperventilation, the next protective measure is to increase the transport of oxygen by increasing the number of red blood cells carrying hemoglobin. We begin to do this very quickly after hypoxia is detected by our sensors: A rapid increase in the *apparent* number of circulating red blood cells occurs due to the loss of fluid from the blood, partly through greater urine output, which concentrates the blood. In addition, for some individuals at high altitude, or under some conditions like strenuous exertion at sea level, fluid leaks out of the small blood vessels into the loose tissues, also decreasing circulating blood volume. This fluid in the tissues becomes apparent in the swelling (*edema*) of feet and ankles and face on wakening. Despite some contrary evidence, it's generally accepted that fluid seeps out of capillaries through tiny pores that have become more permeable from hypoxia.

This loss of fluid from blood into interstitial tissues concentrates the blood so that more oxygen is carried in each milliliter of blood. It does not increase the total oxygen-*carrying capacity,* because the total number of circulating red blood cells has not increased, as it will when the bone marrow makes and releases more red cells. When that happens, both the blood's oxygen *content* and its *carrying capacity* will increase, and acclimatization will be progressing well. I discuss this in more detail in Chapter 4, Moving Blood: Circulation.

Erythropoietin (EPO)

Within hours of becoming hypoxic, a powerful hormone, erythropoietin (EPO), is released from the kidney (and a few other places), and this stimulates the bone marrow to produce more red blood cells and hemoglobin. EPO is a powerful agent, and this stimulation continues, automatically, until an optimum number of red blood cells are circulating, when EPO is turned off. This takes a few weeks. It's interesting that EPO secretion is not increased by all types of hypoxia.

An older belief that the spleen, a reservoir for red blood cells, contracts in response to hypoxia seems to happen only in some animals.

A few attempts to improve altitude tolerance and hasten acclimatization by transfusing blood into the climber high on a mountain have not been effective enough, so far, to justify the risk and difficulties. Several types of "artificial blood" have been produced but transfusing some of these, often valuable in certain medical conditions at sea level, hasn't been studied enough at high altitude. Injections of EPO have been tried, to accelerate acclimatization, but hypoxia is such a strong EPO stimulant that injections don't increase red blood cell production much more at high altitude. To improve competitiveness at sea level, EPO has been used and is not only banned in most arenas but may actually do harm.

Each of the many functions that change in response to hypoxia is affected by the others, and together they produce a stable condition of acclimatization—if, but only if, (1) hypoxia is not too severe, (2) exposure is not too rapid, (3) the individual does not remain too long at the thin edge of survival, which is considered to be at about 23,000 feet, and (4) a predisposition, possibly genetic, does not interfere.

Using a computer model to vary one or many changes, it's possible to calculate roughly how much increase in oxygen delivery to the cells each of the acclimatizing changes may generate. Interestingly, an increase in the arterial oxygen *capacity* is less effective than several others, and less effective than deliberate overbreathing.

In Chapter 3, Moving Air: Respiration, I discuss the oxygen cascade and how it is automatically adjusted to cope with lack of oxygen in the air. These changes are modified slightly during prolonged hypoxia and, together with increased kidney activity, are the basis of acclimatization to high altitude— and to a certain extent to chronic hypoxia from other causes too.

Life depends on an adequate flow of oxygen into each cell, where it is used by the mitochondria, the factories where every life function is energized (see Chapter 5, Cells). Though the number of mitochondria apparently does not increase during acclimatization, their size does, increasing extraction of oxygen from blood before it returns to the lungs.

Myoglobin

Cells, notably muscle cells, must be able to respond to a sudden call for more oxygen. Ordinarily, as we start to exercise and the muscles require more oxygen, the heart speeds up and more blood is pumped to meet this demand. An additional supply of oxygen is available in the muscles, loosely bound to a substance much like hemoglobin called *myoglobin*. During acclimatization, myoglobin increases substantially, and we might think of this as a storehouse or a facilitator of oxygen transfer, even though each molecule of myoglobin holds less oxygen (as does hemoglobin) than at sea level. It's interesting that myoglobin has a left-shifted oxygen dissociation curve, admirably suited for release of a lot of oxygen rapidly when the local supply gets very low. Diving mammals have a large supply of myoglobin from which they draw during long submersion.

In Table 8, we can summarize these major changes in oxygen acquisition, transport, and delivery that tend to bring the oxygen supply to the tissues closer to that available in the lungs.

MAJOR CHANGES IN ACCLIMATIZATION

Table 8.

Increased breathing	Better exchange of air in alveoli
Increased cardiac output	Temporary; more blood is moved
Increased red cells	More oxygen carriers available
More tissue capillaries	Brings blood closer to cells
Increased myoglobin	More oxygen is locally available
Increased urine output	Temporary; concentrates blood

There are many other more exotic changes within each cell; in specialized tissues like the glands, which produce hormones; in the kidneys, which discard bicarbonate as an important contribution to acclimatization; and in the heart. These don't seem to have as much impact in bringing tissue oxygen to levels closer to that in the outside air as do the major changes we have looked at.

How does a person born of generations of high altitude natives differ from the well-acclimatized sojourner? Different races seem to have followed slightly different paths over the centuries, but for most the basic responses are the same, though some may be slightly muted. All involve the same oxygen transport system but emphasize different sections.

Adaptation to High Altitude

In several parts of the world, many generations of altitude natives have been thoroughly at home up to 17,000 feet (elevation of the highest permanently inhabited villages) and can do hard physical work, as Joseph Barcroft wrote after visiting a mine in Peru at 14,000 feet:

> Every few minutes, like a bee out of some hive in cold weather, someone would appear from the mouth of the mine. He would be much out of breath, he would take frequent pauses on the way up, but the weight on his back would be a hundred pounds . . . he would sit for a while to rest and then down into the mine again he would go to bring up another load.

When we look at long-term, Darwinian adaptation to high altitude, we find variations between different races, some of them well recognized, others still unclear or controversial. There's hard evidence that some animals develop larger alveoli if born at high altitude. Less firm evidence suggests that humans born of generations of high altitude residents may have more alveoli.

These adaptations improve oxygen uptake by providing more area for diffusion and are more effective than simply developing a larger chest capable of moving more air in and out, an adaptation found in Andean natives but not in Tibetans.

Sherpas (descendants of generations of high altitude residents) have a healthy response to oxygen lack (brisk HVR) and they have slightly more hemoglobin than do sea level natives. Sherpas are generally physically fit and their maximum exercise capacity is high. They don't lose much weight at high altitude, and they seem to sleep more soundly. Andean natives have larger than normal carotid bodies, and respond more briskly to the hypoxic challenge.

Sherpas have only a little more hemoglobin than their sea level cohorts, but Andean residents have a lot more. However, most Andean studies have been done on Ayamara and Quechua natives, who live at higher altitudes than do the Sherpas. Tibetans are more like Sherpas, but there are some suggestions that Tibetans have a "fast" and a "slow" type hemoglobin—like their versatile servant the yak. Many Sherpas whose forebears lived on the high Tibetan plateau now live at somewhat lower altitude; their oxy-hemoglobin dissociation curves tend to be left-shifted, like the Himalayan bar-headed goose. Sherpas seem able to do more work at extreme altitude than can even well-acclimatized sea level natives, but there are few well-controlled studies to support this. When the chips are down, willpower, motivation, and spirit are arguably the major forces that drive the climber up the last exhausting feet on Everest, where he or she is moving almost automatically. But whether by better genetic heritage or more determination, one Sherpa has summited Everest ten times, and several others have done so four or five times.

Athough a vast amount of research has already been done, it seems to me that many exciting adventures in human physiology are waiting for students of the faraway peoples who have adjusted to altitude (or to cold or heat or drought) along different genetic pathways. I am sure that, from them, many lessons can be learned that could affect all of us.

Acclimatization in Practice

We must now look at some practical aspects of acclimatization: How long does it take? How long does it last? How can it be speeded up or enhanced? And—of special interest—is it helpful to acclimatize at high altitude for competitions held at sea level? To compete at high altitude, where should one train—and how? Training for competition is only peripherally related to mountaineering, so I discuss training in Chapter 14. Only partial answers are available for such questions, and individual variation makes a great deal of difference.

We can say quite confidently that a month of gradual ascent is enough for most people to acclimatize well to 18,000–19,000 feet. We can also say, from a lot of experience, that at above 20,000 feet, deterioration outstrips acclimatization and those who stay so high for many days do not improve with time. No people are known to live for more than a few months above 17,000 feet, but in addition to high altitude, other harsh conditions contribute to their failure to thrive.

How Fast Is Slow Enough?

In Chapter 10, Prevention, I discuss appropriate rates of climb for the unacclimatized sojourner to moderate altitude. In general, taking a few days for the ascent will protect against altitude illness at up to 10,000 feet, and in less than a week most people feel as well as at sea level.

Acclimatizing to Climb the Highest Peaks

Many generations of mountaineers used siege tactics on the highest mountains, slowly building a pyramid of well-stocked camps to within striking distance of the summit. We relied on the daily work of carrying loads up, and returning to a lower camp to sleep.

During a long siege, or after long periods of bad weather kept one in a high camp (a debilitating experience), we would descend to base camp for a rest in richer air. There are many advantages to this approach—but it takes more time and more equipment, and for the last few decades other approaches have been tried.

One is to spend more time at base camp, climbing higher every day or two on mountains nearby, gradually building acclimatization while enjoying the luxuries of base camp. Then, when the climbers feel fit and the weather is good, they may go for the summit, perhaps from base camp or perhaps from a higher intermediate camp. Using this approach, some superclimbers have summited Everest or K2 in less than twenty-four hours.

Always at the mercy of weather, experienced climbers have evolved several different programs for acclimatizing on the highest summits. David Brashears, who has summited Everest four times, recommends going up a few thousand feet a few days after reaching Base camp and returning to Base. Then he may go up to Camp One for a night, and again descend to Base. By then, if acclimatization has well begun, his party may carry loads to Camp Two once or twice, and finally move up to sleep at Camp Three before going to the South Col in promising weather to summit next day. Others have slightly different programs; all rely on a few nights at higher and higher camps for a week or ten days before attempting the summit—and this after several weeks at the 18,000-foot Base.

Other veterans modify siege tactics by setting up a few camps, then retreating several thousand feet for a week or so of real rest. After this, some parties have been able to reach the top in only a few days—if the weather holds. On the highest mountains anywhere, weather is often the most decisive factor.

Any of these plans to go to high altitude during days or even weeks, then retreat to low altitude and return to high altitude, might make the climber vulnerable to re-entry HAPE (see Chapter 8). But apparently the altitude stay usually is not long enough; I haven't heard of such cases.

One extreme approach has not yet been tested: An expert climber, fully fit at sea level, might breathe oxygen night and day above 12,000 feet and, following a prepared track, climb at a reasonable rate of 1,500 feet an hour, reaching the top of Everest and returning in less than twenty hours. It would be risky: should his or her oxygen fail, unconsciousness would be swift and death not far behind. From what we know about acclimatization, this fully oxygenated approach would make the climber only as breathless as at sea level, allow him or her to start out well rested, well fed, and hydrated—but it would not seem to be a very joyful way to go.

For now, different individuals and groups will continue to try various patterns of ascent, work, and rest.

Medication

Will any medication or diet or breathing exercises speed acclimatization? Of these, the only one that makes a real difference is **acetazolamide** (Diamox). This and other means of prevention are discussed in Chapter 10, Prevention. One could call Diamox an "artificial acclimatizer," because it does facilitate the excretion of bicarbonate and normalizes blood pH. Several expeditions have used Diamox every day, but their experiences differ, and there are too many variables to reach any conclusion. From what I know today, I suspect that taking Diamox regularly during a major climb may be more helpful than harmful—if one insists on taking some kind of medicine. There may be a risk: Some of those who have taken Diamox regularly and stopped it abruptly while at high altitude have then developed acute altitude problems rather unexpectedly.

Respiratory stimulants do not seem to speed acclimatization. **Hormones** (steroids, human growth hormone, and others) and **psychotropic drugs** have not been adequately tested.

Changing Hemoglobin

When we try to decide what is an optimal level of hemoglobin, we are on uncertain ground. Crude efforts have been made to improve altitude tolerance by transfusing blood into the acclimatizing mountaineer: The results have been conflicting. Others have tried removing what might be called excess hemoglobin and replacing the blood with plasma. Again, no clear result. Sound theory and a lot of anecdotal evidence suggest that a hematocrit of less than 56 percent to 58 percent is optimal, but we can't conclude from this that removing blood is beneficial to the acclimatized climber.

We know how to convert adult-type hemoglobin to the fetal or fast form—but this is justifiable only in certain serious illnesses and so far no method has been considered for the healthy mountaineer. Undoubtedly, tinkering with the ability of hemoglobin to pick up and release oxygen may help in some situations—but not today, not yet. A few studies of tolerance for hypoxia by persons with a mutant hemoglobin do not seem to have much relevance to mountaineering—but who knows?

Losing Acclimatization

There's not much firm data about how long it takes a person to lose acclimatization once acquired, but most of the changes—even the blood count—revert to normal within a week or two of returning to sea level. It is interesting that shortness of breath on exertion may last for a week at sea level after returning from several weeks at high altitude. This period of "de-acclimatization" has not been studied, but I believe the persistent shortness of breath is due to an increase in sensitivity of the respiratory center to carbon dioxide. In addition, the alkaline reserve (base excess) has been decreased, making the pH of blood more sensitive to small changes in carbon dioxide or to the lactic acid produced by exertion.

Hypoxia Due to Illness at Sea Level

What, if any, relationship does altitude acclimatization have to the changes that make survival possible for persons severely hypoxic from chronic lung disease? What about those who have sleep apnea, or Pickwickian syndrome (*alveolar hypoventilation*), or who have lost a lung to disease or surgery? Or those who cannot breathe adequately due to polio or diseases causing muscular weakness? Are there some solid lessons from high altitudes that apply to these unfortunates?

In Chapter 8, HAPE: High Altitude Pulmonary Edema, I discuss this complicated issue: In some conditions, the defect is an increased barrier between alveolus and pulmonary capillary, increasing the oxygen gradient (and often causing retention of carbon dioxide too). In others the problem is inadequate lung capacity or weakness of respiratory muscles, causing poor ventilation or inadequate respiratory stimulus or inadequate circulation. Each would require a different response by the body, if any is to help.

Finally, what of the longtime high altitude resident who travels to sea level? Will he or she have trouble de-acclimatizing? The answer is firmly "no"—adjustment takes only a few days or a week. The mountaineer coming home from high in the Himalayas is euphoric and elated. Simple things like green grass, flowers, warmth, and space to move about delight him or her. Life is a precious, many-splendored thing, filled with joys and surprises. But within weeks, the trivia of every day intrude: There is money to deal with; the daily round is dull and uninspiring compared to the high drama of a strenuous climb where a single purpose dominates. Life seems to have lost its savor; some climbers become depressed; divorces or broken relationships are common before one adjusts to the daily round. It is tempting to blame these emotional events on lasting effects of severe hypoxia. But men and women returning after great experiences at sea or long trips in the polar or desert regions have experienced similar emotions. It seems to me they are due to shifting gears, rather than to hypoxia.

Acclimatization for Competitive Sports

A vast amount of thought, effort, and money has been invested in the question of sports training. Will you compete better at sea level after acclimatizing to high altitude? If competing at high altitude, should you arrive weeks in advance and acclimatize? How will you fare if you go directly from sea level and at once compete at high altitude?

The enormous and saddening commercialization of most sports (including mountain climbing) has made the answers to these questions potentially worth billions of dollars but, not surprisingly, throwing money at the questions has resulted in more questions than answers. Because it is such a major issue, I discuss training in more detail in Chapter 14, and include in the Bibliography some scientific papers addressing the subject.

△ △ △

ACCLIMATIZATION TO ALTITUDE IS A wondrously complex process wherein many interlocking changes enable survival under extreme conditions. When we look at sea level humans and observe how within seconds they become unconscious when deprived of oxygen, the wonder grows that we are able to get anywhere near the harsh, hostile, and spectacular summit of Everest. We wonder even more that whales and seals can dive without breathing for an hour, that turtles can hibernate for months under water, that the lung fish can go for years without breathing, that some forms of life exist completely without oxygen. Such wonders never cease.

Operation Everest I and II

WHEN THE HEIGHT OF MOUNT EVEREST WAS MEASURED IN 1856, IT excited little interest among mountaineers for forty years because many believed that spending a night above 20,000 feet would be fatal. Besides, Tibet was firmly closed to foreigners. But as the nineteenth century ended, a handful of explorers had climbed higher and slept higher, and the highest summits beckoned. Leading mountaineers wondered: Could Everest be climbed?

After Paul Bert showed that lack of oxygen caused altitude sickness, which could be treated or prevented by breathing oxygen, his colleagues Croce-Spinelli and Sivel died in a hot air balloon when they ran out of oxygen while ascending almost as high as the summit of Everest (see the account in Chapter 12, Acclimatization). To many, this put Everest—without oxygen—beyond reach. Others were optimistic.

Surgeon-mountaineer Clinton Dent thought the climb possible, but barely so. In 1918 chemist-climber Alexander Kellas, projecting from data at lower elevations, agreed. Climaxing the 1924 attempt on Everest, Lieutenant Colonel Edward Norton, one of the more experienced Himalayan climbers, reached 28,300 feet without supplementary oxygen, only 800 feet below the summit, where the oxygen pressure in air is only 2–3 torr higher than on the summit. This was a record that would stand for fifty years. In 1953 Edmund Hillary and Sherpa Tenzing Norgay reached the top breathing supplementary oxygen. Since 1975 more than eighty persons have summited Everest breathing only the air around them, and now there is nowhere higher to climb. But many have died from the combined stresses of high mountains.

Lack of oxygen is not the only problem on high mountains (see Chapter 12, Acclimatization), and by 1940 a new question was asked: How much does the almost unavoidable cold, exhaustion, thirst, fear, and hunger affect performance and even survival on the highest peaks? How could the effect of such additional stresses be measured?

At the end of WW II the large decompression chambers used for training aircrew presented an irresistible opportunity to answer this question by a simulated climb, perhaps even higher than Everest. I had been working in the research unit at the Pensacola Naval Air Station in Florida and saw the two large chambers there as a great chance to study altitude in a controlled environment where hypobaric hypoxia would be the only stress.

In this chapter I describe two studies of acclimatization in which I was involved. Because the data were unique at the time, and may be of interest to scientists reading this book, I have included some details. For the non-scientific reader, this may be hard going, though I've tried to describe in nonmedical words what the two studies mean.

Operation Everest I, 1946

I proposed to the Navy a project, to be called Operation Everest, in which my team would study acclimatization to hypoxia in a warm, comfortable setting. We hypothesized that our findings would be relevant to illnesses causing hypoxia at sea level. Of greater importance to the military, the study would also compare the maximum altitude achievable by *unacclimatized men* breathing oxygen, with that which *well-acclimatized men* also breathing oxygen could reach. Such acclimatization would provide air combat superiority in those days. For mountaineers, we would see if acclimatized men could reach 29,000 feet breathing only the ambient air.

The Navy approved the proposal for Operation Everest five months after it was requested. Four healthy young men volunteered as subjects to live in a cramped decompression chamber for thirty-five days during which the chamber would be gradually decompressed. Recruiting scientists was more difficult because many thought the project either dangerous or foolish.

Our plans called for "climbing" to 8,000–9,000 feet in one or two days and thereafter decompressing the chamber at a rate equivalent to climbing 2,000–3,000 feet a day. When we felt acclimatization was adequate, we would have the subjects taken to 29,000 feet during a long eight-hour "climb." Detailed protocols were prepared for measuring the more important changes we expected and would be able to measure inside the chamber.

A laboratory with the best equipment available at the time was staffed by several experts, and a nutritionist was loaned us by the Navy. The chamber was to be staffed by a crew of thirty enlisted men and petty officers, standing four-hour watches in pairs around the clock. My partner, Dick Riley, and I were to be assisted when needed by student flight surgeons; I lived in a room next to the chamber for the duration.

After the volunteer subjects had been examined and all equipment thoroughly checked, the massive steel door of the chamber was closed on June 28, 1946, and after three days at sea level for control studies, the subjects "took off."

During the next thirty-five days, the chamber was kept warm and humid

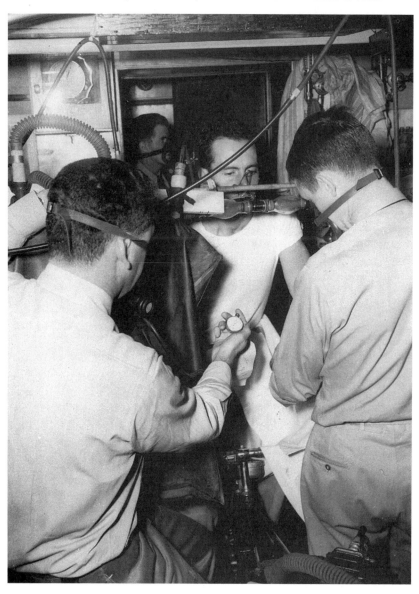

Figure 33. *Operation Everest I decompression chamber*

and continuously ventilated, carbon dioxide was absorbed, and the oxygen percentage in the chamber air was monitored. The barometric pressure in the chamber was measured by aircraft altimeters, calibrated with a mercury barometer to the ICAO (International Civil Aviation Organization) altitude/pressure curve.

Arterial blood and alveolar air samples were taken repeatedly, and pul-

OPERATION EVEREST

The decompression chambers extensively used for training by the armed forces during WWII were a far cry from Hooke's seventeenth-century "barrel" and the small cylinders used in the last decades of the nineteenth century by Paul Bert and Angelo Mosso! But the principles are the same: Air is pumped out of a tightly closed space to simulate the lower barometric pressure at altitude. Modern chambers are large enough for men to live in for several weeks, with a constant flow of air and food and drink brought in, and, by entering through an air lock, scientists can do a wide variety of tests not easily done on a mountain.

The chamber available for the first such project in 1946 was cramped, with barely enough room for four men and some space for scientists. Using what were then state-of-the-art techniques, a large amount of data was obtained to define the process of acclimatization to hypoxia, uncontaminated by the many other obstacles on a very high mountain.

The state of the art changed rapidly due to increasing interest in oxygen and hypoxia, and four decades later, in a pair of chambers three times as large, eight men spent five weeks being taken slowly to 29,000 feet. A much larger database was collected in this controlled environment where ambient pressure was the major difference from a sea level laboratory.

The rate of ascent in both Operation Everest I (1946) and Operation Everest II (1985) was somewhat too rapid for the subjects to acclimatize fully as mountaineers are able to do during many more weeks and with strenuous exercise. But both studies showed that humans could survive briefly on top of Everest—or with an equivalent degree of hypoxia at sea level. OE II clearly demonstrated that the lung rather than the heart would be the limiting factor in extreme hypoxia.

monary ventilation was measured at rest and during and after exercise up to 20,000 feet. Electrocardiograms were recorded every few days and chest X rays taken at seven altitudes. We did not try to do very many studies but to do well those we did. The subjects were well fed and encouraged to take fluids, but neither fluid intake nor output were measured. Three of the four subjects smoked cigarettes. Two exercised every day on a stationary cycle or climbing bars, but the others worked out only sporadically.

During the slow ascent, the subjects said they felt well but with occasional mild headaches, periodic breathing during sleep, and easy fatigue. As seen by observers sitting at sea level, the subjects appeared to be increasingly impaired although they "felt just fine," as the chamber was slowly "climbed."

We worried that, without the hypoxic drive to breathe, they might stop breathing if some emergency required that the chamber be taken abruptly to sea level. We also were concerned that their hearts might dilate, as had been reported by Dr. Somervell on the early Everest climbs.

After four days at 22,000 feet, the chamber was "taken up" at the rate of 1,000 feet an hour. Each subject rode the stationary cycle briefly every hour. At 26,700 feet one man requested oxygen, and a second did so 1,000 feet higher. The other two continued, and after eight hours reached 29,025 feet according to the aircraft altimeter. Both were alert and cycled for a short time, but appeared to be close to their limit. After twenty minutes the chamber descended to 20,000 feet.

These two men had shown that the hypoxia on top of Everest would not rapidly kill acclimatized men. But the eight hours for the final ascent from 22,000 feet had been too fast, and it was obvious that our men could not do the hours of heavy work needed for the actual climb. Nor were they fully acclimatized.

On the following day the two subjects were taken slowly to 50,525 feet breathing oxygen, watched from outside the chamber by sea level observers who could not tolerate that high an altitude, even breathing 100 percent oxygen. Both subjects were alert, weak, and yet able to function moderately well. Because sea level pilots are seriously impaired at 42,000 feet even breathing 100 percent oxygen, we concluded that acclimatization had clearly raised the altitude ceiling of our partially acclimatized subjects. Of great interest at that time, the accomplishment was soon moot because all aircraft would be pressurized to provide a low cabin altitude.

The information collected during OE I was unique because it was the first time humans had been observed, by scientists at sea level, as they acclimatized to increasing altitude. Absent the powerful stresses on a high mountain, these subjects experienced only the hypoxia of decreased barometric pressure, although it's true they were confined and unable to exercise very much.

Some of the observations can be summarized in a few sentences; the full data are given in one of my published papers describing Operation Everest I and II. Pulmonary ventilation increased steadily with altitude as expected. Hemoglobin, hematocrit, and arterial oxygen capacity increased steadily. Arterial carbon dioxide fell and pH rose. When saturation was plotted on the oxy-hemoglobin dissociation curve for the appropriate pH, there appeared to be a shift to the right. Resting pulse rate increased and cardiac output increased two to three times the sea level value. Electrocardiograms and X rays showed no evidence of cardiac enlargement or strain. Of some interest are the Alveolar-arterial oxygen gradients, which decreased with increasing altitude almost to zero at 20,000 feet, the highest point where we drew arterial blood. All A-a gradients increased sharply with exercise.

ALVEOLAR GASES (MEASUREMENTS IN TORR)

	Oxygen	Carbon Dioxide	
Four subjects at 26,000 ft	26, 26, 30, 31	17, 16, 14, 14	Table 9.
Two subjects at 28,200 feet	23, 24	15, 13	
Two subjects at 29,030 feet	23, 21	13, 14	
Same subjects second time	24, 22	13, 14	

As expected, alveolar oxygen pressures decreased with altitude, but were partially sustained at the expense of a fall in carbon dioxide, due to the increasing ventilation. Not shown here is the decrease in work capacity with altitude; although improved by breathing oxygen, it did not reach sea level capacity.

From this study—a "pure culture" of hypoxia without the confounding effects of the mountain environment—we showed that people could live and do light work for a short time at the height of Mount Everest. In fact, the "physiological altitude" at the "summit" in the chamber was about 1,000 feet higher than it would be on the actual mountain, because above 23,000 feet the ICAO calibrated altimeter (which we used) gave measurements several torr lower than those actually measured years later on top of Everest.

We could not measure the extent of acclimatization, but a volunteer brought to 22,500 feet from sea level collapsed in one minute and twenty seconds while riding the stationary cycle after his oxygen mask was removed. In contrast, one of the subjects cycled for twenty minutes until bored.

As the altitude increased, the subjects slowly became less interested in various activities and less inclined to exercise. They had occasional headaches but not the full picture of mountain sickness. None complained of the sore throat or cough so common on high mountains. Appetites declined and they all lost weight. All had periodic breathing, and above 22,000 feet their cyanosis and general appearance during sleep was worrisome enough for us to monitor their pulse rates electronically, and even to keep a flight surgeon in the chamber for a few nights. Having myself spent many days above 24,000 feet, I appreciated how these subjects felt, but was worried by how badly they appeared to us unaffected sea level observers—the first time people at great altitude were watched by those at sea level. In Chapter 8, HAPE: High Altitude Pulmonary Edema, I quote how Haldane appeared to those who were watching him and Kellas from outside the decompression chamber; the subjects in OE I were slightly less affected.

Of special interest to military aviation in that era, we showed that this degree of acclimatization could significantly raise the "ceiling" of pilots breathing oxygen.

We were greatly relieved to see the subjects breathing normally when they descended in a few hours to sea level and showed no ill effects from their exposure. The frequent X rays had shown no sign whatever of cardiac enlargement.

Operation Everest II, 1985

Air warfare in WW II stimulated interest in altitude research, and after the war more studies of high altitude on mountains were done in the next twenty years: Among the many were the Silver Hut expedition near Everest (1960–61), the High Altitude Physiology Studies (HAPS) on Mount Logan (1967–75), and the American Research Expedition (AMREE) to Mount Everest (1981). These and many others added greatly to understanding of acclimatization—in the harsh mountain environment. By 1980 it seemed appropriate to repeat Operation Everest with a more ambitious agenda, in a larger decompression chamber, again in a controlled environment. There we could use modern techniques to study hypobaric hypoxia in a setting in which many sophisticated studies could be done safely and conveniently.

It took five years to recruit scientists and subjects and to find money, but eventually the Army Research and Development Command agreed to cover the anticipated expense. The Army Research Institute of Environmental Medicine (ARIEM) in Natick, Massachusetts provided a large decompression chamber and staff for six weeks. In September 1985, eight male subjects and two alternates completed baseline studies at ARIEM and were approved for the project. Much as we wished to include women subjects, the numbers would be too small, and female hormonal cycles might confound the data and blur our conclusions.

We wanted the rate of ascent to be slower than in OE I, hoping for more complete acclimatization, but a number of factors led to an ascent profile only a little less rapid.

Like the 1946 study, OE II was planned to be a "pure culture" of hypobaric hypoxia, without the cold, privation, and physical and mental stress unavoidable on a very high mountain. Ample water, appetizing meals, and ready access to stationary cycle and treadmill exercise resembled a sea level setting. The chamber was kept warm and humid; entertainments were provided. Although the studies were demanding on both subjects and scientists, the subjects had time for rest and recreation. Most of them exercised regularly and they were watched day and night through ports in the chamber.

The Oxygen Cascade in Acclimatization

In OE II we focused on how the changes in the oxygen cascade (see Chapter 3, Moving Air: Respiration, and Chapter 12, Acclimatization) affected acclimatization. Pulmonary ventilation and diffusion characteristics were measured by standard techniques.

Heart function was assessed by cardiac catheterization done on each subject at three different altitudes, at rest and during and after exertion, and included pulmonary and systemic arterial pressures; mixed venous oxygen was also measured directly. Electrocardiograms and chest echocardiography were done at regular intervals.

Maximal exercise capacity and sustained exercise capability were measured on different days; muscle biopsies were taken during each test of sustained exertion. Vital signs and simple pulmonary function tests, as well as alveolar samples, were obtained every day on all subjects, with occasional simultaneous arterial blood gases. Fluid and caloric intake and output were measured each day.

Above 22,000 feet, most subjects complained of sore throat, which we had not seen in OE I below this altitude. This is particularly interesting because sore throat is a severe problem on very high mountains and has been blamed on the cold, dry air. But because our chamber air was warm and wet, we suggest that a direct effect of hypoxia may be part of the cause.

We realized, as had been true in OE I, that the subjects were not fully acclimatized, but most of the data we collected were new and showed how the process was evolving. All the data have been published in medical papers under the title "Operation Everest II," and have also been assembled in one volume by the Army Institute of Environmental Medicine. Our principal findings can be summarized as follows:

1. The largest improvement in bringing oxygen to the body was the increased ventilation (i.e., moving air from the atmosphere into the alveoli), by increasing both rate and volume of respiration.

2. All subjects developed a consistent and sometimes remarkable ventilation/perfusion mismatch at the higher altitudes, and this was aggravated by exercise, paralleling the rise in pulmonary artery pressure. We believe this was due to accumulation of interstitial fluid in the lungs more rapidly than the lymphatics could remove it. No subject (or scientist) developed full-blown HAPE.

3. The heart functioned well and was not the limiting factor at extreme altitude, as shown by maintenance of cardiac output for a given oxygen uptake. Breathing supplemental oxygen did not increase stroke volume for a given filling pressure.

4. Electrocardiographic changes were compatible with the increase in pulmonary artery pressure. Even maximal exercise at extreme altitude did not cause heart muscle to falter. This is reassuring to everyone.

5. Pulmonary artery pressure increased with altitude; at very high altitude it was lowered by breathing 100 percent oxygen, which did not, however, decrease the calculated pulmonary resistance. This rather puzzling observation was persistent and carefully checked.

6. Alveolar and arterial gases and arterial blood pH were obtained on the

summit, and show higher oxygen and carbon dioxide and lower pH than were found in one subject on the summit during AMREE; that climber told me later that he had been breathing ninety times a minute when he took the sample! This would have caused his very low alveolar carbon dioxide and low pH, indicative of extreme respiratory alkalosis.

7. Maximal exercise capacity decreased steeply at the highest altitudes, as others had found at lower elevations. This suggests that the degree of hypoxia inevitable on the summit of Everest may make that spot close to the highest achievable by even the best-acclimatized human. Some birds go higher, and many animals survive more severe hypoxia using different strategies.

8. As in OE I, all the subjects lost weight despite appetizing, balanced meals, for which they gradually lost appetite. The weight loss could not be explained by balancing energy output against intake, which suggests some malabsorption.

△ △ △

BOTH OE I AND OE II ARE OF INTEREST to mountaineers because, among other things, they showed that our rate of climb was too fast to achieve optimal acclimatization. This may not be especially relevant for some of today's elite mountaineers, who consider siege tactics (i.e., slow, steady ascent) "out" and speed climbing "in," but others can profit from the examples.

Optimal Rate of Climb

Looking at the ascent profiles and symptoms experienced in these two studies, we can cautiously suggest that a healthy young person can go, during the course of three days, to 12,000 feet and not experience more than minor symptoms. Above this, climbing 1,000 or 1,500 feet a day, with a rest every third day, seems appropriate. Above 22,000 feet, our data confirm the belief that one does not acclimatize. The rate of climb above this should be dictated by individual tolerance.

Our finding that not the heart but the lung is the limiting factor at high altitude is reassuring to older persons, but cautionary for those with minor lung problems.

Importance of Operation Everest Studies

For research scientists, OE I and OE II established standards of the effects of hypoxia without the other stresses of a mountain environment, against which data on the real mountain can be assessed. Our data make it possible to separate changes due to hypoxia from those due to cold, dehydration, and other mountain impacts.

Relevance to Everyday Hypoxia

But why are these two complicated studies important to those who have little interest or concern with mountains?

Mostly, I think, because OE I and OE II give us a background against which to appraise persons hypoxic from acute or chronic illness, or injury or long-standing handicap. Our data enable us to estimate which abnormalities are due to hypoxia alone, and which might be caused by the underlying illness or injury. We can approach diagnosis and treatment in many cases more precisely and often more effectively.

Snoring and periodic breathing should be regarded not as a nuisance but a problem that, if not corrected, can lead over time to serious consequences. Mental or personality deviations in patients with severe heart or lung disease may be recognized as partly due to hypoxia—and remedied—rather than due solely to senility or emotional illness. We can be much better informed before we advise people with one or another illness about the benefits and risks of going to the mountains.

In short, these are not simply interesting but unimportant pieces of knowledge, but, to paraphrase Joseph Barcroft, such lessons from high altitude can help us to better understand ourselves at sea level.

CHAPTER 14

Training for Athletic Competition

WHERE SHOULD ONE TRAIN FOR COMPETITIVE ATHLETICS? CAN ONE improve sea level performance by training at altitude? Do high altitude natives surpass sea level natives in competition at sea level? At high altitude?

There's a lot of talk and hundreds of articles about this, but only a few solid conclusions. So intense are competitive athletics today that even the smallest edge is important. But however well motivated, whether one lives at high altitude or goes there from sea level for daily training, one cannot train to the utmost limit at high altitude because even as low as 5,000 feet, maximal work capacity is less than at sea level. So is there any benefit from training at altitude? It's an increasingly important question because of the huge prestige and enormous amounts of money involved.

There might be some advantage from a small increase in hemoglobin, which can deliver more oxygen per unit of blood pumped. This increase comes with acclimatization to moderate altitude, but is partly offset by the slightly decreased alkaline reserve, which results from the small increase in blood pH. This means that the additional carbon dioxide and lactic acid generated by strenuous exercise will have more effect on blood pH and thus on respiration than when alkaline reserve is normal, and the well-acclimatized individual is likely to ventilate more than a sea level rival during the same exertion. To offset this less beneficial effect of acclimatization, elite athletes trained at sea level and were given transfusions of blood, usually their own blood taken earlier, but this is now banned in most sports. Injections of erythropoietin (EPO) stimulate formation of more hemoglobin and red blood cells, but this too is banned. Also, one or two competitors are said to have had an adverse reaction from the artificially added EPO. Too much hemoglobin makes blood sluggish, and the slight advantage gained appears to be offset by those other factors. The bottom line seems to be that adding hemoglobin is not worth the risks.

We should be able to draw conclusions by comparing Olympic performance in 1968 at 7,300 feet in Mexico City with that in Los Angeles in 1984, but even long after the Games, opinions differ about where one should best have trained for those events. At Mexico City the largest number of records were broken in short, intense events (less than two minutes). Runners don't breathe at all during the 100-yard dash—so altitude made only a tiny difference, and that was because thinner air offered a trace less resistance. In most longer events, performance was below that in the Games held at sea level. But it's difficult to compare records set many years apart because of the steady improvement in performance throughout the world of sports during the last fifty years.

One might find an answer by comparing how Denver-based professional teams compare with those from lower altitude, on the assumption that if there were an advantage to training at altitude, the big money involved would so dictate. This has not happened. Our Olympic swimmers and skiers trained at 5,000 feet or higher, but no proven benefits have been forthcoming. On the other hand, Boulder, Colorado (6,000 feet), is a center for world-class cyclists who are convinced that training there gives them an edge. Some runners and prospective expedition mountaineers have trained while breathing low oxygen mixtures for a few hours at sea level each day. This is roughly the same as spending time at simulated altitude in a decompression chamber, but in this country at least, that tactic has not proven of value. Several other countries have tried variations on these programs—anything to get that extra edge.

Kienbaum, East Germany, 1969

An interesting program was carried on for more than a decade at a hidden facility in a village named Kienbaum in East Germany thirty years ago. The secret was so well kept that even the Russians who controlled East Germany during the Cold War were completely unaware of it, at least so I was told when I visited a few years ago.

The facility ran from 1969 until after reunification of Germany, for the sole purpose of training East German athletes for international competition. The operation was based on the conviction that training at altitude improved competitive ability at sea level.

The facility occupies several hundred acres of outdoor track and field courses, dormitories, mess halls, etc., and is at 500 feet altitude. The altitude training building consists of a large domed decompression chamber about the size of a basketball court buried deep beneath a low, innocent-looking mound of grass-covered earth. The interior of the chamber has two levels— the upper one with a circular running track and four treadmills, one for runners and one for cyclists, both wide enough for three abreast, and two smaller ones for one person; all can be set at variable speeds and inclines. A running track goes around the perimeter. The lower level has two large water tanks in which the flow can be controlled, for rowing, canoeing, and swimming. The two chambers operate together and can be taken to a simulated altitude of 12,500 feet, with temperature controllable from +15 to +25 degrees Centigrade.

In 1990 I was invited to visit and given a complete tour and somewhat limited briefing. I was told that the training protocols were adjusted to the sport and to each individual, but usually thirty to thirty-six athletes would work out in the chambers for two to six hours a day at 6,000 to 10,000 feet simulated altitude. They lived and exercised the rest of the day outside the chamber, essentially at sea level. This is just the reverse of today's more widely accepted plan for living high and training low.

One training technique was well ahead of other countries at that time. Measuring devices were part of all equipment to measure the force, speed, and duration of effort expended. On oars of rowers, on pedals of bicycles, and under the treadmill surface, ergometers told the trainer just how effectively the athlete was working. More recently in the United States we began to use an even more efficient measuring program for Olympic swimmer trainees, in the facility in Colorado at 5,500 feet.

Some scientific studies were probably done at Kienbaum but not disclosed to me then or later, and when I pressed, they answered, "Look at our world records compared with other nations." As the world knows, East Germans consistently took more medals than most other nations. Although the East Germans are said to have used hormones and other medications, it seems likely that the Keinbaum program did contribute to their success. It's important to note that though they trained at altitude, they also trained and lived most of the time at sea level. So far as I could tell, they believed that the increased hemoglobin was the principal benefit, but there probably were others as well.

With the end of the Cold War, Kienbaum ceased operations but may have been re-activated recently. It's an especially interesting facility as a testimony to the great expense and effort international competition spawned, even in countries that had limited resources. The lengths to which the East Germans went to keep programs secret from the occupying Russians also has intriguing implications.

Live High, Train Low or Live High, Train High?

Ben Levine, who has done a great deal of work with elite athletes, says it's important to separate "altitude training" into two parts: *acclimatization*, which depends on the altitude where the athlete lives for at least twelve hours every day, and *training*, which is a function of the altitude where the athlete actually works out.

The acclimatization part is planned to stimulate red blood cell and hemoglobin production and thus increase oxygen-carrying capacity. This depends on the altitude, of course, and the availability of adequate iron stores and on the release of erythropoietin (EPO). Other changes of acclimatization are more subtle and contribute less strongly. In a well-controlled study of thirty-nine distance runners who lived at 8,000 feet for four weeks, Levine found an increase of 9 percent in hemoglobin and an increase of 5 percent in maximal oxygen uptake over their low-altitude tests, regardless of where they trained. However, not all retained superior capacity at sea level. When the group lived at 8,000 feet but trained at 4,200 feet, performance in distance running *at 4,200 feet* was better than for those who lived and trained at lower altitude. An influential factor was the increase in EPO, and thus of hemoglobin formation. This study involved distance runners, events where endurance is more important than speed.

The role of altitude in training for other competitive sports is more difficult to evaluate. It's clear from the above and other studies that for endurance events (like distance running, cycling, or skiing), living at high altitude and training at low altitude may improve performance at low altitude. For

CAPACITY FOR EXERCISE DECREASES AS ALTITUDE INCREASES

Figure 34 shows the decline with increasing altitude in maximal work capacity (VO_2MAX), measured in *percentage* of sea-level capacity. At lower altitudes, capacity declines about 3 percent per 1,000 feet, but the decrease is greater the higher one goes. In Figure 34, about 6,400 persons are represented in the 146 data points, each of which shows the mean value of data on all subjects in sixty-five different investigations. Only those studies were included in which altitude, duration of stay, number of subjects, and study techniques were shown.

The thick dark line is a regression curve for all the data, representing thousands of individual tests; the dashed and dotted lines are regression curves for data reported by Buskirk and by Grover, respectively; these are two other major studies.

Chuck Fulco's unpublished paper includes a number of other graphs describing changes in fit and unfit individuals, different lengths of stay at altitude, and different ages. It is the most complete analysis that had yet been done.

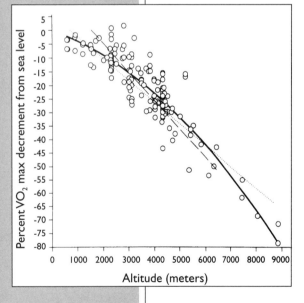

Figure 34. *Fulco's VO₂ MAX graph*

sports requiring both endurance and bursts of intense effort (like football or soccer), the data are not so clear, and benefit if any depends on factors still to be adequately studied. For events demanding short, intense bursts of effort, like sprints, the competitors do not benefit by living or training at altitude because they do not need additional oxygen-carrying capacity.

Levine concluded from several well-controlled studies:

> Combining high altitude acclimatization with low-altitude interval/intense training in well-trained competitive runners results in significant improvements in sea level 5,000-meter time above and beyond those achieved by an equivalent sea level or high altitude control.

My friend Chuck Fulco at the Army Research Institute of Environmental Medicine reviewed hundreds of medical articles describing work at increasing altitude. From these he analyzed the effects of training, the changes that took place after both short and long stays at different elevations, and the effect of altitude on different types of exertion such as rapid, short-duration effort compared to longer endurance work.

His review was written for a textbook of military medicine, which may not be published for several years, but he kindly allowed me to use one of the many interesting graphs and to quote his conclusions. It's likely that a short version of his chapter may be printed in a medical journal, quite likely *Aviation, Space, and Environmental Medicine,* wherein those interested may find it published under his name.

Fulco reached the following conclusions:

> *Training and/or living at altitude can improve altitude exercise performance in athletic events . . . lasting more than about two minutes. . . . Controlled studies do not support a beneficial effect of altitude training on subsequent sea level performance. . . . Living at altitude but training at a lower altitude permits the theoretical advantage of both acclimatization and training without reducing exercise intensity. This paradigm appears promising but is still open to question since altitude natives training at altitude with oxygen supplementation (in effect "living high, training low") did not improve maximal work capacity more than altitude natives training at altitude without oxygen supplementation.*

Alright, What's the Answer?

Though the answers to many important questions about training and altitude are still vague, from the hard data now available we can draw a few conclusions that are widely accepted today, though not without disagreement:

▲ Beginning above 5,000 feet, the maximum work one can do decreases by about 3 percent per 1,000 feet of altitude and improves only slightly during long altitude residence. Endurance or submaximal work may improve slightly over time but does not exceed this limit.

▲ Training at altitude cannot be quite as intense as at sea level and the competitive edge is therefore slightly dulled. Training above 5,000 feet therefore is of doubtful value for sea level competition.

▲ Advantage does come from increased EPO and increased hemoglobin (and thus oxygen carrying capacity), but this is partially offset by the decrease in buffering power that comes with acclimatization and perhaps by the increased viscosity of blood.

▲ Athletes training for short, intense events do not benefit from training at altitude; those planning to compete in endurance events at altitude will probably benefit by training for weeks at that altitude.

▲ Some altitude natives do surpass their cohorts in sea level competition, but others do not, and the explanation is more likely their lifelong dedication to running rather than their level of acclimatization.

One can conclude that if you want to get the edge at sea level, sleep high and train low—except for sprints, for which it doesn't matter.

CHAPTER 15

Gender, Age, and Fitness

ARE THERE IMPORTANT DIFFERENCES BETWEEN THE SEXES IN THEIR susceptibility to mountain sickness, in the ability to work at altitude, or in the ability to acclimatize? Does age make a significant difference? Is physical fitness a factor in acclimatization? From the many articles on these topics, I tried to extract the most important information.

Women Climbers

When the first small parties of mountaineers began to climb in the Alps in the early 1800s, the local people were suspicious: "Why should anyone climb mountains except to find crystals?" they asked. According to Gribble's *The Early Mountaineers,* there was a woman in one of the first party of climbers to visit the Dauphine Alps, and a local chamois hunter declared: "The men are gold-seekers and the woman is a witch they have brought with them to show where the gold is hidden."

Today, of course, the place of women in mountaineering has been firmly established, and dozens have climbed the highest and most difficult peaks around the world, tolerating altitude, cold, and stress as well as men. Women have shown their skill in the Alps for more than a century, though not for several decades did they forgive Alfred Mummery, one of the leading climbers in the Victorian age, for his quite unintended slur (cited in Gribble): "All mountains seem to go through three stages: an inaccessible peak, the most dangerous climb in the Alps, and an easy day for a lady."

Female Physiology

Even after women showed that they could climb as well as men, even after many had climbed the highest mountains and several had summited Everest, there was little systematic study of their responses to hypoxia until recently. Possibly this was because women's cyclic hormone variations might be expected to complicate already complicated responses to hypoxia. Perhaps some male chauvinism persisted even after some female climbers had proven they would gladly participate in such studies. Whatever the reasons, until the last few years data about the effects of female homones at altitude were patchy and incomplete. Now there's a surge of interest, with research grants flowing readily from the U.S. federal government and the military.

INFLUENCE OF MENSTRUAL CYCLE ON MOUNTAIN SICKNESS

For some women the menstrual cycle alters the salt and water balance and often causes edema, which might be expected to increase susceptibility to acute mountain sickness. But there isn't much agreement among the few studies on this. Lorna Moore has been leading a team that is examining the various hormones involved: estradiol (in the premenstrual phase), luteinizing hormone (in the luteal phase), and progesterone (during the resting phase). The hormones are measured in minute amounts, picograms (abbreviated pg) and nanograms (abbreviated ng) per milliliter, and their combined effects are complex.

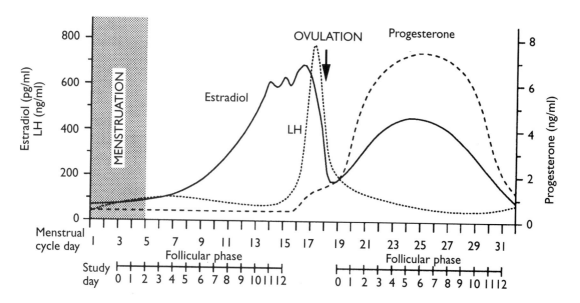

At any altitude, women's ventilation increases slightly during the luteal phase of the menstrual cycle (see Figure 35), due to the release of both estradiol (estrogen) and progesterone. This increases ventilation (and thus the alveolar oxygen) somewhat, and one might expect this to decrease the incidence of acute mountain sickness (AMS). Administration of progesterone to either men or women does in fact increase ventilation and decrease AMS

Figure 35. *Menstrual cycle*

slightly. But no statistical study has been published to confirm any relationship of AMS or HAPE to the natural cycle. In fact, five studies have shown that the incidence of AMS is slightly less frequent in women than in men, but the incidence of HAPE is five times greater in men. None of these studies was able to correlate menstrual cycle to incidence. Nor has the occurrence of altitude illness in women taking contraceptive pills (that contain progesterone) been established, although several groups are studying this.

Both plasma aldosterone and atrial natriuretic protein fluctuate during the menstrual cycle, but these affect ventilation and fluid retention in opposite directions, and need more study.

The hypoxic ventilatory response (HVR) tends to be slightly lower in women, but when the data are corrected for body size, the HVR turns out to be slightly higher than men's.

Women may burn food somewhat differently than do men, but the limited data suggest that women have about the same energy requirements as men and, given the same fuel, can accomplish the same amount of work, though usually at a somewhat slower pace. Their maximum work capacity is less than men's, but women can train up as well as men. Like men, those women who start with a higher maximum oxygen uptake at sea level may be better off at altitude, where both men and women function at a percentage of sea level capacity that decreases proportionately as altitude increases. A few studies show that women's pulse rate and blood pressure, and thus the "double product" or approximate load on the heart, at altitude is as variable as men's. Women may acclimatize faster than men, and they don't lose as much weight during an altitude stay.

Men also release a sex hormone, but the testosterone cycle is weak and irregular. Testosterone secretion decreases during long exposure to altitude, with aging, and in chronic obstructive pulmonary disease (COPD).

Pregnancy

When the Spanish conquistadores occupied the territory of the Incas in the sixteenth century, the Catholic priests who lived and traveled widely in the region commented on the high fertility of the natives and blamed the high infant mortality on cold. The Spanish women became pregnant apparently at a normal rate, but for decades all pregnancies ended in miscarriage or stillbirth. Not for fifty-three years did the first child of Spanish ancestry survive birth at altitude. Whether this was due to the altitude is unclear: There were many other adverse factors. But soon—and ever since—many newcomers to altitude go down to sea level during the last trimester of pregnancy.

Today libido and fertility are reported to be normal in altitude residents, but in both residents and newcomers, complications of pregnancy, such as toxemia, uterine hemorrhage, premature delivery, miscarriages, and stillbirths, are more common at altitude. Newborns have a lower birth weight and gain weight more slowly. In children conceived and born at altitude, the small artery between the aorta and pulmonary artery (which is open while in the womb), fails to close after the child is born. This *ductus arteriosus* allows some blood to bypass the lungs and if open must be closed surgically within a few months after birth. This defect is five times as common in infants at altitude as in infants of similar ancestry at sea level. A few other congenital defects are slightly more common at altitude. A persistent rumor maintains that a child was conceived by a French couple during a storm at 25,000 feet, but the outcome is not reported!

Can a pregnant woman go to altitude without harming herself or the child she is carrying? One might expect the fetus of a woman going from sea level to altitude in the first three or four weeks of pregnancy might be damaged by hypoxia. This does not seem to happen, but the higher incidence of miscarriage may mask it. Many authorities suggest that a woman go to lower altitude—as many do—during the last trimester to avoid complications, including congenital defects, though these would have developed earlier.

It's been suggested that placental circulation is such that a fetus lives in an oxygen environment equivalent to that on top of Everest, but the presence of fetal hemoglobin (see Chapter 4, Moving Blood: Circulation) and a greatly increased red blood cell mass, as well as increased circulation, result in an oxygen carrying capacity and oxygen content closer to normal. Nature has protected the growing fetus against hypoxia.

Most authorities agree that a pregnant woman can safely go to moderate altitude, say, 8,000 feet, without fear for the baby, though some put the ceiling lower. Few would consider it safe or appropriate to climb high in the Andes or Himalayas after the first trimester—but some have done so.

Other Hormonal Differences

Menstrual hormones are not the only operative differences between men and women at any altitude. Men also have hormonal fluctuations in testosterone release, though neither as marked nor as regular as the female cycles. The effect of these male cycles on altitude tolerance has not been adequately studied, but increased testosterone has been linked to sleep apnea. Genetically, males receive from their parents one X and one Y chromosome, while females receive two X chromosomes, but the genetic factors influencing oxygen transport and use are only now beginning to be explored. Maternal DNA may be more influential than paternal.

Other hormones common to women and men, like human growth hormone, change at altitude and fluctuate with time, but in the same general direction in each sex. Circadian rhythms almost certainly affect acclimatization and hypoxia tolerance each day because most of the powerful hormones in the adrenal glands normally are secreted at around 4 or 5 in the morning, toward the end of sleep. These affect salt and water balance among other things, and have not been studied adequately at altitude. One can only speculate what effect circadian rhythms might have during climbs at night or during several continuous days, especially when the climbers are superstressed.

Unlike men, women often have hidden iron deficiency, which becomes more important as the body is called on for more iron to make more red blood cells as a part of acclimatization. Women recover their sea-level blood volume faster than men, but seem to be slower in forming red cells during acclimatization; whether this is due to low iron stores or some other factor is unknown. But if they are deficient and take supplementary iron, the response to hypoxia improves.

Most women tend to have less muscle mass than men, but they can double their strength by training without noticeable change in bulk. Though women are almost as strong as men in trunk and legs, their arm strength, even with training, is less than that of men.

Women who engage in prolonged strenuous physical activity, be it ballet, marathon training, or long mountain expeditions, tend to have scanty menses or even to stop menstruating. This is not due to altitude but to physical work, and normal cycles resume after a while once the strenuous efforts have decreased. But there's a lot of variation among women, some continuing with normal cycles throughout strenuous exertion like a long mountain expedition.

Aging

Thirty years ago Ross McFarland, a pioneer in many aspects of oxygen and altitude medicine, suggested that the effects on the brain of hypoxia and aging were similar. He based his hypothesis on the following: (1) immediate recall, span of concentration, and increased reflex time are impaired with age and altitude; (2) sensitivity of vision in dim light decreases with age just as it does with altitude; (3) acuity of hearing decreases with age as with altitude. He added that "calculations are unreliable, judgment faulty, and emotional responses unpredictable" both with age and at altitude. Acknowledging great individual variation, one may be impressed by this concept.

Aging changes everything, and rarely for the better: imperceptibly at first, then slowly, but soon the slope becomes steeper. Fortunately, *as with hypoxia,* we don't notice much change. We believe we are as young as we feel, not as old as we act. Still, to paraphrase what a patient once told Walter Alvarez: "Age keeps taking little bites of me."

Memory

Memory, declining with age, troubles us older folks. At any age one may have difficulty recalling a name, a date, a fact, but often within minutes, hours, or even days, the brain pops out the answer, unrequested! It's gratifying that this happens at any age. Weakened memory or poor recall is also one of the troubling effects of high altitude, even though memory might be normal at sea level. What is particularly interesting to the climber is that those who have acclimatized to high altitude once or twice apparently do so more easily and completely next time. Is this surprising? We remember how to ride a bicycle, play a tune, recognize a smell years and years after the first experience. Why should not the brain remember how to acclimatize?

Exertion and Breathing

With age, muscular strength and endurance decrease, which is only slowed for a time by vigorous training. Maximal work capacity decreases along with maximal breathing capacity. Reflexes are slowed, increasing the time of response to any stimulus, even if only slightly.

The maximum achievable heart rate (MAHR) declines with age, but for many people both systolic and diastolic blood pressure slowly increase. Pulmonary artery pressure increases slightly with age, and peripheral circulation, including to the brain, is decreased. The hypoxic ventilatory response (HVR) is blunted, and the normal values of pulmonary function tests must be adjusted for age.

A fit and healthy seventy-five-year-old man spent a week at 12,000 feet and then climbed slowly in one day to 14,000 feet. He was very short of breath after even light exertion but had no headache, edema, cough, or sputum. During the night he had a profuse diuresis but was still very dyspneic next morning, and turned back.

A fit seventy-seven-year-old man walked in seven days from 6,000 to 14,000 feet. The path was long and difficult, the weather hot; after five days he became weak and increasingly dyspneic when climbing. He reached 14,000 feet with difficulty, but was able to move about on the level. He had mild headache, no edema or other evidence of AMS, and no cough, but felt slight "rattles" in his chest. He remained forty-eight hours before descending, but had slight dyspnea going downhill and for a few days thereafter.

In these two cases, several explanations are available. First, both individuals may have acquired somewhat more interstitial fluid than is usual, and might have developed HAPE if they had gone higher or continued heavy work. Interstitial fluid increases the urge to breathe. Another possibility is an increase in the number of unventilated alveoli due to weakness or even collapse of terminal bronchioles. Shunts, normally few and small, may have increased, sending more underoxygenated blood to the body (including the carotid bodies).

Stories like these are not uncommon among older persons, even those familiar with mountains and in good physical condition. Pulmonary function at any age is slightly less at altitude but the decrease is larger in older persons, and decreases even more after exertion.

As McFarland suggested, many similar changes are likely to appear with aging, and it should not be surprising to find that the responses to altitude of most old folks are additive to those due to age. Most elders climb more slowly and carefully, most grow less ambitious as they find the spirit as willing as ever but the flesh weaker. There are many exceptions: hundred-year-old men and women who walk up Mount Fuji (12,395 feet), the rare veteran climbers who summit Everest though over sixty, many even older who climb fourteen-thousanders with pleasure if not ease. And hundreds of thousands of elders throng to mountain resorts at 8,000–10,000 feet, or trek in the Andes or Himalayas.

It's reassuring that several good studies have shown that at moderate altitudes, the incidence of acute mountain sickness (AMS) decreases linearly with age: Young folks are more likely to be sick, for whatever reason—speed, overactivity, or exuberance—than their elders.

Because older individuals have higher pulmonary artery pressure, which increases with hypoxia, one might expect them to have high altitude pulmonary edema (HAPE) more frequently. But not so: The incidence is higher in children under ten, and lower in older adults than in younger adults. HAPE is far more frequent in males than in females, though AMS is equally distributed. However, pulmonary function at altitude, already lower in older persons, is more sharply decreased after strenuous exertion at altitude, suggesting that more interstitial edema than usual has accumulated. This could, of course, be an early warning of HAPE.

Fitness

Most of us aspire to be physically fit; we feel better, sleep better, think better when fit, or so we believe. Fitness and good health go hand in hand, and around the world men and women spend vast sums of money and great chunks of time exercising. In many countries health spas are part of the culture and include fitness programs along with beautification, mineral waters, medicated baths, and "fat farms." Many European industries give employees paid leave to attend health spas where fitness is stressed. Apparently they believe it pays.

Fitness, achieved by whatever level and form of exercise is appropriate to age and environment, is difficult to measure. Maximum work capacity (VO_2MAX) decreases about 1 percent a year after the forties, but this decline can be slowed or arrested, possibly even reversed, by regular exercise. But VO_2MAX does not measure endurance or ability to do prolonged moderate work. Is this important? It depends on what you want to do.

All our reflexes slow almost imperceptibly with age but this can be compensated for, though not improved, by practice and regular exercise. Bone loss in men and even more so in women begins around age fifty and increases slowly in many people; this can also be halted, and lost bone, like muscle, can even be rebuilt to some extent with regular exercise. Many other functions worsen with age—and few improve. But for many functions, the decrease can be slowed by staying fit.

Few would argue that getting and keeping fit is a good way of life. Does it delay aging and death? Does it improve mental processes, creativity, sexuality? What do the hard data show? Perhaps most of us would say "yes, amen" to all of these and others, and the scattered data, some of it well controlled, tend to support the belief. Today a majority of us make some effort to stay fit, for whatever reason.

Does fitness at any age decrease mountain sickness? Can one climb higher, more easily and safely, and be less likely to develop AMS, HACE, or HAPE? Regrettably, there's little or no hard data to answer these questions conclusively. Physical fitness does not equate with better altitude tolerance at any age.

But wait a moment! The fit athlete at any altitude moves and works more easily, uses less oxygen per unit of work done in a fixed time, and is generally more oxygen- and fuel-efficient. This certainly suggests, if it does not prove, that a fit climber might do better in the low oxygen atmosphere on high mountains. Logically and theoretically this is true, but there's little statistically significant data to prove that fitness decreases mountain sicknesses. It's equally true that the experienced and skillful climber moves more easily and with less oxygen and fuel consumption than the amateur, but this does not necessarily mean that one is less fit than the other.

And, obviously, by being able to climb more rapidly, the fit and experienced climber will be in harm's way for a shorter time.

In short, staying fit is good medicine for living, but it may not protect you from mountain sickness.

CHAPTER 16

The Mountaineer's World

THIS BOOK IS MOSTLY ABOUT MOUNTAINS, AND HOW LACK OF OXYGEN affects the many *thousands* of men and women who go to high altitudes. In Chapter 9, Hypoxia in Everyday Life, I discuss some of the many acute and chronic illnesses that cause hypoxia for many *millions* of people throughout the world. I haven't touched on the other animals who live—briefly or throughout their lives—with little or no oxygen. Many species of single-celled animals, large amphibians, diving mammals, and hibernators survive and thrive for hours, months, or years in environments without oxygen. This is a vast and wonderful area of adaptation from which we feeble humans have not yet learned all we can.

The sad stories with which I begin this book (see Chapter 1, The Air About Us) are examples of many others, less dramatic but just as tragic, due to the mountain environment that can so often be hostile. On very high mountains, several elements combine to cripple or kill. Often hypoxia, particularly disruptive of the higher faculties of the brain, degrades judgment and initiative, and may even erode one's ethics or morality. Thousands of words have failed to justify or explain the events on Everest in 1996, on K2 in 1986, and on Nanga Parbat in 1934.

Most of those involved on Everest in 1996 had been strangers only a few weeks before and did not have the strong bonds between them and the sense of brotherhood that are essential in the extreme situations described earlier. Some qualified for such a climb more because of wealth than experience.

On K2 1986 some climbers had changed from one expedition to another, only a few shared a common language, and most were strangers to others. Fixed ropes on both Everest and K2 allowed climbers to move alone over much of the route, not roped to a climbing partner, often at night. Gone was the "Fellowship of the Rope."

The heart-rending deaths of the Russian women on Pic Lenin in 1974 is a story of grace under pressure from cold and privation. They chose to stay together, rather than to save themselves. It was an example of the best tradition of mountaineering. Their decision to go on to the summit despite increasing storm, and to bivouac had been an error of judgment. Perhaps nothing could have prevented some or all of the deaths, but poor decisions, perhaps due to hypoxia, certainly contributed.

Make no mistake: Many other smaller, less well-known tragedies have happened on smaller mountains too. Together, all show that great mountain ventures carry great risks. Who is to judge whether the game is worth the price so often paid?

Smaller Mountains

The mountain environment can be harsh even on much smaller mountains like 6,400-foot Mount Washington, the highest mountain east of the Rockies, where hypoxia is no problem but the weather every bit as severe as on Everest, K2, Nanga Parbat, and Pic Lenin. Sudden violent winds sweep across Washington's barren summit at any season, and temperatures plummet. When visitors have ignored what may happen to the unwary on that "small" mountain, cold, hunger, thirst, and exhaustion have killed more than 160 persons over the years—*more than 160*—on a "small" mountain.

Problems Encountered in the Mountain World

From 1921 through 1996, 391 expeditions consisting of about 4,400 climbers attempted Everest; 679 climbers summitted and 148 died. These numbers are the best now available, but they differ depending on who is writing and often do not include all the Sherpas. Most of the deaths have been during descent. Several of the Sherpas who had made the top three or more times survived the events of 1996.

In 1997 more men and women attempted the summit and more died. Even as I write (June 1998), major expeditions are on Everest and already several dozen have summited and six are dead.

Since 1903, some 20,000 persons have attempted Mount McKinley (20,300 feet) and half have succeeded, while 87 have died from the same causes that killed climbers on Everest, K2, Nanga Parbat, and Pic Lenin. On Mount McKinley, which is now more often called Denali, meaning the "Great One" in the ancient Athapascan Indian language, altitude illnesses have been a frequent cause of death. Denali has the most severe weather of any great mountain. Few places ever get colder: "The cold chilled my soul," said one veteran. Storms strike with little warning, as they do on Everest, but often last much longer, tempting the impatient climber to start out before the snow and weather have settled. "Allow one month for McKinley," advises Brad Washburn, director of the Boston Museum of Science, distinguished photographer and mapmaker, who knows more about Mount Washington and Denali than anyone else. "You cannot rush McKinley; some who have tried have died."

On Everest in 1996, all of those involved during that ghastly period were well acclimatized by the weeks they had spent reaching Base Camp and climbing higher. By the time they had reached their high camp at 26,000 feet, their bodies had already adjusted as well as humans can—but they had stayed so long above 20,000 feet that "deterioration" had begun. This is what gives the name "Death Zone" to altitudes above 20,000–22,000 feet, and fits Hans Selye's General Adaptation Syndrome (see Figure 30), but we do not have data to define what happens any more clearly than to say "everything runs down."

Every aspect of mountaineering has changed so tremendously in the last few decades that the alpinists of a century ago would be amazed and appalled. Before the Golden Age of Himalayan climbing began in 1950, only a few of the greatest mountains had been attempted or even visited, while today there are few if any ranges, however remote, that have not seen climbers. On very high, remote peaks, routes and techniques thought impossible a few decades ago are commonplace today. The dangers are great and do not change over the years.

Lack of Oxygen

Of these dangers, the impact of lack of oxygen on the brain at high altitude has been the root cause of the great catastrophes like those on Everest in 1996 and K2 in 1986. Many less dramatic tragedies have been directly due to hypoxia because it weakens judgment, fosters indecision or bad decisions, fractures morality, and impairs the very skills most needed in climbing.

Because they are usually acclimatized during the approach, climbers on high mountains don't often have symptoms of AMS, HAPE, or HACE. Even so, some healthy climbers—who should know better—die of HAPE and HACE each year on the highest mountains. Falls, rock and ice avalanches, and frostbite are more frequent, but altitude hypoxia kills one just as dead.

For several years trekkers in the Himalayas have been reported to have about the same incidence of mountain sickness as tourists in the Rockies have today. This began when, in place of the two- to three-week approach march, trekkers were flown to 11,000 feet and began the trek from there. Better education and better planning have reduced mountain sicknesses—but illnesses and deaths among tourists are still a problem, especially in the Everest region, which draws some 15,000 visitors a year. In 1950 there were only the six of us.

Supplementary Oxygen

Breathing bottled oxygen increases the percentage, and thus the partial pressure, of inhaled oxygen (see Chapter 3, Moving Air: Respiration), in effect "taking the climber down" several thousand feet. In 1996 most of those who went for the summit on Everest were using supplementary oxygen during the final climb; for many, their oxygen supplies ran out at various times during the descent. For them, the altitude had a greater impact than on those who had not used oxygen. With oxygen they had been at an altitude equivalent to about 22,000 feet, but when the supply suddenly ran out, they were breathing the much thinner air near Everest's top (29,028 feet).

One of the guides who died had been ill for a day or two; some suggest that he may have had HAPE and/or HACE but persisted in trying to reach the summit to take care of his clients. Too late he turned back and died with one of them. It is difficult to doubt that his judgment and ability to make hard decisions were flawed by hypoxia. The guide (Anatoli Boukreev), who had argued he would be safer without oxygen, after summitting with his group still had strength and will to attempt rescue three times during that awful night. Because he is known to be a very strong and experienced climber, no conclusions can be reached from this, but his argument against supplementary oxygen has some validity.

Many of the survivors have described their feeling of dissociation from their bodies and from each other, and the replacement of pain with total fatigue. Even their reasons for being there near the summit were hazy, replaced by an animal instinct to go on, to survive.

Hypothermia

Hypothermia mimics hypoxia. As the body chills, the brain falters, judgment and perception are blurred, and the victim does not realize what is happening. Mental confusion and hallucinations soon follow. Reflexes slow, muscles seem stiff, and movements are awkward and clumsy. The combination of cold and altitude is very powerful; together, the impact of each is perhaps doubled.

At a core body temperature of 95° Fahrenheit (rectal), hypothermia is serious; at 89° death is probable unless heroic treatment is provided; few victims survive a body temperature of 85°. Wind increases the rate of cooling by the square of wind velocity; the wind-chill is much colder than the actual air temperature and more dangerous because it cools one faster.

Even the best down- or fiber-filled clothing in a windproof breathable shell cannot protect completely against wind-chill for long. Muscular exertion is the major heat producer and if the victim stops moving and shivering, hypothermia will begin.

This is what happens on high mountains: The exhausted climber stops "to rest," sits or lies down, and usually will not rise again. But one of the 1996 Everest survivors did lie down for many hours and did survive. A companion never roused. Another spoke on the radio for many hours, slowly losing consciousness, and finally was silent. The Russian women on Pic Lenin in 1974 died slowly during three awful days, while one by one those remaining described their plight. Their immense fortitude and courage to the end could not mitigate the impact of cold and altitude.

Hypothermia is said to be the foremost killer in outdoor winter sports. Twenty percent of the deaths on Denali are due to cold and exhaustion, as are most of those on Mount Washington. Even at low altitude or sea level, tens of thousands of people, mostly the poor and elderly sitting alone in unheated rooms, become hypothermic even when the outside temperature is not extremely cold. It's said that 25,000 elderly die annually in the United States from hypothermia, often misdiagnosed. The danger of hypothermia is that it is so subtle, so insidious that the victim is unaware of the slow slide toward unconsciousness. On high mountains, hypothermia and hypoxia together pack a double whammy.

After the exhausted rescuers had left two climbers on Everest in 1996, believing them too near death to attempt the desperate carry-out, one of them roused next morning. He believes he had been hypothermic, and of course he was. But few people survive deep hypothermia when they lie down for very long; it's more likely that he slept, exhausted. When the sun rose, he somehow gathered will and strength to stagger several hundred yards down to camp, where he collapsed. The other exhausted climbers expected him to die and did little more for him than provide warm coverings and some hot drinks. Next day he recovered enough strength to be helped down the mountain, terribly frostbitten but alive. His story powerfully shows the truth of the maxim "the hypothermic patient is not dead until warm and dead."

Hypoglycemia

Strenuous exertion combined with little or no food drains the reserves of fuel, notably of carbohydrate. Some of the signs of the resulting low blood sugar resemble those of hypoxia and hypothermia: Confusion, bizarre behavior, clumsy walk and hand motions, even paranoid hallucinations aren't uncommon, especially in diabetics. Most of us are familiar with the shaky feeling, perhaps cold sweats, we experience after skipping a meal or two; we're aware that just before lunch often isn't the best time for a complicated discussion or decision. When cold is causing the body to burn more fuel (mostly glucose), hypoglycemia complicates life for the climber at any altitude. In the rush of excitement on a summit day, too many "can't eat" or won't, and pay for it later. "Brain waves" recorded by the electroencephalogram (EEG) during hypoglycemia resemble those recorded during hypoxia.

Though it may not be a major hazard, hypoglycemia adds to the odds against one on a high mountain; many of those on Everest in May 1996 had not eaten for many hours and this contributed to their danger.

Dehydration

Dehydration is common on mountains because so much water is lost in overbreathing and in sweat (which is often imperceptible because it evaporates instantly in the dry air). The climber must drink water to keep the blood from becoming too thick and sluggish, allowing the red blood cells to pile up like plates, decreasing the surface for picking up or releasing oxygen, thus adding to tissue hypoxia. The kidneys require water to form urine to eliminate bicarbonate (part of the acclimatization process described in Chapter 12), as well as to excrete waste products.

On high mountains the air is cold and completely dry. As inhaled air passes through nose or mouth, it is warmed and humidified, sucking both heat and water from the body, and these are not recovered during exhalation. On the highest mountains where breathing is so greatly increased, this heat and water loss cannot be sustained for very long. Dehydration exaggerates the impacts of hypothermia and hypoxia.

Sleep Deprivation

Recent studies have shown that when a night's sleep is repeatedly interrupted, even for only a few seconds, mental processes are impaired next day, at any altitude. The fragmented sleep most climbers experience at the highest camp add to the likelihood of confusion, poor judgment, and bad decisions next day.

One of the survivors on Everest in 1996, Jon Krakauer, described his experience as he reached the summit:

> I hadn't slept in fifty-seven hours. The only food I'd been able to force down over the preceding three days was a bowl of soup and a handful of peanut M&Ms . . . so little oxygen was reaching my brain that my mental capacity was that of a slow child . . . I was incapable of feeling much of anything except being cold and tired.

Each of these environmental impacts adds to the effect of the others and the combination produces the "sick man walking in a dream," as George Mallory described a climber high on Everest. (Mallory, with Andrew Irvine, was last seen near the summit of Everest in 1924, but whether they made the summit is unknown.) Several of the survivors in 1996 eloquently described their sense of isolation and loss of normal perception.

Except for lack of oxygen, these influences are operative in many extreme situations, like long-distance runs or ski races, and being lost for several days in a strange and often hostile environment. They can be lethal if the warnings are ignored.

Health Conditions
That May Cause Problems at Altitude

Bearing in mind these environmental risks, are there some individuals who should not go to altitude? The mountain world is attracting more and more people, and not only to small mountains but also to big ones, not only to hike but also to climb, ski, explore, or simply visit. Getting to the mountains has become much easier and faster in most parts of the world, and millions of men, women, and children of all ages are going to potentially dangerous altitudes.

Almost anyone can go to 5,000 feet without noticing any effects. Above 8,000 feet, one of every five visitors is likely to have symptoms due to altitude, and what happens above this depends on the rate of climb and altitude reached, as I discuss in Chapter 6, AMS: Acute Mountain Sickness.

But what about persons with some illness or disability? How shall doctors advise a pregnant woman, a man in his sixties with heart disease, or someone with diabetes, epilepsy, or asthma? Hundreds of people are asking their doctors these questions and many more, as thousands who never would have dreamed of it a few decades ago are going up into the mountains.

A sixty-two-year-old woman wishes to take a six-day trip in the Andes, going as high as 12,000 feet after a rather rapid ascent. She had asthma as a child and smoked heavily until recently. Years ago she had an eosinophilic granuloma (an unusual malignant tumor) in her lungs and in her brain. The lungs healed slowly; the granuloma was removed from the brain surgically. She had several seizures after the operation and has taken dilantin ever since. A year ago she had a breast cancer removed and was given a course of radiotherapy. She has no symptoms, is moderately active in sports, and is not excessively short of breath. Her arterial oxygen saturation is 96 percent. Chest X ray shows little scarring, EKG is normal, but her pulmonary function tests show greatly reduced maximal breathing capacity with no improvement after medication.

S is a fifty-one-year-old mother of three who has rapidly progressive Lou Gehrig's disease (amyotrophic lateral sclerosis). She wishes to visit her family's home at 9,000 feet while she still is able. Her arterial oxygen saturation is below 85 percent at sea level. Her neurology specialists advise her not to go, but if she insists, they urge that she not go outside!

The first woman has several strikes against her. Her asthma did not leave any damage, but years of smoking did. The tumor in her lungs probably left some scarring, and X ray treatment after her breast cancer was removed may have also caused fibrosis of lung tissue, even though carefully monitored. I warned her that she probably would have problems, and she decided not to go on the altitude part of the trip.

As for S, I told her that the low arterial oxygen saturation suggests that her ability to breathe is limited because her respiratory muscles are compromised. This means she would lose one of the best defenses against hypoxia even as low as 9,000 feet and might have a serious problem. The advice not to go outdoors is silly. I told her that if she breathed supplementary oxygen during the flight and drive to the resort, and all the time while there, she should not be at greater risk than at sea level. But her respiratory paralysis increased rapidly, and soon it was too late for her to travel.

Cancer

A seventy-year-old veteran mountaineer developed widespread bone metastases from multiple myeloma. Powerful treatments relieved his pain somewhat and apparently arrested further spread. A few months after finishing his treatment, he climbed a 14,000-foot mountain faster and more easily than his partner.

I don't know of any evidence that going to high altitude has a bad effect on cancer. In fact many years ago Al Barach, a visionary physician, proposed treating certain cancers by having the patient breathe oxygen at half sea level partial pressure, which is equivalent to going to 18,000 feet. The justification was that fast-growing cancer cells require more oxygen than do normal cells, and their growth might be slowed. Only a few limited studies were done, but the concept has been revisited recently. A promising new treatment for cancer is based on depriving the tumor of oxygen and also of food by decreasing its blood supply. Since cancers grow more rapidly than normal tissue, they are more susceptible to oxygen lack and "starvation." Unless anemia or some other impediment decreases oxygen delivery to cells, as far as I am concerned, someone with a disease likely soon to be terminal should grasp every pleasure he or she can.

Advanced Age

In Chapter 15, Gender, Age, and Fitness, I discuss the many things that age does to slow us down. In deciding whether an elderly person can or should go to altitude, the doctor should pay extra attention to several of these. Vital capacity—the largest breath we can take—decreases slightly but steadily with age, thus decreasing one of the best ways of dealing with hypoxia. The Maximum Achievable Heart Rate (MAHR) decreases with age, so the older we get, the less increase we can expect in the rate and output of the heart when pushed. We may, hopefully, grow wiser, but memory, along with reflexes, work capacity, and strength, all worsen. On the other hand, the older one is, the less likely is acute mountain sickness, at least up to 10,000 feet, which is about as high as most older persons want to go. Still, many men and women over seventy have climbed to 18,000 feet and higher, and several who were over ninety have walked up Mount Fuji (12,395 feet). A very few over seventy have summitted even higher peaks.

I tell people that age by itself is not a deterrent—if you think you can, and if you long to climb or just visit the mountains, age alone shouldn't stop you.

High Blood Pressure

Systemic blood pressure usually increases slightly with altitude but soon tends to level off or return to sea-level values. Persons who already have hypertension are likely to increase their blood pressure more than others do, even at moderate altitude. If one is taking hypertensive medication, it's prudent to have blood pressure checked a few times after arrival, and perhaps to increase the medication—but with caution and advice. High blood pressure alone is not a contra-indication to a visit to the mountains, though the individual had better not try one of the major summits. It's important to remember that a single blood pressure reading in any setting is often misleading because blood pressure is so labile and changes so much and so quickly in different circumstances.

Pulmonary artery pressure (PAP) also increases with age and increases further with cold and altitude, but this does not seem to increase the risk of HAPE in the elderly. The increased PAP may cause more breathlessness than expected, which suggests that some fluid is collecting in the lung interstitial space, but this happens in many people without progressing to HAPE. Unless one's activity at sea level is limited due to lung disease, this is not a reason not to go to altitude—where the air is fresher, and actually easier to breathe because it's thinner.

This is good news for asthmatics, most of whom tolerate altitude well unless they have badly hurt their lungs over the years:

R. P. had very severe asthma throughout his childhood. This ended in his late teens and he became an active climber and hiker. Attempting Denali at age thirty-one, he (and others in the party) turned back at 19,000 feet and during descent his breathlessness grew worse. Back at sea level he was still weak and breathless, and for four days coughed up sputum suggestive of infection; he improved slowly with antibiotics. One year later a similar episode happened at 17,500 feet on another mountain, again lasting five days even with antibiotics after return to sea level. Now R. P. is anxious to try Denali again. There's nothing remarkable in his physical examination; his blood pressure is normal, though hypertension runs in his family. His lab work is all normal, as are his pulmonary function tests, chest X ray, and cardiogram. He exercises regularly. He asks if he can make it to the top of Denali this time.

Judging from his story, it's likely that R. P. developed rather more interstitial fluid in his lungs than most people do; he may actually have had early HAPE. The strenuous work at an altitude where this is a danger, even though he had not climbed unusually fast and had taken Diamox, may have triggered this. On top of this, he probably got some infection that responded only slowly to descent and antibiotics. Perhaps he falls into the recently recognized category of persons unusually susceptible to HAPE, known as HAPE-S. Because he does not appear to have structural damage to his lungs, I suggested that, after a test dose to see how his systemic pressure is affected, he take nifedipine during the climb and try again—but be prepared to go down quickly if problems appear. Steroids and Diamox do not protect HAPE-S climbers adequately.

Heart Disease

Many people with known heart disease, or those who might be at risk for various reasons, ask about going to the mountains. Herb Hultgren, a distinguished cardiologist who had studied high altitude for forty years, was conservative in his published articles and recent book (*High Altitude Medicine)* in which he described several cases, which I have paraphrased as follows:

A seventy-year-old physician with stable angina required several nitro-glycerine tablets daily, plus several cardiac drugs. He flew to 8,000 feet, where he had repeated episodes of angina for thirty-six hours, but these decreased and by the end of a week he was having no more episodes than at sea level. On return home his former condition was unchanged.

An elderly businessman had slowly worsening angina for twenty-two years after a heart attack; this limited his activity. He flew to Denver (5,280 feet), and drove over a 12,000-foot pass and down to a resort at 8,200 feet. His angina was very severe on the pass and continued at the resort, forcing him to return home. He did not show evidence of further heart damage.

As I interpret these stories, the first patient tolerated the altitude reasonably well despite his coronary artery disease. This is not unusual and in fact some patients actually have less angina at moderate altitude. In the second individual, the coronary disease was more serious and he was fortunate not to have precipitated another heart attack.

In fact myocardial infarcts are uncommon at altitude, some believe less frequent than in a comparable population at sea level. David Shlim reported that of 148,000 trekkers in Nepal who went to 9,000–17,000 feet, about 10 percent were over fifty; six left a trek early because of "heart symptoms" but there were no deaths due to heart disease. Maggiorini's large survey of climbers and hikers in the Alps showed no evidence of increased heart disease (see Table 2). But despite these encouraging studies, the belief that moderate hypoxia actually dilates coronary arteries and improves angina is, unfortunately, a myth.

Ben Levine, a practicing cardiologist as well as an active researcher in high altitude physiology, reported a well-controlled study of fifteen men and five women visiting a resort at 8,200 feet for five days. They averaged sixty-eight years of age, and 35 percent of them had known coronary heart disease and an additional 50 percent were considered at high risk of undetected underlying heart disease. They tolerated the altitude and daily treadmill exercise well. One man had a myocardial infarct after exercise on the fifth day, but the night before he had experienced severe angina, which he did not mention before the test. Forty-five percent of the group had symptoms of mild mountain sickness. A battery of heart studies led the researchers to conclude:

> Patients with coronary artery disease who are well compensated at sea level are likely to do well at moderate altitude, although with acute exposure ischemia may be provoked at . . . lower work rates.

So what should an older person with heart symptoms do if he or she wants to go the mountains? Everything depends on the individual's condition, and evaluation by a cardiologist who understands more than a little about high altitude. A careful history and physical examination plus a few of the more appropriate tests are necessary and should lead to good advice.

In general, recognizing that individuals differ and the differences may be crucial, I believe a person with angina due to mild coronary artery disease who is active at sea level can probably go safely to moderate altitude and do somewhat less than his or her usual sea level activities.

Congestive heart failure, whether compensated or not, is evidence that the heart has been damaged or is an inadequate pump. The additional load of moderate hypoxia may not be well tolerated even with medication, and my advice, again considering the individual, usually is not to take the risk.

Congenital heart disease, valvular disease, valve replacements, enlargement of the heart, and frequent rhythm disturbances may be added risks and require careful evaluation. When feasible, marginal cases can be evaluated by exposing the patient to at least six hours of mild hypoxia, but this is hard to arrange.

Older and recent exercise protocols for testing at sea level are unreliable predictors of altitude tolerance.

What about cardiac bypass? After a patient has had a successful bypass, function usually returns to normal and the surgeons like to consider the heart to be, if not "as good as new," at least nearly so. Although some disagree, many believe that a fully recovered bypass patient can safely go to altitude. In fact several have gone very high in the Himalayas within a few weeks after bypass without difficulty. The outlook after dilatation of a plugged coronary artery by balloon angioplasty or by one of the newer techniques may not be quite so favorable, but here too, each person must be individually evaluated.

Blood Problems

Anemia exaggerates the impact of altitude because there's less hemoglobin to transport oxygen, and the heart tries to make up for this by faster, more forceful beats. One can tolerate mild anemia at altitude, but not if hemoglobin is less than about 8 grams. Leukemia might pose a problem, as would any illness that interferes with oxygen transport; I mention carbon monoxide in Chapter 4, Moving Blood: Circulation.

An uncommon red cell problem is sickle cell anemia and **sickle cell trait**, also discussed in Chapter 4. Persons with sickle cell trait or thalassemia (a similar mutant hemoglobin) are likely to have problems if they go to altitude:

V. F. is a black social worker who lives in Denver (5,280 feet). She learned she had sickle cell trait after the birth of her third child, but had few symptoms. During the next twenty years she often went to 7,500 feet without difficulty. Then, on going to 8,000 feet, she became very short of breath and tired and feverish, but recovered promptly on return home. Three years later the same symptoms occurred soon after going to 9,100 feet, and she also developed abdominal pain. She returned to Denver, and after some difficulty explaining her problem to the emergency room staff, she was diagnosed as having a spleen infarct and treated with oxygen. Since then she has limited her activities and takes oxygen with her when she goes to 8,000 feet. Her blood shows that she has Beta-thalassemia, an unusual variant of sickle cell.

This woman had a bad experience with a problem that at the time was not often diagnosed. Since then many similar cases have been reported, with estimates that half of the persons with sickle cell will have sickle crisis if they go above 10,000 feet. Several dozen persons have experienced crises during very long aircraft flights in which the cabin is pressurized only to 7,500 feet, or sometimes higher.

Not all persons with sickle cell or thalassemia experience crises. I'm not aware of any black high altitude mountaineers, but there are several ski clubs of black men and women who regularly ski at high mountain resorts. It's also clear that some who develop sickle crises do not have known or acknowledged black ancestry; Mediterranean ancestry might include that trait, far back in time.

Pulmonary Disease

In Chapter 9, Hypoxia in Everyday Life, I discuss how persons with some of the several lung problems like chronic obstructive pulmonary disease (COPD) adjust to hypoxia. Of the 16 million people with COPD in the United States, one group will tolerate moderate altitude quite well—

notably the "pink puffers," who often have a nearly normal arterial oxygen pressure and saturation, although their carbon dioxide is low and pH on the alkaline side. They are able to maintain good oxygenation at sea level by automatically overbreathing all the time. If blood studies and the usual pulmonary function studies and chest X rays confirm this diagnosis, many can go safely to 8,000–9,000 feet. In fact many veteran miners have COPD from years of dust inhalation—yet are able to live and work even higher than this.

By contrast, "blue bloaters" breathe less than a healthy person, but rely on increased hemoglobin to sustain oxygen delivery. These people do not adjust to altitude and if they go much higher than 5,000 feet without supplemental oxygen, they will be at risk of HAPE and perhaps even right-sided heart failure. Those with advanced COPD don't tolerate air travel well. However, breathing oxygen will help such a patient considerably and enable him or her to fly in commercial aircraft and even to visit altitude, providing that additional oxygen is breathed at all times. "Blue bloaters" usually have a high pulmonary artery pressure, and HAPE could be a significant risk without the extra oxygen.

Other Illnesses

As climbing and skiing became more popular, many persons with chronic illnesses began to go to mountain resorts and then to higher and higher mountains. A good deal of reliable information has come from experience and from a few careful studies, but we need more—and no two individuals are quite the same.

Epilepsy is not a contra-indication if it is well controlled, and hypoxia doesn't seem to increase the frequency or severity of attacks. Obviously, someone who is taking medicine should be careful to not stop taking it.

There's little or no evidence that **mental illness** is worsened by altitude, and in fact the calm beauty of mountains has soothed many disturbed persons. I have a well-described story of a man with manic-depressive illness who took steroids to prevent acute mountain sickness during a climb on Denali; he stopped the steroids and a day later had a major paranoid breakdown, but whether stopping steroids caused this is certainly not clear.

Diabetes isn't a contra-indication, but may be more difficult to control during a climb. Exertion will use up blood and liver sugars and thus decrease the need for insulin, and even cause insulin shock. At altitude, however, some people show an increase in blood sugar during or after exertion, indicating that the insulin dose might need to be increased for some people. Persons with severe or "brittle" diabetes planning to exercise in the mountains might be wise to take frequent fingertip blood samples and adjust insulin accordingly. Insulin is not damaged by freezing.

Scuba Diving at High Altitude

Scuba diving is very popular, and diving on mountain lakes poses an extra risk because of the greater change in pressure after surfacing. At a depth of 34 feet, the diver is exposed to one atmosphere of pressure in addition to the pressure at the surface. So when the diver returns to the surface, at, say, 15,000 feet in the Andean lakes, where the atmospheric pressure is about eight and a half pounds per square inch or 0.56 atmospheres, the pressure change is more likely to cause bends (*aero-embolism*), which can be serious. (One atmosphere equals fifteen pounds per square inch, or 760 torr.) This pressure change is more risky than if diving at sea level and then flying home. It would be prudent to wait thirty-six hours before flying after a dive at any altitude, and one should surface even more slowly when diving at altitude. Bends can be very serious.

Taking Medications

There's little authoritative information about the use of medications at altitude. We are a pill-taking culture and although the chemistry and the actions and interactions of many drugs are well documented, we don't know much about how hypoxia affects them.

Diamox and dexamethasone are discussed in Chapter 11, Treatment. Several of the people on Everest in 1996 carried syringes loaded with dexamethasone and some were given the injection in the belief it would quickly give them a little extra strength in the crisis.

Progesterone has been used to increase ventilation and prevent AMS, with little benefit or adverse effect for short-term use. **Nifedipine**, like other cardiac calcium channel blockers, lowers both systemic and pulmonary blood pressure, and is good treatment for HAPE. For those who have had HAPE or are considered HAPE-susceptible, a small dose of nifedipine before (and perhaps during) a trip above 10,000 feet is a good preventive measure; it is not advisable for non-susceptibles.

The use of **birth control pills** (BCP) at altitude is controversial: Some believe they may increase the risk of thrombosis and embolism, already increased by the thickened blood and by the release of biologically active substances by hypoxia (see Chapters 7 and 8). Those BCPs that contain progesterone may help slightly.

Aspirin and non-steroidal anti-inflammatory drugs (NSAIDs) may cause stomach irritation and even a little bleeding, but they're less irritating when taken with food. At one time it was thought that by preventing platelet clumping, aspirin might alleviate some altitude illness, but this hasn't proven to be the case. NSAIDs are of some help in relieving altitude headache but have no other effect on hypoxia.

I've heard a few stories that **tricyclic anti-depressants** have caused a severe reaction to hypoxia, and in fact one patient with severe COPD died from respiratory arrest in hospital allegedly because he was given an anti-depressant. **Barbiturates and tranquilizers** have a greater and more prolonged effect when taken at altitude than they do at sea level, and are unwise, certainly above 18,000 feet, because the small, persistent effect may further blur judgment. One of the very short-acting sedatives is thought to have precipitated hallucinations and brief mild mental changes on a few occasions. Most climbers believe—and with firsthand experience—that **alcohol** is more powerful on a mountain where "one drink does the work of two."

Stimulants like tea and coffee are part of contemporary life at any altitude; high on a mountain, disrupted sleep may be further disrupted by **caffeine** if one has taken gallons of tea. In place of boiling, water is often sterilized by adding **iodine**, which will not affect altitude tolerance. **Amphetamines** have been used for extra energy in a crisis: In 1950 Maurice Herzog is said to have taken dexedrine on top of Annapurna, the first 8,000-meter peak to be climbed. The resulting euphoria may have caused the careless loss of his gloves and severe frostbite, but it may also have saved his life. Just how much extra energy amphetamines provide during a crisis such as the one on Everest in 1996 is hard to determine. Certainly amphetamines, like other stimulants, are not to be taken casually anywhere.

Medicines prescribed for high blood pressure are likely to need dose adjustment at altitude, and other **cardiac drugs** may also need to be changed. It would be prudent to consult a local doctor at altitude if possible. These are individual issues that should be addressed by your own doctor before a trip—though he or she may not have guidelines any more definite than these!

The bottom line is that although we know a great deal about the chemistry of medications and their metabolic and degradation pathways, we have very little good information about their effects and effectiveness at altitude. Many drugs are broken down and eliminated by the liver, which has a high demand for oxygen, and some laboratory studies indicate that these, and perhaps others, are not well handled at altitude or during chronic hypoxia.

Using Illegal Drugs

Many climbers have used **marijuana** on mountains and, depending on who you ask and how candid the responses, the effects may be called great, indifferent, or bad. Marijuana does blur awareness, especially of unpleasant stimuli, which is one reason it's taken. If it disturbs reaction times or judgment, that would not be helpful on a difficult climb. **Morphine and other opiates** blunt the respiratory drive and can be expected to increase the likelihood of AMS, HAPE, and HACE. Nevertheless, morphine is valuable as a last resort for treating HAPE. I've never heard of **hallucinogens** and other mind-altering drugs being used at altitude, but I have been told about one man who had a serious LSD flashback during a climb.

In general it's probably safe to assume that any medication will be more potent at altitude—which may be good news or bad.

△ △ △

IT'S AN OXYMORON TO SAY THAT THE mountain environment is different! Below 10,000 feet the difference may be noticeable but not dangerous. The higher one goes, the more powerful is the combined impact of cold, exhaustion, and lack of oxygen, food, water, and sleep. Each of these may be moderated but not eliminated. Together they make very high mountains potentially lethal. Terrible in beauty, awesome, fickle in weather, the mountain environment can truly be a death zone.

But approached with experience, educated caution, humility, and reverence, mountains have been and always will be a reservoir of beauty and inspiration.

As for the mountaineers, Walter Lippman, philosopher-cum-journalist, wrote in the *New York Times* many decades ago:

The world is a better place . . . because it contains human beings who do . . . the useless, brave, noble, divinely foolish, and the very wisest things that are done by man. And what they prove . . . is that man is no mere creature of his habits, no automaton in his routine, but that in the dust of which he is made there is also fire, lighted now and then by great winds from the sky.

GLOSSARY

A-a gradient: The difference in the partial pressure of oxygen between alveolar air and arterial blood in the lungs.

Acapnia: Literally, no carbon dioxide. Often used to describe a condition in which the partial pressure of carbon dioxide in the blood is lower than normal. See also *Hypoecapnea.*

Acclimatization: Changes responsive to altitude that develop in weeks or months.

Accommodations: Changes responsive to altitude that are struggle responses.

Active transport: The process by which cells "pump" a substance across the cell membrane against a higher concentration.

Adaptation: Changes responsive to altitude that take generations.

Adenosine diphosphate (ADP): One of the adenosine molecules that glucose is enzymatically converted to.

Adenosine monophosphate (AMP): One of the adenosine molecules that glucose is enzymatically converted to.

Adenosine triphosphate (ATP): One of the adenosine molecules that glucose is enzymatically converted to.

Adult Respiratory Distress Syndrome (ARDS): A type of pulmonary edema that results from severe trauma or toxic shock.

Altitude: Geographers and cartographers use feet or meters to define height above sea level. Physiologists prefer to express altitude in terms of barometric pressure, using torr or millimeters of mercury (mm Hg).

Alveolar: Pertaining to the air sacs in the lung.

*Alveolus (*plural, *alveoli):* The tiny air spaces in the lung where oxygen and carbon dioxide pass between air and blood.

Ambient: Relating to the environment surrounding us. Customarily refers to air, temperature, or humidity.

Anoxemia: Literally means no oxygen in blood. See also *Hypoxia.*

Anoxia: Literally means no oxygen. See also *Hypoxia.*

Ataxia: Customarily refers to staggering gait, but also applies to clumsiness with arms, hands, or fingers.

Atmospheric: Pertaining to the air that envelops the earth.

Atrio-natriuretic peptide (ANP): A hormone secreted by small granules in the muscle fibers of the atria of the heart. Has a powerful effect on salt and water balance.

Atrium (plural, atria): A heart chamber; there are two atria, the left and the right. Also known as auricle.

Autonomic nervous system: The part of the the brain and peripheral nerves that automatically controls the functions we cannot willfully control—among them the heart and blood pressure and movement of the muscles that control breathing.

Barometer: A device developed by Torricelli, from Gaspar Berti, to measure the weight of the atmosphere that envelops the earth, commonly expressed as torr or millimeters of mercury (mm Hg) barometric pressure.

Basement membrane: The part of a cell that, with a single layer of epithelial cells, separate it from the interstitial space. See also *Membrane.*

Bronchus (plural, bronchi, bronchioles): Branches of the trachea or windpipe; they lead from each bronchus, at the bifurcation of the trachea, and subdivide into progressively smaller tubes through which air moves in and out of the alveoli.

Buffer: A salt formed by the combination of a weak acid with a strong base (or vice versa) that is able to absorb hydrogen ions with little change in pH (acidity or alkalinity). Buffering power describes the amount of buffer in blood.

Capillaries: Tiny thin-walled vessels that form a network that carries blood from the smallest arterioles to precapillaries and capillaries that connect to the smallest veins and venules, taking blood back to the heart.

Carbonic anhydrase: An enzyme that facilitates conversion of carbon dioxide to carbonic acid in red blood cells and to bicarbonate in the kidneys.

Carboxy-hemoglobin: The compound formed when carbon monoxide attaches to hemoglobin, displacing oxygen.

Carotid: Large artery on each side of the neck, supplying the head with blood. Each has a smaller bulge called the carotid sinus, which monitors blood pressure. A collection of specialized cells adjacent to each artery (*carotid body,* aka *glomus*) monitors oxygen in blood.

Carrying capacity: The amount of oxygen that the blood can carry when fully saturated. Usually described in volumes percent, i.e., the number of milliliters of gas in 100 milliliters of blood.

Cerebrospinal fluid (CSF): The fluid that bathes the brain and spinal cord. In patients with HACE, the worse the symptoms, the higher the CSF pressure is likely to be.

Cerebro-vascular accident (CVA): See *Stroke.*

Chronic Mountain Sickness (CMS): Also called Monge's disease.

Computerized tomography (CT): A scanning X-ray procedure used for diagnosis.

Cotton wool spots: Whitish areas seen in the retina of the eye, indicating swelling or edema, without bleeding.

Cyanosis, cyanotic: A bluish color of lips and nailbeds (and, in extreme cases, of skin) due to lack of oxygen in the blood, which leaves some of the hemoglobin in the unsaturated form.

Diffusion: The movement of one substance through another, for example, of a gas through a barrier such as a cell wall, or of a gas or a dissolved substance throughout the gas or liquid in which it is dissolved.

Diuretic: A substance, either natural or synthetic, that increases the formation of urine.

Edema: Fluid that accumulates in the loose tissue between the cells, or within cells, or within the alveoli or interstitial space of the lungs.

Embolus (plural, *emboli*): An abnormal particle (as an air bubble) circulating in the blood.

Endothelins: A family of substances, released by endothelial cells; one of the endothelins constricts blood vessels in direct opposition to nitric oxide.

Endothelium: The lining of small precapillary vessels.

Endothelium-derived relaxing factor (EDRF): A powerful agent that was soon identified as a simple chemical substance, nitric oxide (NO).

Epithelium: Cells that line the alveoli and cover skin.

Hematocrit (HCT): The percentage of whole blood occupied by cells (mostly red blood cells). Describes the red cell mass.

Hemoglobin (Hgb): A complex substance containing four iron atoms (which combine loosely with oxygen), and a protein (a species-specific globin) that determines the type of hemoglobin. Different animals have a metallic ion other than iron and different proteins.

Hypercapnia: Excessive carbon dioxide in blood.

Hypoecapnea: Insufficient carbon dioxide in blood. This term is more precise, though less often used, than *acapnia*.

Hypoxia: Lack of oxygen. This has largely replaced the older, less accurate term *anoxia* (literally, "no oxygen"). *Anoxemia* refers to inadequate oxygen in the blood and is used instead of the more precise but clumsy word *hypoxemia.*

Hypoxic ventilatory response (HVR): The change in rate and/or depth of breathing dictated by a decrease in the partial pressure of oxygen in the inspired air. It is an index of the sensitivity of the respiratory center to oxygen lack.

Intercellular: Literally, between cells.

Intermittent upper airway obstruction (IUAO): A big name for simple snoring.

Interstitial: Pertaining to loose tissue (less accurately "interstitial space") between cells.

Intracellular: Literally, within cells.

Macula: The area of central vision.

Magnetic resonance imaging (MRI): A scanning X-ray procedure used for diagnosis.

Maximal breathing capacity (MBC): The largest volume of air one can breathe in one minute.

Maximal oxygen uptake: The amount of oxygen one can acquire while working at peak capacity. It indicates the volume of air one can move, as well as the volume of oxygen passing from lungs to blood, and is the standard measurement of fitness and work capacity. Often abbreviated as VO_2MAX.

Membrane: A thin, single-cell-thick covering for cells or organs. The characteristics of each membrane have developed to match its function. See also *Basement membrane.*

Membrane potential: Each living cell membrane carries a minute electric charge (bioelectric potential) that maintains the cell's integrity and enables it to fulfill its particular function. Cell death occurs when the membrane potential falls to zero.

Metabolic rate: The amount of oxygen consumed per minute. Usually measured under basal (resting, fasting) conditions, corrected for body surface area, called BMR.

Mitochondria: Small bodies within every living cell that perform the functions of that cell. They are the factories of the body and require a large supply of oxygen.

Oxy-hemoglobin ($HgbO_2$): The combination of oxygen and hemoglobin, used to define the dissociation curve relating partial pressure of oxygen to percentage of hemoglobin saturated with oxygen.

Oxygen carrying capacity: See *carrying capacity.*

Oxygen cascade: Shorthand description of the progressive decreases in partial pressure of oxygen as that gas moves from outside (ambient) air into lungs (alveoli), into blood, and finally into the cells, where it is used by the mitochondria.

Oxygen content: The amount of oxygen in blood, usually defined as milliliters of oxygen in milliliters of blood. When hemoglobin is fully saturated, oxygen content equals carrying capacity. But when less saturated, capacity is greater than content.

Oxygen transport system: Rather loosely used phrase that describes the process of acquisition of oxygen by breathing in, the passage of oxygen from lungs into blood, carriage of oxygen throughout the body by hemoglobin, and, finally, passage of oxygen from blood into the cells.

Parasympathetic nervous system: Part of the autonomic nervous system that transmits signals to and from the brain.

Partial pressure: The pressure that one gas in a mixture of gases would exert if it were the only gas present. The number of molecules of the gas present, divided by the total number of molecules in the mixture, gives the percentage of the gas, and that percentage multiplied by the total pressure of the gas mixture gives the partial pressure. Because we know the percentage of oxygen in air (20.93 percent), if we know the barometric pressure, we can easily determine the partial pressure of oxygen at that pressure and thus at that altitude.

Perfusion: Flow of blood through tissues or organs, such as the lungs.

pH: A logarithmic term used to define degree of acidity or alkalinity.

Plasma: Liquid portion of blood.

Pulmonary artery pressure (PAP): Blood pressure in the pulmonary arteries. Increased PAP is a hallmark of HAPE.

Pulmonary function tests (PFT): A battery of tests used to measure the physical characteristics of the lungs, the efficacy of respiratory muscles, and the physiology of air exchange. Especially useful in detecting and defining the causes of many breathing problems. See also *Vital capacity.*

Respiration: Term commonly used to describe the process of breathing (inspiration and expiration). Sometimes used to define the entire process of getting and using oxygen. Or, more narrowly, used to refer to the consumption of oxygen and formation of carbon dioxide by cells or tissues.

Respiratory equivalent, respiratory quotient (RQ), respiratory exchange ratio (RER): Carbon dioxide output divided by oxygen input.

Respiratory center: A collection of highly specialized cells located in the lower part of the brain (the midbrain) that controls the rate and depth of breathing in response to blood carbon dioxide and/or pH. Primarily controlled by carbon dioxide.

Retina: The layers of nerve tissue, blood vessels, and receptor organs in the back of the eye.

Retinopathy, retinal hemorrhages: Abnormalities in the retina; at high altitude due to increased blood flow and high altitude retinal hemorrhages (HARH).

Secretion: Formation of a substance by specialized glands. Also used to describe active transport across cell membranes.

Signs and symptoms: Signs are indications that can be seen or heard by an observer; symptoms are sensations perceived only by the affected individual. The former are objective; the latter are subjective.

Sino-atrial node (S-A node): Located in the wall of the right atrium of the heart; stimulates the heart to beat at its own intrinsic rate.

Sodium-potassium pump: An electrical activity of cell membranes that constantly pushes sodium ions out of the cell while retaining potassium ions within the cell. It is one of many "pumps" that maintain proper concentrations of ions within cells by active transport across the membrane.

Stroke: Caused either by blood clot or cerebral hemorrhage; also called cerebro-vascular accident (CVA).

Sympathetic nervous system: Part of the autonomic nervous system that transmits signals from the brain.

Thorax: The chest wall.

Thrombosis: The formation or presence of a blood clot within a blood vessel.

Thrombus (plural, thrombi): A blood clot formed within a blood vessel.

Torr: See *Barometer.*

Trachea: The windpipe.

Transient ischemic attack (TIA): Small, "silent" stroke.

Ventilation: Movement of air in and out of the lungs.

Ventilation-perfusion mismatch: Imbalance or inequality between alveolar ventilation and circulation; also called $\dot{V}/Q$ *inequity*.

Ventricle: A heart chamber; there are two ventricles, left and right.

Vital capacity: Volume of air in a maximal exhalation after the fullest inspiration. Timed vital capacity refers to the volume that can be exhaled in a specific time, usually thirty seconds or one minute. See also *Pulmonary function tests.*

VO₂MAX: See *maximal oxygen uptake.*

SELECTED BIBLIOGRAPHY

Abelson, A.E. "Altitude and Fertility." *Human Biology* 48 (1976): 83–91.

Acosta, I. "Of some mervellous effects of the windes, which are in some partes of the Indies." In *High Altitude Physiology*, edited by J. B. West, 10–15. Stroudsberg, Pa.: Hutchinson Ross, 1981.

Adnot, S., B. Raffestin, and S. Eddahibi. "NO in the Lung." *Respiration Physiology* 101 (1995): 109–20.

Alexander, J. K. "Coronary Heart Disease at Altitude." *Texas Heart Institute Journal* 21 (1994): 261–266.

———. "Coronary Problems Associated with Altitude and Air Travel." *Cardiology Clinic* 13 (1995): 271–8.

Alvarez, A. "Sleep." *New Yorker* (1992): 85-94.

Alvarez, W. C. "The Migrainous Scotomata as Studied in 618 Persons." *American Journal of Ophthalmology* 49 (1960): 489–504.

Anand, I. S. and Y. Chandrashekhar. "Subacute Mountain Sickness Syndromes: Role of Pulmonary Hypertension." In *Hypoxia and Mountain Medicine*, edited by J. R. Sutton, G. Coates and C. S. Houston. Burlington, Vt.: Queen City Press, 1992.

Anand, I. S., R. M. Malhotra, Y. Chandrashekhar, H. K. Bali, S. S. Chauhan, S. K. Jindal, R. K. Bhandari, and P. L. Wahi. "Adult Subacute Mountain Sickness: A Syndrome of Congestive Heart Failure in Man at Very High Altitude." *Lancet* 335, No. 8689 (1990): 561–565.

Anonymous. "La Grotte du Chien." *Bulletin de Societé Meridionale de Speleologie et de Prehistoire* 22, Nos. 93–95 (1982).

Anonymous. "The Lake Louise Consensus on the Definition and Quantification of Altitude Illness." In *Hypoxia and Mountain Medicine*, edited by J. R. Sutton, G. Coates and C. S. Houston, 327–330. Burlington, Vt.: Queen City Press, 1992.

Appenzeller, O. "Altitude Headache." *Headache* 12 (1972): 126–129.

Arias-Stella, J. and H. Kryger. "Pathology of High Altitude Pulmonary Edema." *Archives of Pathology* 76 (1963): 43–53.

Arregui, A., J. Cabrera, F. Leon-Velarde, S. Paredes, D. Viscarra, and D. Arbaiza. "High Prevalence of Migraine in a High-altitude Population." *Neurology* 41 (1991): 668–1670.

Asahina, K., M. Ikai, Y. Ogawa, and Y. Kuorda. "A Study of Acclimatization at Altitude in Japanese Athletes." *Schweiz Z Sportsmed* 14 (1967): 240–247.

Asmussen, E., and H. Chiodi. "The Effect of Hypoxemia on Ventilation and Circulation in Man." *American Journal of Physiology* 132 (1941): 426–436.

Aste-Salazar, H. and A. Hurtado. "The Affinity of Hemoglobin For Oxygen at Sea Level and at High Altitudes." *American Journal of Physiology* 142 (1944): 733–743.

Astrand, P. O. "The Respiratory Activity in Man Exposed to Prolonged Hypoxia." *Acta Physiologica Skandinavica* 30 (1954): 343–368.

Astrup, P. "Some Physiological and Pathological Effects of Moderate Carbon Monoxide Exposure." *British Medical Journal* 4 (1972): 447–452.

Atkins, J., B. Honigman, C. S. Houston, and R. C. Roach. "Elderly Population Has Decreased AMS Incidence at Moderate Altitude (Abstract)." In *Hypoxia and Molecular Medicine*, edited by J. R. Sutton, G. Coates and C. S. Houston. Burlington, Vt.: Queen City Press, 1993.

Baker, P. T. "Human Adaptation to High Altitude." *Science* 163, No. 3872 (1969): 1149–1156.

Balke, B., J. T. Daniels, and J. A. Faulkner. "Training for Maximum Performance at Altitude." In *Exercise at High Altitude*, edited by R. Margaria, 179–186. New York: Excerpta Medica, 1967.

Balke, B. and J. G. Wells. "Ceiling Altitude Tolerance Following Physical Training and Acclimatization." *Journal of Aviation Medicine* 29 (1958): 40–47.

Banchero, N., R. F. Grover, and J. A. Will. "Oxygen Transport in the Llama (Lama Glama)." *Respiration Physiology* 13 (1971): 102–115.

Barach, A. L., R. A. McFarland, and C. P. Seitz. "The Effects of Oxygen Deprivation on Complex Mental Functions." *Journal of Aviation Space Environmental Medicine* 8 (1937): 197–207.

Barbashova, Z. I. "Studies on the Mechanisms of Resistance to Hypoxia: A Review." *International Journal of Biometeorology* 11, No. 3 (1967): 243–254.

Barcroft, J. "Mountain Sickness." *Nature* 2855, No. 114 (1924): 90–92.

———. *Respiratory Function of the Blood. Part I: Lessons from High Altitude.* New York: Cambridge University Press, 1925.

Barcroft, J., M. Camis, and C. G. Mathison. "Report of the Monte Rosa Expedition of 1911." *Philosophical Transcripts of the Royal Society of London (Series B)* 206 (1914): 49–102.

Barcroft, J., A. Cooke, H. Hartridge, T. R. Parsons, and W. Parsons. "The Flow of Oxygen through the Pulmonary Epithelium." *Journal of Physiology* 53 (1920): 450–472.

Bärtsch, P., B. Merki, B. Kayser, M. Maggiorini, and O. Oelz. "Controlled Trial of the Treatment of Acute Mountain Sickness (AMS) with A

Portable Hyperbaric Chamber (Abstract)." In *Hypoxia and Mountain Medicine*, edited by J. R. Sutton, G. Coates, and C. S. Houston. Burlington, Vt.: Queen City Press, 1992.

Bärtsch, P., S. Shaw, M. Francioli, M. P. Gnadinger, and P. Weidmann. "Atrial Natriuretic Peptide in Acute Mountain Sickness." *Journal of Applied Physiology* 65 (1988): 1929–1937.

Baume, Louis. *Sivalaya*. Seattle, Wa.: The Mountaineers, 1980.

Beall, C. M., K. P. Strohl, B. Gothe, G. M. Brittenham, M. Barragan, and E. Vargas. "Respiratory and Hematological Adaptations of Young and Older Aymara Men Native to 3600m." *American Journal of Human Biology* 4 (1992): 17–26.

Bean, W. B. "Physical and Toxic Agents." In *Pathologic Physiology*, edited by W. A. Sodeman, 291. Philadelphia: Saunders, 1961.

Benoit, H., M. Germain, J.C. Barthelemy, C. Denis, J. Castells, D. Dormois, J. R. Lacour, and A. Geyssant. "Pre-Acclimatization to High Altitude Using Exercise with Normobaric Hypoxic Gas Mixtures." *International Journal of Sports Medicine* 13 (1992): S213–S215.

Bernier, Francis. *Travels in the Mogul Empire*. London: Pickering, 1826.

Bernstein, M. H. "Avian Respiratory Physiology and High Altitude Performance." In *Hypoxia: The Adaptations*, edited by J. R. Sutton, G. Coates, and J. E. Remmers, 30–40. Philadelphia, Pa.: BC Dekker, 1990.

Bert, P. *Barometric Pressure*. Bethesda, Md.: Undersea Medical Society, 1978.

Billings, C. E., R. E. Brashears, R. Bason, and D. K. Mathews. "Medical Observations During 20 Days at 3,800 Meters." *Archives of Environmental Health* 18 (1969): 987–995.

Blaschko, H. *Mountain Sickness, Handbuch des Offentlicher Gesundheitswesens*. Berlin: Herman Eulenberg, 1882.

Bligh, J., and D. Chauca. "The Effect of Cold and Hypoxia on the Pulmonary Arterial Pressure and Its Possible Significance in the Occurrence of High Mountain Sickness." Unpublished paper, 1982.

Block, A. J., P. G. Boysen, J. W. Wynne, and L. A. Hunt. "Sleep Apnea, Hypoecapnea and Oxygen Desaturation in Normal Subjects." *New England Journal of Medicine* 300, No. 10 (1979): 513–517.

Bohr, C. "The Influence of Section of the Vagus Nerve on the Disengagement of Gases in the Air Bladder of Fishes." *Journal of Physiology* 15 (1894): 494–500.

Bortz, W. M. "Disuse and Aging." *Journal of the American Medical Association* 248, No. 10 (1982): 1203–1208.

Boukreev, Anatoli. *The Climb*. New York: St Martin's Press, 1997.

Boycott, A. E. and J. S. Haldane. "The Effects of Low Atmospheric Pressures on Respiration." *Journal of Physiology* 37 (1908): 355–377.

Boyle, R. "Two New Experiments Touching the Measure of the Force of the Spring of Air Compress'd and Dilated." In *High Altitude Physiology*, edited by J. B. West, 70–75. Stroudsberg, Pa.: Hutchinson Ross, 1981.

Bradwell, A. R., A. D. Wright, C. Imray, and R. Fletcher. "Progesterone in Acute Mountain Sickness." In *Hypoxia and the Brain.* Edited by J. R. Sutton, C. S. Houston, G. Coates. Burlington, Vt.: Queen City Press, 1995.

Bradwell, A. R., A. D. Wright, M. Winterborn, and C. Imray. "Acetazolamide and High Altitude Diseases." *International Journal of Sports Medicine* 13 (1992): S63–S64.

Brendel, W., J. R. Weingart, and L. R. Haas. "Medical Statement Analysis of 3200 High-altitude Climbers." *Medical Science and Sports Medicine* 19 (1985): 180–191.

Brooks, M. M. "Effect of Methylene Blue on Performance Efficiency at High Altitudes." *Aviation Space and Environmental Medicine* 16 (1945): 251–262.

———. "Methylene Blue, An Antidote to Altitude Sickness." *Journal of Aviation Space and Environmental Medicine* 18, No. 3 (1948): 298–299.

Broome, J.R., M. A. Stoneham, J. M. Beeley, J. S. Milledge, and A. S. Hughes. "High Altitude Headache: Treatment with Ibuprophen." *Aviation Space and Environmental Medicine* 65 (1994): 19–20.

Brown, P. "Cheyne-Stokes Respiration." *Journal of Medicine* 30 (1961): 849–860.

Campbell, E. J. "The Evolution of Oxygen." In *Hypoxia: Man at Altitude*, edited by J. R. Sutton, N. L. Jones, and C. S. Houston, 2–7. New York: Thieme-Stratton, 1982.

Chang, K. C., C. G. Morrill, and H. Chai. "Impaired Response to Hypoxia After Bilateral Carotid Body Resection For Treatment of Bronchial Asthma." *Chest* 73 (1978): 667–669.

Cournand, A. *The Historical Development of the Concepts of Pulmonary Circulation.* In *Pulmonary Circulation*, edited by: W. R. Adams and I. Veith. New York: Grune and Stratton, 1959.

Coward, F. A. "Mountain Sickness As Observed in the Andes." *Journal of the South Carolina Medical Association* 2 (1906): 123–125.

Creel, D. J., A. S. Crandall, and M. Swartz. "Hyperopic Shift Induced By High Altitude After Radial Keratotomy." *Journal of Refractive Surgery* 13 (1997): 398–400.

Curran, Jim. *K2: The Story of the Savage Mountain.* London: Hodder and Stoughton, 1995.

———. *K2: Triumph and Tragedy.* London: Hodder and Stoughton, 1987.

Curran, W. S. and W. G. B. Graham. "Long Term Effects of Glomectomy." *Annual Review of Respiratory Diseases* 103 (1970): 566–8.

De Saussure, H. B. In *A General Collection of the Best and Most Interesting Voyages and Discoveries in All Parts of the World,* edited by J. Pinkerton. London: Longman, 1813.

Dent, C.T. "Can Mount Everest Be Ascended?" *The Nineteenth Century* (1892): 604–613.

Dill, David B. *Life Heat and Altitude*. Cambridge, Mass.: Harvard University Press, 1938.

Dill, D. B., H. T. Edwards, A. Folling, S. A. Oberg, A. M. Pappenheimer, and J. H. Talbott. "Adaptations of the Organism to Changes in Oxygen Pressure." *Journal of Physiology* 71 (1931): 47–83.

Douglas, C. G., J. S. Haldane, Y. Henderson, and E. C. Schneider. "The Physiological Effects of Low Atmospheric Pressure As Observed on Pikes Peak, Colorado." *Proceedings of the Royal Society of London (Series B)* 85 (1912): 65–67.

Druml, W., H. Steltzer, W. Waldhausl, K. Lenz, A. Hammerle, H. Vierhapper, S. Gasic, and O. F. Wagner. "Endothelin-1 in Adult Respiratory Distress Syndrome." *Annual Review of Respiratory Diseases* 148 (1993): 1169–73.

Fa-Hsien. *The Travels of Fa-Hsien (399-414 AD)*. Cambridge, Mass.: Cambridge Unversity Press, 1923.

Fishman, A P. "Pulmonary Hypertension—Beyond Vasodilator Therapy." *New England Journal of Medicine* 338, No. 5 (1998): 321–322.

Fitzgerald, M. P. "Further Observations on the Changes in the Breathing and the Blood at Various High Altitudes." *Proceedings from the Royal Society of London (Series B)* 88 (1914): 248–258.

Fitzgerald, W. G. "How High Can We Climb?" *Technical World Magazine* December (1907): 383–391.

Fleming, D. "Galen on the Motions of the Blood in the Heart and Lungs." *Isis* 46 (1955): 13–21.

Freshfield, D. W. "The Conquest of Mount Everest." *Alpine Journal* 1924, 1–11.

Fulton, J. F., and L. G. Wilson. *Selected Readings in the History of Physiology*. 2d. ed. Springfield, Ill.: Charles C Thomas, 1966.

Giaid, A., and D. Saleh. "Reduced Production of Endothelial Nitric Oxide Synthase in the Lungs of Patients with Pulmonary Hypertension." *New England Journal of Medicine* 333, No. 4 (1995): 214–221.

Gibbs-Smith, C. H. A. *A History of Flying*. New York: Praeger, 1953.

Gilbert, D. L. "The First Documented Description of Mountain Sickness: The Andean or Pariacaca Story." *Respiration Physiology* 52 (1983): 327–347.

———. "The First Documented Report of Mountain Sickness: The China or Headache Story." *Respiration Physiology* 52 (1983): 315–326.

———. *Oxygen and Living Processes*. New York: Springer-Verlag, 1981.

Gillespie, Charles. *Dictionary of Scientific Biography*. Sixteen vols. New York: Scribners, 1980.

Gippenreiter, E. G. and J. B. West. "High Altitude Medicine and Physiology in the Former Soviet Union." *Aviation Space and Environmental Medicine* 67 (1996): 576–584.

Gordon, B. L. *Medicine Throughout Antiquity*. Philadelphia, Pa.: F.A.Davis, 1949.

Gribble, Francis. *The Early Mountaineers*. London: T. Fisher Unwin, 1899.

Hackett, P. H. "Medical Research on Mt. McKinley." *Annual of Sports Medicine* 4, No. 4 (1989): 232–244.

Hackett, P. H., R. C. Roach, R. B. Schoene, F. Hollingshead, and W. J. Mills. "The Denali Medical Research Project, 1982–85." *American Alpine Journal* 28, No. 2 (1986): 129–137.

Hackett, P. H., R. C. Roach, R. A. Wood, R. G. Foutch, R. T. Meehan, D. Rennie, and W. J. Mills, Jr. "Dexamethasone for Prevention and Treatment of Acute Mountain Sickness." *Aviation Space and Environmental Medicine* 59 (1988): 950–954.

Hackett, P. H., P. R. Yarnell, R. Hill, K. Reynard, J. Heit, and J. McCormick. "High Altitude Cerebral Edema and MR Imaging: Clinical Correlation and Pathophysiology." *Journal of the American Medical Association*. In Press (1997).

Haider, M. "A History of the Moguls of Central Asia." In *The Tarikh-I-Rashida*, edited by N. Elias. Lahore, Pakistan: Book Traders, 1896.

Haldane, J. S. "Acclimatisation to High Altitudes." *Physiological Review* 7, No. 3 (1927): 363–383.

———. *Respiration*. Oxford: Clarendon Press, 1935.

Haldane, J. S., A. M. Kellas, and E. L. Kennaway. "Experiments on Acclimatisation to Reduced Atmospheric Pressure." *Journal of Physiology* 53 (1919): 181–206.

Hannon, J. P. "High Altitude Acclimatization in Women." In *The Effects of Altitude on Physical Performance*, edited by R. F. Goddard, 37–44. Chicago: Athletic Inst, 1966.

Harvey, William. *De Motu Cordis*. Springfield, Ill.: Thomas, 1957.

Heath, D. *Man at High Altitude*. Edinburgh: Churchill Livingstone, 1989.

Hebbel, R. P., J. W. Eaton, R. S. Kronenberg, E. D. Zanjani, L. G. Moore, and E. M. Berger. "Human Llamas: Adaptation to Altitude in Subjects with High Hemoglobin Oxygen Affinity." *Journal of Clinical Investigation* 62 (1978): 593–600.

Hecht, H. H. "A Sea Level View of Altitude Problems." *American Journal of Medicine* 50 (1971): 703–708.

Hecht, H. H., H. Kuida, R. L. Lange, J. L. Thorne, A. M. Brown, R. Carlisle, A. Ruby, and F. Ukradyha. "Brisket Disease, II. Clinical Features and Hemodynamic Observations in Altitude-Dependent Right Heart Failure of Cattle." *American Journal of Medicine* 32 (1962): 171–183.

Henderson, Yandell. *Adventures in Respiration*. Baltimore, Md.: Williams and Wilkins, 1939.

————. "Life at Great Altitudes." *Yale Review* 3NS (1914): 759–773.

Honigman, B., M. K. Theis, J. Koziol-McLain, R. C. Roach, R. Yip, C. S. Houston, and L. G. Moore. "Acute Mountain Sickness in A General Tourist Population at Moderate Altitude." *Annals of Internal Medicine* 118, No. 8 (1993): 587–592.

Houston, C. S. and Bengt Kayser. *Proceedings of the Hypoxia Symposia 1977-1997.* Computer Disc, 1998.

Hultgren, Herb. *High Altitude Medicine.* Stanford, Calif.: Hultgren, 1996.

————. "High Altitude Pulmonary Edema at A Ski Resort." *West Journal of Medicine* 164 (1996): 222–227.

————. "High Altitude Pulmonary Edema: Current Concepts." *Annual Review of Medicine* 47 (1986): 267–284.

Hultgren, H.N. and W. Spickard. "Medical Experiences in Peru." *Stanford Medical Bulletin* 18, No. 2 (1960): 76–95.

Hurtado, A. "Chronic Mountain Sickness." *Journal of the American Medical Association* 120 (1942): 1278–1282.

————. *Life at High Altitudes.* Washington, D.C.: Pan American Health Organization, 1966.

Hurtado, A. "Studies at High Altitude. Blood Observations on the Indian Natives of the Peruvian Andes." *American Journal of Physiology* 100 (1932): 487–505.

Kamio, S., and S. Ohmori. "Hematological, Biochemical, and Immnunological Study During 24 Hour Japan Mountaineering Stamina Race." *Japanese Journal of Mountain Medicine* 17 (1997): 77–82.

Kayser, B. "Acute Mountain Sickness in Western Tourists Around the Thorong Pas (5400 M) in Nepal." *Journal of Wilderness Medicine* 2 (1991): 110–117.

Kellogg, R. H. "La Pression Barometrique: Paul Bert's Hypoxia Theory and Its Critics." *Respiration Physiology* 34 (1978): 1–28.

————. "Some High Points in Altitude Physiology." In *Environmental Stress: Individual Human Adaptations*, edited by L. J. Folinsbee, J. A. Wagner, J. F. Borgia, B. L. Drinkwater, J. A. Gliner, and J. F. Bedi, 317–324. New York: Academic Press, 1978.

Keys, A. "The Physiology of Life at High Altitudes; The International High Altitude Expedition to Chile, 1935." *Scientific Monthly* 43 (1936): 289–312.

Khan, D. A., M. Aslam, and Z. U Khan. "Changes in Plasma Electrolytes During Acclimatization at High Altitude." *Journal of the Pakistani Medical Association* 46, No. 6 (1996): 128–131.

Khoo, M. C. K., J. D. Anholm, Song-wan Ko, R. Downey, A. C. Powles, J. R. Sutton, and C. S. Houston. "Dynamcs of Periodic Breathing and Arousal During Sleep at Extreme Altitude." *Respiration Physiology* 103 (1996): 33–43.

Kimmelberg, H. K. "Current Concepts of Brain Edema." *Neurosurgery Journal* 83 (1995): 1051–1059.

Klausen, T., H. Christensen, J. M. Hansen, O. J. Nielsen, N. Fogh-Andersen, and N. V. Olsen. "Human Eythropoietin Response to Hypocapnic Hypoxia, Normocapnic Hypoxia and Hypocapnic Normoxia." *European Journal of Applied Physiology* 74, No. 5 (1996): 475–480.

Klausen, T., T. D. Poulsen, N. Fogh-Anderson, J. P. Richalet, and O. J. Nielsen. "Diurnal Variations of Serum Erythropoietin at Sea Level and Altitude." *European Journal of Applied Physiology and Occupational Medicine* 72, No. 4 (1996): 297–302.

Kleger, G. R., P. Bärtsch, P. Vock, L. J. Roberts, and P. E. Ballmer. "Evidence Against An Increase in Capillary Permeability in Subjects Exposed to High Altitude." *Journal of Applied Physiology* 81, No. 5 (1996): 1917–23.

Krakauer, Jon. *Into Thin Air*. New York: Villard, 1997.

Krogh, A. "The Supply of Oxygen to Tissues and the Control of Capillary Circulation." *Journal of Physiology* 52 (1919): 457–474.

Kronecker, H. "Mountain Sickness." *The Medical Magazine* 4, No. 7 (1895): 651–666.

Lafflen, D., D. Poquin, G. Savourey, P. A. Barraud, C. Raphel, and J. Bittel. "Cognitive Performance During Short Acclimation to Severe Hypoxia." *Aviation Space and Environmental Medicine* 68 (1997): 993–997.

Landon, Perceval. *The Opening of Tibet*. New York: Doubleday, Page, 1905.

Last, H. "Empedocles and His Klepsydra Again." *Classics Quarterly* XVIII (1924): 169–173.

Lavoisier, A. *Elements of Chemistry, Book I, Great Books Foundation*. Chicago: Henry Regnery, 1949.

Leeuwenhoek, A. *Antony van Leeuwenhoeck and His Little Animals*. New York: Harcourt Brace, 1932.

Lieberman, P., A. Protopapas, and B. G. Kanki. "Speech Production and Cognitive Deficits on Mt. Everest." *Aviation Space and Environmental Medicine* 66 (1995): 857–864.

Longstaff, T. G. "Mountain Sickness and Its Probable Causes." Doctoral Thesis, Edinburgh, 1906.

Lowenstein, C. J., J. L. Dinerman, and S. H. Snyder. "Nitric Oxide, A Physiologic Messenger." *Annals of Internal Medicine* 120 (1994): 227–237.

Marx, J. L. "Neurobiology: Researchers High on Endogenous Opiates." *Science* (1976): 1227–9.

Mayow, J. "Medico-Physical Works." In *Alembic Club Reprints - No. 17*. Edinburgh: E&S Livingston, 1957.

Menon, N. D. "High Altitude Pulmonary Edema." *New England Journal of Medicine* 273, No. 2 (1965): 66–73.

Middleton, Dorothy. *Victorian Lady Travellers*. Chicago: University of Chicago Press, 1982.

Middleton, W. E. K. *The History of the Barometer*. Baltimore, Md.: Johns Hopkins University Press, 1964.

Monge, Carlos. *Acclimatization in the Andes*. Baltimore, Md.: Johns Hopkins University Press, 1948.

Mooney, Blake. *Altitude-related Places: A Medical Atlas*. New Orleans, La.: McNaughton and Gunn, 1993.

Morse, W. K. *Chinese Medicine*. New York: Hoeber, 1934.

Mosso, Angelo. *Life of Man on the High Alps*. London: T. Fisher Unwin, 1898.

Mummery, A. *My Climbs in the Alps and Caucasus*. London: T. Fisher Unwin, 1894.

Murray, Hugh. *Historical Account of Discoveries and Travels in Asia from the Earliest Times to the Present*. Edinburgh: Constable, 1820.

Naeje, R. "Pulmonary Circulation at High Altitude." *Respiration* 64 (1997): 429–434.

Needham, J. *Science and Civilization in China*. Vol. 2; History of Scientific Thought. New York: Cambridge University Press, 1969.

Noakes, T. D. "Hyponatremia During Endurance Running." *Medicine and Science in Sports and Exercise* 24, No. 4 (1992): 403–405.

Pearce, W. J. "Mechanisms of Hypoxic Cerebral Vasodilatation." *Pharmacologic Therapeutics* 65, No. 1 (1995): 75–91.

Perkins, J. F. "Historical Development of Respiratory Physiology." In *Handbook of Physiology, Section 3, Volume 1: Respiration,* edited by W. O. Fenn and H. Rahn. Washington, D.C.: American Physiological Society, 1964.

Pinker, Stephen. *How the Mind Works*. New York: Norton, 1997.

Pinkerton, J. *A General Collection of the Best and Most Interesting Voyages and Travels In All Parts of the World*. London: Longman, 1808.

Poirier, J-P. *Lavoisier: Chemist, Biologist, Economist*. Philadelphia: University of Pennsylvania, 1996.

Priestley, J. *The Discovery of Oxygen, Alembic Club Reprints No.7*. Edinburgh: E&S Livingston, 1961.

Prioreschi, Plinio. *A History of Medicine: Roman Medicine*. 1st ed. Three vols. Vol. Three. Omaha, Neb.: Horatius, 1998.

———. *A History of Medicine: Greek Medicine*. Second ed. Three vols. Vol. Two. Omaha, Neb.: Horatius, 1996.

Pugh, G. "Cardiac Output in Muscular Exercise at 5800 m (19,000 ft)." *Journal of Applied Physiology* 19, No. 3 (1964): 441–447.

Ravenhill, T. H. "Some Experiences of Mountain Sickness in the Andes." *Journal of Tropical Medicine and Hygiene* 16, No. 20 (1913): 313–320.

Renniek, I. D. B. "See Nuptse and Die." *Lancet* II (1976): 1177–1179.

Richalet, J.P. "High Altitude Pulmonary Edema: Still A Place For Controversy?" *Thorax* 50 (1995): 923–929.

Roach, R.C., C. S. Houston, B. Honigman, R. A. Nicholas, M. Yaron, C. K. Grissom, J. K. Alexander, and H. N. Hultgren. "How Well Do Older Persons Tolerate Moderate Altitude?" *Western Journal of Medicine* 162 (1995): 32–36.

Samaja, M. "Blood Gas Transport at High Altitude." *Respiration* 64 (1997): 895–899.

Scherrer, U., L. Vollenweider, A. Delabays, M. Savcic, U. Eichenberger, C. R. Kleger, A. Fikrle, P. E. Ballmer, and P. Bärtsch. "Inhaled Nirtic Oxide for High-Altitude Pulmonary Edema." *New England Journal of Medicine* 334, No. 10 (1996): 624–9.

Schoene, R. B. "Control of Breathing at High Altitude." *Respiration* 64 (1997): 407–415.

Shlim, D. R., and J. Gallie. "The Causes of Death Among Trekkers in Nepal." *International Journal of Sports Medicine* No. 13, Suppl. 1 (1992): S74–S75.

Singh, I. et al. "Acute Mountain Sickness." *New England Journal of Medicine* 280 (1969): 175–184.

———. "High Altitude Pulmonary Edema." *Lancet* 1 (1965): 229–232.

Speer, S. T. *On the Physiological Phenomena of Mountain Sickness.* London: T. Richards, 1853.

Stager, C. "Killer Lake." *National Geographic* September (1987): 404–420.

Stamler, J.S., L. Jia, J.P. Eu, T. J. McMahon, I. T. Demchenko, J. Bonaventura, K. Gernert, and C. A. Piantadosi. "Blood Flow Regulation By S-Nitrosohemoglobin in the Physiological Oxygen Gradient." *Science* 276 (1997): 2034–2036.

Stickney, E. J. Van Liere and J. C. *Anoxia, Its Effects on the Body.* Chicago: University of Chicago Press, 1962.

Tate, R. M., and T. L. Petty. "Primary Pulmonary Edema (ARDS)." *Annual Review of Medicine* (1984): 471–493.

Torricelli, E. "Torricelli's Letters On the Pressure of the Atmosphere." In *High Altitude Physiology*, edited by J. B. West, 60–63. Stroudsberg, Pa.: Hutchinson Ross, 1981.

Torrington, K.G. "Recurrent High Altitude Illness Associated with Right Pulmonary Artery Occlusion From Granulomatous Mediastinitis." *Chest* 96, No. 6 (1989): 1422–24.

Tschudi, J. J. *Travels in Peru.* London: David Bogue, 1847.

Voelkel, N. "Appetite Suppressants and Pulmonary Hypertension." *Thorax* No. 52, Suppl. 3 (1997): S63–S67.

Walsh, M. N., and W. M. Boothby. "The Demonstration of Air Bubbles in the Spinal Fluid Under Atmospheric Pressures Produced in A Low Pressure Chamber Simulating Those Obtaining During Rapid Ascents in

Airplanes." *Proceedings of the Staff Meetings of the Mayo Clinic* 16, No. 15 (1941): 225–228.

Ward, Michael P., James S. Milledge, and John B. West. *High Altitude Medicine and Physiology*. London: Chapman and Hall, 1995.

West, John. *High Life: A History of High-altitude Physiology and Medicine*. New York: Oxford University Press, 1998.

West, J. B. "Alexander M. Kellas and the Physiological Challenge of Mt. Everest." *Journal of Applied Physiology* 63, No. 1 (1987): 3–11.

———. *Everest: The Testing Place*. New York: McGraw Hill, 1985.

———. *High Altitude Physiology*. Stroudsburg, Pa.: Hutchinson Ross, 1981.

———. "Oxygen Enrichment of Room Air to Relieve Hypoxia of High Altitude." *Respiration Physiology* 99 (1995): 225–232.

Wilson, L. G. "Erasistratus, Galen, and the Pneuma." *Bulletin of the History of Medicine* 33, No. 4 (1959): 295–314.

Wilson, L.G. "The Transformation of Ancient Concepts of Respiration in the Seventeenth Century." *Isis* 51, No. 3 (1960): 161–172.

Woodworth, J. A. "Brief Notes and Bibliography of History of Mountain Medicine." *Appalachia* (1976): 81–93.

Workman, W. H. "Some Altitude Effects at Camps Above 20,000 feet." *Appalachia* 13 (1908): 350–359.

Zanger, T. "The Danger of Railway Trips to High Altitudes for Elderly People." *Lancet* June 20, 1903 (1903): 1730–1735.

Zuntz, N. and A. Loewy. *High Altitude Climates and Walking in the Mountains*. Berlin, 1906.

APPENDIX:
Historical Figures
in Altitude Physiology

Trying to discover who did what, and when, is one of the most fascinating aspects of research. The deeper you dig, the further you look, the more likely you are to find unsung heroes—persons whose work precedes, often by many years, that of those now better known. Fame often seems to be capricious in its choice of whom to anoint. Often those whose names have endured are those who have sifted the work of others and put together many pieces to make something new and important. Most of us are able to reach however high we do because we stand on the shoulders of those who have gone before.

Here I have noted the names and brief biographies of some well known and some obscure persons whose intuition, labor, courage, genius, or ability to bring together the observations of others enabled them to expand our knowledge and our skills. Only a few are here: I have omitted most of those in our century, and regretfully left out many others. Certainly there are many I never found.

△ △ △

Anaxagoras (500–428 B.C.). One of the philosophers during the Golden Age of Pericles in Athens, Anaxagoras built on the principles advanced by Empedocles, holding that matter was infinitely divisible, and that all things were held together in an apparently uniform and motionless form. He wrote only one important paper and has not had much permanent impact.

Aristotle (384–322 B.C.). Of all the great philosopher-scientists in the Golden Age of Greece, Aristotle is one of the best known. His scientific concepts were based on logic: He believed the universe to be finite and centered about the earth. Outside of his universe there could be nothing; inside of it there could be no emptiness, i.e., no vacuum. He believed in the four basic elements of fire, air, water, and earth as defined by Empedocles, but rejected the latter's atomic theory. Some consider Aristotle the founder of anatomy because of his studies of the heart and circulatory system. He believed that the pulsation of the heart was due to "boiling" of the blood, which then flowed to the lungs to be cooled. Because of the way he prepared his animals for study, he did not recognize that there were four rather than three chambers in the heart, nor did he distinguish between arteries and veins or recognize the existence of the heart valves. His influence on all of the sciences endured for a thousand years, being challenged successfully only during the Renaissance.

Baliani, Giovanni Batista (1582–1666). Although trained in the law and following the career of a public servant, the Italian Baliani was a gifted and imaginative amateur in physics, whose correspondence with Galileo in 1630 explained why lift pumps and siphons were limited in the height at which they could function. Baliani's concept of atmospheric pressure was correct but rejected by Galileo, while Torricelli agreed, after Berti had described his first barometer.

Barcroft, Joseph (1872–1947). Together with Paul Bert, Bruce Dill, and John S. Haldane, Barcroft's name is most closely associated with studies of high altitude. Born in England, he graduated with a doctorate in physiology from Kings College, Cambridge, and remained there as professor of physiology until his death. For some years he studied glands of internal secretion with Ernest Starling, and for a time with Haldane, soon developing better techniques for measuring gas exchanges. After several discouraging years studying oxy-hemoglobin dissociation, Barcroft was the first to show how the concentration of different salts, temperature, and acidity affected the shape of the curve. Brought up as a Quaker, he disagreed with their stand during WW I, and served with distinction in the medical corps. Experience with troops gassed with chlorine led him to respiratory physiology, revisiting the question of oxygen secretion in the lungs, wherein he disagreed with Haldane. He soon became interested in altitude sickness and made several mountain expeditions, for which he is best known among altitude specialists today. He also showed that the spleen serves as a reservoir for blood, releasing a significant amount when needed to restore circulating volume.

Beeckman, Isaac (1588–1637). Primarily interested in physics, mechanics, and meteorology, Beeckman was a progressive and influential Dutch thinker much concerned with teaching physics and mathematics to the common man. He believed that the universe was infinite, he subscribed to the atomic theory, and he came close to understanding the circulation of the blood. He challenged convention by proclaiming that air had weight, and seems to have understood how pumps worked, and perhaps accepted the possibility that a vacuum could exist.

Bernard, Claude (1813–1878). Although Bernard became one of the best-known French physiologists, he was an average student, passing examinations only with difficulty. Fortunately he came under the influence of some of the great physicians of his time, fell in love with physiological experimentation rather than medical practice, and received many honors for his studies of digestive enzymes, liver function, and the autonomic nervous system. He was a great experimenter, and as his studies advanced, his horizons widened and the concept of the constancy of the internal environment became central to most of his experiments and writing. Apparently he was the first to recognize that carbon monoxide kills by replacing oxygen in blood, and he was a pioneer in the study of both toxic and and beneficial medications. His great contribution was the principle of homeostasis—the tendency of organisms to maintain their internal stability.

Bert, Paul (1833–1886). Truly the father of altitude physiology, Bert was also a zoologist, a physiologist, and a pioneer in transplant surgery, and his textbooks on natural history, zoology, and the physical sciences were widely printed and translated. His countryman Claude Bernard had the greatest influence on Bert's career, and was largely responsible for his major work on barometric pressure. Although less well known than his work at high altitude, his studies of hemoglobin and how it combines with oxygen were even more important, as they explained how oxygen is carried to the tissues from the lungs. Deeply saddened by the death from acute hypoxia of two of his young colleagues during the flight of the balloon *Zenith,* he gave up research. He then became more active and prominent in French politics, and was appointed governor general of Indo-China, where he died soon after.

Berti, Gaspar (1600–1643). Although this Italian professor of mathematics was primarily interested in astronomy and physics, his major contribution to science was the apparatus that led to the modern barometer, which he built sometime between 1640 and his death in 1643. None of Berti's own writing has survived, and what we know of his work comes from secondary sources. At first he could not believe that a vacuum existed above the water column in his crude barometer because the sound of a bell could be heard ringing in the space, but his friend and biographer Emmanuel Maignan showed him that the sound was transmitted by a metal arm holding the bell! Berti described the device to Torricelli, who made it practical.

Black, Joseph (1728–1799). In addition to having a busy and distinguished medical practice in Edinburgh, Black was a brilliant and popular chemistry teacher, lecturing without notes, demonstrating his experiments with unfailing success, and attracting students from all over the world. His experimental methods were very precise, and he was the first to describe the qualities of carbon dioxide, which he called "fixed air" and recognized as a product of animal metabolism. His experiments with heat were even more important. Black recognized that air was necessary for all forms of combustion, was quite ambiguous in his treatment of the phlogiston theory, and, after Lavoisier's work was known,

gradually abandoned the phlogiston theory.

Boerhaave, Hermann (1668–1738). Holding three of the five professorships in the medical school at Leiden in the Netherlands, Boerhaave was one of the great teachers of his time, attracting students from all over Europe. He not only lectured for four or five hours a day, but he was also a brilliant bedside teacher and established the modern system of history, physical examination, diagnosis, course of illness, and outcome. He did not have a clear concept of red blood cells, and his somewhat ambivalent interest in alchemy is indicative of the confusion that still existed in science in Europe during that time. With extraordinary patience, he studied the possibility of transmutation of elements; for example, distilling a portion of mercury 500 times, shaking a sample of mercury continuously for eight and a half months and then distilling it repeatedly, and even boiling one sample of mercury for fifteen and a half years.

Borrichius (Borch), Olaus (1626–1690). Ole Borch, a Dane, studied medicine first but became better known as a professor of botany and chemistry. He had a large and busy medical practice and wrote extensively about a wide variety of subjects. In one of his many experiments, in 1678 he decomposed potassium nitrate to generate oxygen, but, like many others before him, did not realize the importance of what he had done.

Boyle, Robert (1627–1691). Born in Ireland, Boyle achieved major influence through his extraordinary work in philosophy, chemistry, and physics and as a founder and principal influence in the Royal Society of London. Of his wide interests, his best-known work is in the physics of air. By 1650 he had heard of Guericke's air pump, adopted an improved design by Hooke, and confirmed the observations of Torricelli and Berti. He demonstrated that sound could not be transmitted in a vacuum. Throughout his life, Boyle studied the behavior of gases, the vacuum, and the properties of matter. He supported the concept of atomic structure of all matter, although he used the less specific term "corpuscle." He was a great experimenter, and described all of his experiments in immense detail so that others might repeat them.

Cesalpino, Andrea (1519–1603). Cesalpino was an Italian philosopher and physician, a follower of Aristotle, and a pioneer in the study of circulation. He realized that the heart pumped blood throughout the body through the arteries, and received blood from the veins. He described the valves of the heart and pulmonary vessels, although he failed to put together a coherent picture of circulation as Harvey later did.

Dalton, John (1766–1844). Son of an English Quaker weaver, Dalton was entirely self-educated in physics and chemistry. After several stints of teaching in small schools and giving private lessons, he was drawn to examine the properties of gases and liquids, specifically of atmospheric humidity and rain. He kept meticulous daily meteorological records, and after five years published his first description of the individual properties of each gas in a mixture of several gases. After some controversy, this was formulated as Dalton's law of partial pressures and became fundamental to all studies of atmosphere and physiology.

Empedocles (490–430 B.C.). This early Greek philosopher originated the four-element theory of matter, believing that earth, water, air, and fire were the "roots of all things" and that there were two forces—love and hate—that moved humankind. He believed that animals developed both by chance and by natural selection, and Darwin quoted his work as cited by Aristotle. Only a few of his writings have survived and most are overlaid with legend. He is said to have stopped an epidemic by diverting two rivers, to have changed the climate in a valley by building a wall across a gorge, and to have revived a woman who had been without pulse or respiration for thirty days. His alleged fatal leap into the volcanic crater of Etna may be myth, or—impelled by belief in his immortality—a fatal prank!

Fabricius, ab Aquapendente (1537–1619). This Italian surgeon (usually called Hieronymus) is best known for his outstanding studies of anatomy and embryology. He succeeded his teacher Gabriel Fallopius as professor of surgery at the University of Padua, and his fame spread throughout Europe. Among his many works is a description of the valves in veins, which permit blood to flow in only one direction. This observation, along with a beautiful engraved illustration, was picked up by William Harvey as an essential part of his description of the circulation of the blood twenty years after he had studied under Fabricius.

Galen (129–199). Few physicians have more profoundly influenced medicine than did this Roman who served as physician to the gladiators after completing twelve years of medical studies. He believed in a "fourfold scheme" that included the four humors of the body, the four elements, the four seasons, the ages of man, and other factors in a harmonious whole. His greatest work was titled *Anatomical Procedures* but was based on observation rather than dissection. He accepted the view of Erasistratus that blood entered the right ventricle from the veins and was prevented from returning by the tricuspid valve. From the right ventricle it went to the lungs by the pulmonary artery and nourished the lungs. He felt that the heart worked like a bellows, actively dilating and passively contracting. He showed that the heart and vessels always contained blood, while Erasistratus had thought that sometimes they could contain air. Galen is best known for his immense pharmacopeia, which dictated medical treatment for many centuries.

Galilei, Galileo (1564–1642). His is one of the most famous names in mathematics, physics, and astronomy. This Italian was a firm supporter of Copernicus, and for this he was examined by the Inquisition and condemned to prison, but the sentence was commuted to house arrest for life. His most famous studies were made possible by the thirty-power telescope he developed in 1609, and he is best known for his work in astronomy and in the motions of falling bodies. Galileo treated the existence of a vacuum in a curious way. Having been told that suction pumps and siphons could not lift water beyond a certain height, he explained this with the theory that water had its own inner limited tensile strength, just as a rope or wire will break of its own weight if it's long enough. He failed to understand that the weight of the atmosphere was the cause of the siphon phenomenon, and rejected it even after Giovanni Baliani had clearly explained it to him.

Guericke, Otto von (1602–1686). Born in Hamburg, he was destined for politics and studied law, but was attracted by the concept of space and soon became a convert of Copernicus. He wondered about the possibility of a vacuum, how heavenly bodies might affect each other across the emptiness of space, and whether space was indeed bounded or limitless. In 1647 he made the first functioning suction pump and ten years later constructed the famous Magdeburg Sphere, which consisted of two hemispheres made of heavy copper, fitted tightly together with a gasket, and then evacuated. Teams of horses could not pull the hemispheres apart until a valve was opened, which convincingly demonstrated the pressure of the atmosphere.

Hales, Stephen (1677–1761). Born to an old and distinguished English family, Hales took a general education at Cambridge, where he was strongly influenced by Newton's heritage and by the distinguished scholar William Stukeley. Throughout his life he was a clergyman. Although he had no formal medical training, his curiosity and ingenuity led him into pioneering studies of blood pressure and circulation, for which he was made a member of the Royal Society. At the time, the magnitude of the arterial blood pressure was unknown, some contending that it was very large and might actually power muscle contraction. Hales's simple measurement of the arterial blood pressure in a mare ensured him permanent fame, and led him to further studies of the heart, the veins and capillaries, and the mechanics of blood flow. He was very versatile, and his most original—though less known—work involved the force that could raise the sap in plants and trees often to great heights. He demonstrated transpiration, showing that leaves give off not only moisture but also tiny bubbles of gas. This led him to study the gas laws and the composition of air as defined by Hooke, Mayow, and Boyle. He repeated Mayow's experiments, placing either a candle or a small animal under a bell jar and demonstrating that some element in air was consumed before the candle was extinguished or the animal died. Taking this a bit further in a series of rebreathing experiments on himself, he showed that some element of air was consumed and another gas produced by the body, which would not support life. This convinced him that "fresh air" was essential to health and led him to invent ventilators for purifying the air in hospitals and on shipboard, a major advance in public health.

Harvey, William (1578–1657). After undergraduate studies at Cambridge, Harvey left England to complete his medical degree under some of the great anatomists in Italy. Upon returning to London, he became a distinguished physician and an important influence in the Royal College of Physicians, doing his historic work on circulation in his free time. He had broad interests and a wide circle of friends outside of the sciences, and was untiring in his studies of the entire animal world, though he is best known for his "discovery" of the action of the heart and circulation. Most of his papers on other areas of natural history were lost in the Great Fire of London. Though Harvey followed Aristotle rather than Galen, his unique contribution came from his ability to put together many theories and observations of others and his own dissections and calculations to produce the first complete and accurate explanation of the coursing of blood through arteries, veins, and tissues, impelled by the heart as a pump. Many others had accurately described parts of the system—Galen's concept of the greater circulation was one bit, and Renaldo Colombo's description of the circulation through the lungs another, but Harvey was the first to make a coherent description of the whole. The logical steps through which he reached his conclusions are fascinatingly detailed in his great book *De Motu Cordis*, a first edition of which is said to be the most expensive book in the world!

Hooke, Robert (1635–1702). Although described as sickly all of his life, Hooke was a precocious genius whose talents included mathematics, mechanics, and physiology. Before he was eighteen he had mastered geometry and playing the organ, and described thirty ways of flying; he then entered Oxford, where he was befriended by some of the most brilliant men of his time. As assistant to Robert Boyle, he built an improved version of Guericke's air pump, and undoubtedly contributed importantly to formulating Boyle's famous gas laws. By 1660 he had invented a method for using a spring instead of a pendulum to drive a clock, and actually drew up a patent for this, although Christian Huygens built the first spring watch in 1674. He was made a member of the Royal Society, becoming curator responsible for several new scientific demonstrations for each weekly meeting. He published his most important book, *Micrographia*, in 1665, containing hundreds of observations made through a beautiful microscope that he had specially made to his specifications. Less well known are Hooke's studies of

air, combustion, and respiration. He showed that the function of breathing was to supply fresh air to the lungs rather than to cool or to pump blood and, along with Mayow, Boyle, and Lower, came close to isolating oxygen. He was a tireless inventor, producing brilliant and innovative ideas and a variety of scientific instruments. He was described by his contemporaries as a difficult man in an age of difficult men whose life was punctuated by bitter quarrels that refused to be settled.

Ibn-al-Nafis (circa 1208–1288). Only in the last thirty years has the work of this great Egyptian physician been rediscovered, and even today his contributions to medicine are inadequately recognized. In his early thirties he planned a comprehensive 300-volume medical text of which eighty volumes were published. Primarily a surgeon, he defined three stages for each operation: diagnosis, during which a patient entrusts the surgeon with his life; the operation; and, finally, postoperative care. His most extraordinary contribution was his description of the pulmonary circulation in 1242, centuries before Servetus, Colombo, and Harvey. He wrote:

This is the right cavity of the two cavities of the heart. When the blood in this cavity has become thin, it must be transferred into the left cavity, where the pneuma is generated. But there is no passage between these two cavities, the substance of the heart there being impermeable. It neither contains a visible passage, as some people have thought, nor does it contain an invisible passage which would permit the passage of blood, as Galen thought. The pores of the heart there are compact and the substance of the heart is thick. It must, therefore, be that when the blood has become thin, it is passed into the arterial vein (pulmonary artery) to the lung, in order to be dispersed inside the substance of the lung, and to mix with the air. The finest parts of the blood are then strained, passing into the venous artery (pulmonary vein) reaching the left of the two cavities of the heart, after mixing with the air and becoming fit for the generation of pneuma. . . .

It is said that his religion and compassion prevented him from dissection, which might have led him to an accurate definition of the total circulation. Whether or not reports of his work reached and influenced his successors is hotly debated today.

Lavoisier, Antoine-Laurent (1743–1794). Although best known for his studies of oxygen (and he is sometimes credited with having been the first to make it), this Parisian was a distinguished chemist, geologist, and social reformer as well, and it was indeed his activity as a humanitarian and reformer that led to his execution during the Reign of Terror in the French Revolution. In his mid-twenties he first became interested in the properties of air, which led in 1775 to his "discovery" of oxygen, some two years after he had received a letter from Scheele describing how to make that gas. Hales, Black, Priestley, and others were also studying the atmosphere, and although Lavoisier at first knew little of their work, he recognized the significance of Priestley's work as soon as he learned of it. His own description of oxygen, its preparation, and its properties was published in 1775, a few weeks after Priestley's.

In 1782–83, following some leads from Cavendish and Priestley, Lavoisier showed that water was not a simple material but a combination of "inflammable air" (hydrogen) and "dephlogistigated air" (oxygen). He immediately understood the importance of the Montgolfier balloon ascents in 1783, and during the next two years made a number of hydrogen balloons that rose even better, but his interest in balloons was soon displaced by work on his monumental chemistry textbook, completed only shortly before his death on the guillotine.

Lower, Richard (1631–1691). Lower became one of the most distinguished practitioners of medicine in London and was also recognized as among the finest English physiologists after Harvey. He became interested in the attempts by Christopher Wren to infuse blood and medication directly into veins, and performed the first successful blood transfusion between dogs in 1665, and between humans in 1667. These studies led to extensive work in cardiopulmonary physiology, and in 1669 he published definitive experiments showing that the bright red color of arterial blood was due to the oxygenation of dark red venous blood during its passage through the lungs. Thus he rounded out Harvey's work and laid the basis for much of what would follow.

Malpighi, Marcello (1628–1694). Italian-born Malpighi received his doctorates in medicine and philosophy at the age of twenty-five, and has since been known as the father of microscopic anatomy, although he also practiced medicine throughout his life. Giovanni Borelli, a distinguished naturalist, was his lifelong friend, and stimulated his interest in the physiology of plants and animals. He was the first Italian to be elected to the Royal Society of London, and in 1669 was made an honorary member. Malpighi acquired one of the new microscopes made by Robert Hooke, with which he examined capillary blood flow. This enabled him to show the connections between arteries and veins in the lung, providing the linkage that William Harvey had not been able to make decades before. He founded the study of histology.

Mayow, John (1643–1679). Born in London and educated at Oxford, Mayow accomplished a great deal in his short life. By the age of twenty-seven he had published two important books on respiration. His studies of the "nitro-aerial spirit" did more than those by others to show that something in air was necessary for, and consumed by, both living animals and a burning candle. He perceived too that a gas (which, a century later, was identified as oxygen) entered the blood through the lungs. Some consider Mayow the most important investigator in the distinguished English group who made such advances in the seventeenth century.

Mosso, Angelo (1846–1910). At twenty-four Mosso graduated summa cum laude from the University of Turin medical school in Italy and studied physiology under several distinguished scientists, becoming professor of physiology in 1879 at Turin. His Institute of Physiology established a station in the Alps to study human physiology at high altitude in 1895. Some of his most important work was the invention of scientific instruments, notably a plethysmograph for measuring blood flow and pressure, and an ergograph for measuring muscle activity and fatigue. In 1904 he developed locomotor ataxia and was forced to give up his physiological and political activities, but turned to archaeology, where he made equally noteworthy contributions.

Paracelsus, Theophrastus (1493–1541). The real name of this extraordinary Swiss was von Hohenheim. Where or even whether he took formal medical training is unknown, but he did serve as a military surgeon, and he understood that most diseases were of external origin, describing silicosis and tuberculosis as occupational diseases, and recognizing for the first time that syphilis could be congenital. He understood and used the anesthetic and sedative qualities of certain volatile liquids similar to ether, and used mercury and other chemicals as medications. He was a great and pioneering physician, an able chemist, but uncompromisingly destructive toward tradition.

Pascal, Blaise (1623–1662). Born in France and brought up and educated by his father, a widower, young Pascal became interested in mathematics and physics, and before he was twenty published several new mathematical concepts. He invented and built a mechanical device to do simple addition and subtraction, which

enjoyed limited success. By 1646 he had repeated Berti's experiment and was corresponding with Torricelli about barometers, and expanded the study to prove that a vacuum was possible. After being caught up in the controversy over his alleged role in Perier's demonstration that barometric pressure decreases as altitude increases, he returned to mathematics and published more books and papers, for which he is best known.

Priestley, Joseph (1733–1804). Born in England and educated for the ministry, it is not surprising that Priestley's initial writings were theological discussions of the nature of matter. They aroused great controversy, but throughout all of his work runs a vein of religious conviction that occasionally confuses or obscures his great original contributions. He began to study gases at the age of thirty-seven and became one of the outstanding gas chemists of the world, making many new gases, such as ammonia and sulfur and nitrogen, and of course working on oxygen. He seems to have cultivated the role of poor scientist, in contrast to Lavoisier, with whom his competitive rivalry sharpened with time. In 1770 he began publication of a series of six important books on gases that were widely studied and influential, and show a strong influence of Stephen Hales. Priestley's major clash with Lavoisier came over the latter's demonstration of the composition of water and claim for priority in discovering oxygen. Priestley clung to the phlogiston theory even after his voluntary exile to Pennsylvania because of his support of the French Revolution. His demonstration that green plants can convert carbon dioxide to oxygen was beautifully designed and explained why atmospheric oxygen was not wholly consumed by combustion and life on earth.

Ravenhill, Thomas (1882–1952). This Englishman is best known for his work as physician to a mining company in the Andes, where he saw and described three forms of mountain sickness.

He served as surgeon in some of the worst action of WW I and was so physically and mentally broken by his experiences he never returned to medicine. His single publication (1908) is comprehensive and accurate, and after long obscurity has become widely known and cited. Ravenhill became a well-known artist after that war.

Saussure, Horace-Benedict de (1740–1799). Although de Saussure is best known for his interest in Mont Blanc, his degree in philosophy from Geneva was in physics, and he was a distinguished mathematician, botanist, and geologist as well. This Frenchman made studies of the transmission of heat and cold, electricity, and magnetism on Mont Blanc, and observed his own pulse and respiration on all his mountain ascents. His extensive studies of geology, meteorology, and physiology were published in his four-volume work *Voyages dans les Alpes*, a collector's item until reprinted recently. In 1760 he made his first visit to Chamonix and became passionately interested in Mont Blanc, and the reward that he offered to the person who would reach the summit first undoubtedly hastened the ascent.

Scheele, Carl Wilhelm (1742–1786). Born, educated, and living his entire life in Sweden, Scheele was primarily a pharmacist and chemist whose ingenuity, curiosity, and persistence made him one of the most distinguished scientists of his time. Before he was twenty years old, he challenged the phlogiston theory and undertook a series of experiments on plants and animals that convinced him that life was supported by some element in air that was converted in the animal to a gas that would not support life. Although he took voluminous notes, he was slow to publish, and his notebooks have only recently been deciphered. On September 30, 1774, he wrote to thank Lavoisier for one of the latter's books and in his letter gave detailed instructions on how to prepare oxygen, together with basic information on its chemical and physiological properties—the

earliest-known written description of oxygen. Scheele knew that some English scientist was following similar studies, and sent to the printer in December 1775 a manuscript in which he described the preparation of oxygen, which would support combustion, and of nitrogen, which would not. Publication was delayed for various reasons, and by the time his book appeared in July 1777, others had published, and credit for Scheele's discoveries went to them. He did important work in both organic and inorganic chemistry, but is almost unknown for his most important contribution.

Servetus, Michael (1511–1553). Servetus was born and first educated in philosophy in Spain, where his religious studies raised in him doubts about the Holy Trinity that made him a fugitive and later led to his execution. He went to France and studied law, where he published his most heretical work, for which he was most criticized. He became a proofreader for a publisher, and this aroused his interest in medicine, which he studied in Paris and later practiced. His most important book was a theological text, important mainly because in one section of this he describes the circulation of the blood from the heart through the pulmonary artery to the lungs and back to the heart. Servetus understood that some "vital spirit" entered the lungs, passed into the blood, and was carried back to the heart and throughout the body. He was on the threshold of comprehending the circulation of the blood, but his text was primarily a religious one, and all but three copies were destroyed when he was burned at the stake for heresy, seventy-five years before Harvey's announcement.

Stahl, Georg Ernst (1660–1734). Allegedly intolerant and narrow-minded, and undoubtedly controversial, Stahl was an outstanding and active German physician and academician, a chemist, and a natural philosopher. He devoted much of his attention to distinguishing between the living and the nonliving and the anima that separates them. He preached preventive medicine and felt that doctors had to deal with the entire body and mind rather than individual organs. Strongly influenced by the chemist J. I. Becher, Stahl apparently originated the name "phlogiston" to define combustibility. Although he recognized that phlogiston and air were related, he believed that phlogiston was an element rather than a quality, and considered carbon as almost pure phlogiston. Although the phlogiston theory was wrong, it stimulated much of the essential study that was to follow in the next century.

Starling, Ernest (1866–1927). Born in Jamaica, part of the British Commonwealth, Starling made major contributions to human physiology. He pioneered modern understanding of the balance throughout the body tissues, and factors that affect the balance of salts and water across the semipermeable membranes of blood capillaries. His hypotheses are the basis of what we understand about edema. He coined the word "hormone" for substances that are secreted by what we know as glands of internal secretion, and carried throughout the body to affect functions. During his studies of poison gas in WW II, he prepared functioning heart-lung organs, and from these derived his "Law of the Heart" describing the relationship between inflow and outflow of the beating heart.

Sylvius, aka Franciscus de la Boe (1614–1672). Born in the Netherlands, this physician-anatomist's work helped to change the reliance of medicine from mystical speculation to a rational application of basic chemical and physical laws. Sylvius believed that the important processes of life and of illness occur in the blood, and therefore diseases could be treated chemically. He was a distinguished influential professor and was ahead of his times in understanding the process of respiration.

Torricelli, Evangelista (1608–1647). This Italian physicist and mathematician is memorialized in the term "torr," which is commonly used as a measure of barometric pressure. Whether he influenced Gaspar Berti's great experiment is unclear, but once he learned of it, he had the wit to see its importance and to use mercury in place of water, thereby making the first true barometer.

Vesalius, Andreas (1514–1564). Born in Brussels, Vesalius revolutionized medicine by the dissections he made on hundreds of human cadavers and publishing the first textbook of anatomy. These studies and his public lectures led him to challenge many of Galen's conclusions as based on animal rather than human observations. This plus beautiful engravings of parts of the human anatomy in his textbook make him the father of human anatomy. Vesalius's demonstration of the valves in human veins predated Harvey by twenty years, and Harvey may have studied under him in Padua. His textbook was so well done and became so influential that Vesalius was appointed to the court of Philip II, King of Spain.

INDEX

ABOUT THE AUTHOR

An M.D., scientist, mountaineer, and teacher, Charles S. Houston is one of the leading authorities on high-altitude medicine. He began climbing in 1925, organized a British-American expedition to Nanda Devi in 1936, and led expeditions which almost climbed K2 in 1938 and 1953. He began his study of the effects of high altitude as a Naval flight surgeon during World War II and in the mid-1940s directed Operation Everest—an acclimatization study that used a decompression chamber to simulate an altitude of 29,000 feet. From 1967 to 1975 he directed high-altitude studies in the Canadian Yukon, and in 1985 was the principal investigator for Operation Everest II.

As an internist he practiced family medicine and later taught medicine at the University of Vermont (until 1979). Houston believes strongly that medical knowledge can be made accessible and interesting to the general public. He has written almost a hundred scientific papers, co-authored four books, and written extensively for mountaineering journals. He lives in Burlington, Vermont.

Outdoor
Books
by the
Experts

Whatever the season, whatever your sport, The Mountaineers Books has the resources for you. Our FREE CATALOG includes over 350 titles on climbing, hiking, mountain biking, paddling, backcountry skiing, snowshoeing, adventure travel, natural history, mountaineering history, and conservation, plus dozens of how-to books to sharpen your outdoor skills.

All of our titles can be found at or ordered through your local bookstore or outdoor store. Just mail in this card or call us at 800·553·4453 for your free catalog. Or send us an e-mail at mbooks@mountaineers.org.

Name_____

Address_____

City_____ State _____ Zip+4 _____ - _____

E-mail_____

580-8

Outdoor
Books
by the
Experts

Whatever the season, whatever your sport, The Mountaineers Books has the resources for you. Our FREE CATALOG includes over 350 titles on climbing, hiking, mountain biking, paddling, backcountry skiing, snowshoeing, adventure travel, natural history, mountaineering history, and conservation, plus dozens of how-to books to sharpen your outdoor skills.

All of our titles can be found at or ordered through your local bookstore or outdoor store. Just mail in this card or call us at 800·553·4453 for your free catalog. Or send us an e-mail at mbooks@mountaineers.org.

Please send a catalog to my friend at:

Name_____

Address_____

City_____ State _____ Zip+4 _____ - _____

E-mail_____

580-8

BUSINESS REPLY MAIL
FIRST-CLASS MAIL   PERMIT NO. 85063   SEATTLE, WA

POSTAGE WILL BE PAID BY ADDRESSEE

THE MOUNTAINEERS BOOKS
1001 SW KLICKITAT WAY STE 201
SEATTLE WA 98134-9937

BUSINESS REPLY MAIL
FIRST-CLASS MAIL   PERMIT NO. 85063   SEATTLE, WA

POSTAGE WILL BE PAID BY ADDRESSEE

THE MOUNTAINEERS BOOKS
1001 SW KLICKITAT WAY STE 201
SEATTLE WA 98134-9937

NO POSTAGE
NECESSARY
IF MAILED
IN THE
UNITED STATES